For Alexander.
Thanks also to Ena, for years of support and to Cathy Jonas
for her careful editing.

Thanks to Christine, for lending me her spirit guides and
for patiently teaching a reluctant student.

First published in Australia in 1999 by
Simon & Schuster (Australia) Pty Ltd
This edition published by Academy Publishing, Sydney 2017

© 1991 / 2017 Paul Fenton-Smith

National Library of Australia
Cataloguing-in-Publication data

Fenton-Smith, Paul.
A secret door to the universe.

ISBN: 978-0-9581534-5-4

1. Psychic ability. I. Title.

133.8

Cover design and interior layout: Tracey Honig
Set in: Legacy Serif, 11pt
Illustrator: Nadia Turner

10 9 8 7 6 5 4 3 2 1

Contents

Preface 6
1   Glimpsing the Big Picture 8
2   The Physical Journey 13
3   In Search of a Holiday 20
4   The Journey Homeward 28
5   Spirituality and Religion 43
6   Giving Psychic Readings 46
7   Your Spiritual Energy Channel 49
8   Fear and Desire 53
9   Karma 61
10 Psychic Energy Cords 67
11 Psychic Cords to the Chakras 80
12 Becoming Centred Before Meditation 91
13 Learning to Visualise 93
14 The Purpose of Meditation 99
15 Awakening to the Light Meditation 105
16 Meditation Procedure 110
17 Simple Meditations .116
18 Your (Astral) Traveller Body 121
19 Procedure for Cutting Cords 125
20 Spiritual Protection 133
21 Spiritual Cleansing .140
22 Maintaining Energy Balance 143
23 Symbols for Protection 147
24 Energy Dumping 151
25 Spirit Guides 156
26 Clairvoyants 168
27 Clairvoyants and Meditation 172
28 The Senses 178

29   Retrieval of the Senses 185
30   Rewards of Being Centred 197
31   Finding Your Master 203
32   Organised Religions and Philosophies 210
33   Psychic Attack 213
34   A Journey through Love .217
35   Confirmation of Accuracy 228
36   Paths up the Mountain; a metaphor 234
37   Spiritual Healing 242
38   The Energy of Beliefs 249
39   Guilt and Auric Awareness 255
40   Your Journey 259
41   Twenty Years Later 262
42   Glossary 266

Illustrations

Figure 1:   The energy channel 54
Figure 2:   A psychic cord 74
Figure 3:   The main chakras of the body 76
Figure 4:   Psychic cords to the chakras 88
Figure 5:   The energy channel aligned with the physical body.
           A cord from the heart chakra. 100
Figure 6:   Channeling energy through meditation 144
Figure 7:   Spirit guides 182
Figure 8:   How clairvoyants use psychic cords 198
Figure 9:   Your spiritual master is found above your guides in
           your channel. 238

Preface

We are all spiritual masters in the making. This book offers practical avenues for spiritual nourishment for each individual's unique journey through life and beyond. It illuminates one of many paths to inner peace and bliss. Long term plans for a spiritual journey beyond this life require skills and preparation. A Secret Door to the Universe provides insight to where we go beyond this life and ways to prepare for your unique spiritual journey.

This book describes one man's voyage to discover where we might go after we die. Although the body dies, the spirit lives on to continue a longer passage home. This book reveals some of the groundwork necessary to build solid foundations for such an important journey.

A Secret Door to the Universe reminds us that we are spiritual beings in human bodies and that it is important to tend to our spiritual, mental, emotional and physical needs. The specific techniques offered here help resolve past situations and people who have negatively influenced your spiritual direction, diverting you from personal deeper spiritual purpose. Move from our to you. Should the last sentence continue our?

Within each person there are exclusive answers to individual questions about one's own life and purpose. This book demonstrates ways to access those unique answers. If a person lacks purpose or is less present in life than previously, specific meditations can help to retrieve those parts that may have been lost along the way.

By resolving the past and being centred in the present to pursue a unique spiritual destiny, it is possible to open a door within that leads to the universe. With spiritual guidance; one can more fully understand the consequences of personal actions. This connection provides more perspective, allowing readers to assess whether or not their life directions are leading towards or away from their spiritual purpose.

Are you ready to clarify and pursue your deeper spiritual purpose? Are you prepared to open your spiritual door and explore the universe? If so, be prepared to become the spiritual master you were meant to be.

1

Glimpsing the Big Picture

While travelling through England in the 1980s I found myself working as a palmist and clairvoyant ten hours a day, six days a week for a pittance. My plans to explore Europe seemed a distant memory when my days consisted of train and tube travel, bustling crowds and lunch at my desk.

Not long before I left London to travel further and before my return to Australia, my employer took a fortnight's holiday and was replaced by another clairvoyant, Christine. She was a short, plump woman from London's East End who enjoyed good conversation and a cup of tea. She was a powerful channel for spiritual energy and when working with her I found myself opening up spiritually and receiving information faster than ever before.

After I'd worked with Christine for three days I was giving detailed readings that had previously been impossible for me to do. I was suddenly detailing names, dates, full descriptions of the clients' loved ones and having clear conversations with deceased relatives. I thought that I had reached a point where I could be proud of my abilities. I had a lot to learn.

On the fifth day of working with Christine I found myself in trouble and had to seek her help. I had been reading for a woman who had requested that I contact someone on the 'other side'. I blithely agreed to do so and tried to find someone to converse with.

In my mind's eye I saw a man. He was tall, dark-haired, with a large build, straight nose and a tight expression on his face. He lay on a stretcher bed with his eyes closed. I said 'hello' to him but received no response, so mentally I moved a little closer to him. I described his mid-1960s style black suit and his physical features to my client.

She told me the description fitted her late father. I moved a little closer to the man in my vision but still received no response. I was squirming at this point, having given a physical description to my client but no further information. I visualised opening my third eye wider, allowing my psychic awareness to increase. I mentally sent a stream of energy across to him, reasoning 'a little zap to give him a boost'. He seemed disoriented but sat up and we began to talk. I kept it fairly short, thanked him and then left him alone again.

As I emerged from the trance I found my client crying quietly. She confirmed that her father had died in 1965. After she left, I read for two more people before resuming a long conversation I had been having with Christine. Our discussions had begun on our first day working together and had been interrupted only by clients and the telephone. Each time we resumed our talking, it seemed to flow on from where it had stopped.

I learned early on that Christine couldn't sit and talk without a cup of tea in one hand, so if I completed a reading before her I made her tea. She'd amble out of the consulting room and easily resume our conversation between sips of tea. The next few hours were quiet and our dialogue was interrupted only by my groaning with stomach discomfort. As we sat together my stomach had been bloating to look like a heavily pregnant woman.

My abdominal area was extremely painful. I asked Christine if she could assist me in removing any negativity I may have collected from clients during the day. My usual cleansing techniques for clearing energy seemed suddenly ineffective. Negative energy is easily collected when giving psychic readings, as the reader is open to information on a physical, emotional, mental and spiritual level. Often emotions are left behind by the clients when they depart. Many people leave a reading feeling lighter or relieved, in the same way that we feel lighter when sharing a secret or a problem that has been bothering us.

Christine looked at me briefly and launched into a routine of puffing and blowing, a method she employed to shift her awareness for better psychic vision.

"You've picked up a spirit," she said.

"What?" I asked blankly. I began to feel invaded and slightly paranoid at this point.

"It's a man," she continued. "He's been over quite a while." ('Over' means he is in the spirit world, or deceased.)

"He is an older man, who is quite tall, with a funny suit on. Like he's all dressed up."

She went on to clearly describe the man in the black suit I had seen in my meditation. I explained what I had seen during the reading and that I'd given him a little zap of energy to enliven him. That's when my real lessons began.

"You shouldn't do that. He's gone over without any spiritual beliefs and he's got himself stuck. A part of him knows that he's got to find his way home now but the rest of him doesn't have a clue where or what home is.

"He's spent his whole life in the pursuit of material pleasures and now he finds he's not equipped to make it back. You've come along, sticking your nose in and splashing a bit of energy about and he thinks, 'Oh there's the light; there's the way back home,' she said. "He followed the light to its source, which is you and he climbed aboard."

"So what happens now?" I asked, with a sense of panic engulfing me.

"Well in most cases, he'll just settle there with you. He could move on if you spend time in the presence of someone who has a brighter light than you, someone who has a stronger connection with spirit than you. That person may not look or act any different from you but a lost spirit like that man sees the difference.

"If the other person is wide open, such as during a psychic reading or a meditation, this spirit may move towards them, especially if you're physically close to them. The spirit interprets the brighter light as being a step closer to home."

"But surely I can simply go into meditation and pass the spirit over to the other side or give it back to its spiritual home?"

"You can if you know how. A lot of people think that they can do this, when in fact they aren't doing anything more than visualising that they are doing this.

"Here, let me do it for you," she said and spent the next five minutes huffing and blowing. My distended stomach gradually returned to normal within ten minutes.

"If you're going to do this work, you better find out what it is you're bleedin' doing," she advised.

I resolved immediately to do exactly that. Had I known then what I was letting myself in for, I may not have been quite as eager but my enthusiasm compensated for a lack of wisdom. Christine taught me the true meaning of a spiritual connection. All the years I'd spent in 'meditation' were valuable but never quite as deep or clear as I experienced under her guidance.

In the weeks we spent together I asked many questions, probed, challenged, listened and made over a hundred cups of tea. I confess that there were times when I even dissuaded potential clients from having a reading, so that Christine and I might continue our conversation.

I returned to Australia and resumed my career as a clairvoyant, gradually losing the skills I had learned from Christine. I hungered for that perfectly still connection with spirit but lacked the discipline to meditate every day. Although I'd meditate for clients as part of a clairvoyant reading, this is not a perfectly still spiritual connection, as I'm continually searching for information and relaying it to the client. When meditating alone I sometimes experienced blissful timelessness, where sitting still for an hour felt like five minutes. In those meditations I was happy, content and restful. The past and the future ebbed away from me as I embraced the present moment.

This isn't possible when reading for clients, as the client sitting before me has questions, fears, dread or anticipation. I can sense silent requests for information and the pressure takes me away from a centred stillness I experience when alone in meditation. It's no different from the pressure I give myself when meditating to find answers to question I have about my own current circumstances or life issues. Some of the deepest contemplations occur when information or answers are not the primary goal of the meditation. The conscious mind tends to lift a person out of deeper meditative states when practical questions or issues needing clarity are presented.

2
The Physical Journey

In 1991 my partner Amanda and I returned to England specifically to study meditation and spiritual development with Christine, who still lived in East London. We set six months aside, closed up our house, packed a few belongings and departed.

Christine was reluctant to teach us at first but eventually she consented. She showed us how to find our energy channels and how to gain a good clear connection with spiritual energy through meditation. It took ten weeks of the six-month stay to establish a home base, which interrupted our studies. However, we still managed to squeeze in periodic visits to Christine.

We had moved about 25 miles out of London and as Christine lived in the city it was difficult to pop in for a quick chat. I telephoned regularly but soon became concerned about the escalating phone bills, so I kept our calls as short as possible. This was not simple as Christine loves a good conversation. During our regular calls we often spent 40 minutes listening, learning, laughing and talking before we realised how long we had been talking.

One afternoon, I offered Christine a tarot reading using my method of clairvoyance and she accepted. I read for her for an hour or so in the upstairs living room of a friend's flat in London. I gave her a vague reading, as I couldn't seem to 'see' (clairvoyantly) very much. She laughed at my clumsy methods, as she was able to clairvoyantly 'see' how I was receiving my information, which was not by the most direct route.

A few days later she read for me and mentioned my spirit guides to me. She described them as being Indian, Chinese as well as some nuns. I told her that I had never seen any of the guides she had described, yet I could still 'see' clairvoyantly. She suggested I release my need to have white Anglo-Saxon guides and take information from those who were there in spirit for me because they had known me from previous lives.

We argued while I steadfastly refused to believe that this group of spirit guides was actually hanging about in spirit, waiting to help and advise me. I had, after all, been giving clairvoyant readings with guides for at least three years. My guides, despite all being Caucasian, had served me well until then. I felt that Christine was insisting that I see what she could see around me.

I have always been sceptical when clairvoyants tell me "I can see that you have an Indian guide with war paint and feathers ..." It is often followed by trite explanations such as "It stems from a past life you shared in Egypt around 3000 years ago when you were in a temple together." I usually switch off or ask "Why is it that people always describe past lives of unbelievable heroism or glory and never a life of drudgery or rountines. Where are all the past life prostitutes and street sweepers? What has become of all the past life Ancient Roman viaduct builders?"

I accept the existence of many lifetimes for soul evolution but have reservations about the type of past life small talk found at dinner parties after the third bottle of wine. Christine backed off immediately, deciding not to force the issue. She simply said, 'I can see two doors. You have taken one previously, in other lives and you know what lies beyond that door. The other door is the way I am telling you about.'

As silence fell, I began to panic. I have always disliked the idea that I might miss out on something, so I asked Christine more about what lay on the paths beyond these two doors.

"Tell me about the path I have previously taken," I ventured.

"It was the path of magic," she stated. "It dealt with palmistry, tarot, astrology, the occult and magic. It was a path of knowledge but it ended and when it ended you were not fulfilled or complete."

She was telling me that this path offered knowledge but not necessarily wisdom. As I had previously chosen it and had come back to choose again, perhaps it was not a viable long-term path to spiritual fulfilment. Our conversation ended. Christine had not entirely convinced me but now I was not as strongly opposed to her path. I simply needed time to think it over.

In the weeks that followed Christine showed me how to connect with the spirit world through meditation. For the first time I could truly feel light and love enter my head and pour throughout my whole body, filling every cell. This was the first occasion I found I was not restless during meditation but peaceful, still and deeply connected.

I felt light, whole and contented within. With surplus energy and enthusiasm I felt very positive about life. Meditation was nurturing me emotionally and spiritually like nothing else I had ever experienced. During meditation a deep stillness descended over me and the urge to rush around subsided. With this newfound contentment, there was no need to strive.

Christine was my perfect teacher because she left subjects until I encountered a problem related to them. This happened one morning when I woke with a tightness in my throat. It was sore and felt as though someone had been working on it with a nail file all night. I attempted to re-balance my energies but there was no change. I put the problem aside and later drove over to visit her. During the first cup of tea she casually asked how my throat was.

"It's sore actually. Why do you ask?" She hesitated. "Why is it sore do you think?"

"Oh I don't know. I'm probably uncentred or something." I replied.

"Why don't you go into meditation and find out?" she asked me.

"Look, I went into meditation before I came over and tried to re-centre myself but nothing has changed." I was impatient to change the subject. Christine persisted in a calm but determined manner.

"A part of your energy is not present in your physical body. It has been with me since yesterday and it linked with my throat. Because I was uncentred last night you are feeling the effects of what I was experiencing. That's what's causing your sore throat."

"What do you mean?" I asked.

"When you left here yesterday, you unconsciously left a part of your awareness behind. I was working in the throat chakra (energy centre) area and that part of you that was left behind is experiencing the disturbance I am experiencing in this area."

"How did you know part of me was here with you?"

"I saw an image or manifestation of you."

"Why didn't you simply send it home?" I asked.

"Because I want you to see for yourself that what I am saying is real." I immediately felt guilty for doubting her.

"Don't feel bad," she continued, "see it and understand it."

I sat down and looked within myself to see a cord of etheric energy reaching out to Christine. I then pulled it back by returning my awareness to myself, as it was my thoughts that had previously sent my awareness out to her in the first place. (The process of doing this is explained in chapter 29).

I was learning directly about the fine cords of psychic energy that connect us and how to centre myself to avoid dissipating too much personal energy through these energy cords to others. These invisible cords are naturally formed when we interact with others and when we desire someone or the attention of another person. This simplest way to test cords is to stare at someone in a crowd when you're in a café, on a train or sitting at the airport. That person is likely to sense your stare and look around to meet your gaze.)There is more information on energy cords in Chapter ten).

We regularly meditated at Christine's flat and no sooner had she described something than I'd have confirmation of what she had been saying. She'd say, "As soon as you bring down the light into your body through your channel, the darkness follows. As soon as you get a good clear connection in meditation, that's the time the phone or the doorbell rings. Others want the energy that you are experiencing."

An hour later we entered meditation together and within 20 seconds the phone started ringing. Minutes later there was a loud knock at the front door. Later she mentioned that she had a neighbour who unconsciously knew when to drop in to say 'hello' and collect some clean energy.

"It's a case of when you're up, the world connects with you and when you're down, you're down alone," she said. "When you are up and your chakras are open, you are easily linked to the whole world."

It is very difficult to close your chakras or energy centres (see Chapter 11, Psychic Cords to the Chakras; and Fig. 4) while parts of your awareness are out with other people, situations or even in the past.

While working in a healing centre in London I had direct opportunities to see how giving psychic readings could uncentre me. The act of reading for others refocused my awareness and spiritual energy away from myself. One afternoon I exchanged a reading for an osteopathic treatment with a fellow practitioner. I gave her a general reading and she asked her questions before we completed the session.

Later in the day she gave me a treatment and worked awhile around my neck and head areas. An osteopath is usually my best friend when I travel, as planes, trains and lumpy sofa beds all take their toll. I felt unusually vague and unable to concentrate when I left for the day but thought no more of it. Upon my arrival home I showered to cleanse myself of the day's energies, ate dinner and began to meditate.

I couldn't open up to spirit or bring down the light through my crown and throughout my body. It was as though there was a layer of concrete tied to the top of my head. I tried several times but to no avail. It was past midnight when I gave up trying and fell asleep.

The next afternoon I was still unable to open up to the light, so I telephoned Christine and explained it to her. She decided not to link in to me (to send out a cord to me to explore the causes) but instead suggested that I summon up all of my energy and create a mental whirlwind of energy to drill through the block and then up to the light. She then suggested that when I once again had a source of light, to drill a wider hole in the block, gradually breaking it up before examining it.

I did as she suggested and saw in my mind's eye a cord that I mentally followed, leading back to my osteopathic treatment the previous day. This cord was like a thin beam of light, stretching out before me. Upon reflection it all became clearer to me. During my treatment she had said, "I'd love to be able to read people the way that you do." I realised that this was an openly stated desire.

Her hands on and under my head, as I lay on the bench, were the easiest way for her to pass a cord through to me. She was probably unaware of any cords. I appreciated that she helped me inadvertently to discover a technique that I never knew existed, of using whirlwind energy to break through barriers (more on this technique in chapter 19).

The head is a very sensitive area that needs to be protected. This is not to suggest that osteopathic treatments, haircuts or dental work are to be avoided but caution is needed to ensure that you have closed down psychically before these treatments. It is also worthwhile to check yourself carefully afterwards in meditation.

Closing down is simply the act of minimising personal awareness of surrounding circumstances. Like closing the windows before leaving home for the day, you can close down easy entry points for curious people to access your energy field. A more effective closing down procedure is to close the chakras or energy centres of the body. (more details on closing the chakras can be found in chapter 11).

A natural and instant reaction to circumstances triggering someone to close down occurs when a person walks through a spider's web at night. The first thought is often about where the spider might be and if it is in your hair or still in the web. In response to this fearful thought, you instinctively pull your energy field close in to your body in an effort to protect yourself.

In a more controlled way it happens when a person sees someone he wants to avoid. There is a conscious effort to become invisible to the other person despite the close proximity. Closing down also means not being curious about others to the point where you open up your energy field while attempting to glean information about other people.

If you meditate regularly it's important to close down the main body chakras before the end of the process so that you're not energetically wide open when you travel to work, go shopping or mix with others who might not be so diligent with psychic development or personal cleansing. Just as you might close the car windows and air vents when entering a long tunnel, it's important to close down your chakras when stepping out of the house or entering a crowd of people.

3

In Search of a Holiday

Our time in England was passing and we wanted to take a brief trip to Europe before returning to Australia. Unfortunately we planned this first trip logically. France seemed a perfect place to visit in the summer, so we set aside 12 days. We encountered a few obstacles to our plans but blithely pushed ahead anyway, ignoring all warning signs.

It was the worst trip I have ever experienced. It was August, the holiday season, so we queued for everything. We travelled hundreds of kilometres in search of an available campsite. I soon realised that, with my intolerance to dairy products, France was not an ideal choice of culinary vacation. I didn't eat dairy, drink alcohol, eat much meat and spoke very little French, so France probably should have been one of my last choices for a holiday. Platters of cheeses? No thanks. Trout grilled in butter? No thanks and on it went.

Christine laughed heartily when we returned with our miserable travel tales.

"I saw that the signs were against it but you've got a strong will and were not to be stopped. You see, when you want to do something and you have three setbacks, it is usually best to stop and reflect. Three setbacks indicates that either the goal is wrong or that you are going about it incorrectly."

It was true. Even when we finally landed again in England, our motorbike lost its steering and we had to complete the journey in a tow truck. Upon our return, we needed a holiday more than before we'd left.

Several years later Jacinta, described a day when she set out to purchase some flowers for the house and never made it beyond the front gate. At first the car wouldn't start. Then, when she had borrowed another car, the remote control button wouldn't operate the front gate. Next she lost the remote control button and at this point she realised that perhaps she had better stay at home.

Several hours later, when she was ready to attend a function, the car started first time and the gate opened easily. The reason why she took the warning of the obstacles was that, in the past when she went against life's signs, it had cost her a considerable amount of money.

Abandoning pursuit of a goal when encountering three obstacles contravenes western belief that persistence brings success. However, in western philosophy success is often counted in material terms rather than spiritual contentment.

When arranging the next holiday I was much more careful. I went into meditation and asked a spirit guide where would be the perfect place spiritually for us to holiday at this point.

The guide thought for a moment and then replied, "Poros."

"Paros? Where's that?" I asked him.

"It's an island in Greece," he replied.

I awoke and promptly scanned the newspapers for the travel advertisements. I telephoned three large travel agencies, each time without success. One woman hadn't heard of Paros and another said that they no longer offered Paros as a destination but suggested Hydra or Santorini as possible alternatives.

I had received three setbacks and I was not about to push my luck. I returned to meditation and asked the guide to spell the name of the destination.

"P - O - R - O - S," he said.

From Paros to Poros; I was scanning the papers again. I looked for Poros in an atlas but couldn't locate it. Yes, the was the early 1990's and before easy Internet access. I telephoned two more travel agencies and on the second call the woman laughed and said, "Would you believe it? We have Poros on our lists and we are currently offering a special. Two weeks for the price of one. The next flight leaves on Saturday."

Amanda, Christine and I took that flight. It was a freezing overcast morning in England when we boarded the plane for Athens. My hands and feet were numb with the cold and I was glad to leave, if only for two weeks. We landed, transferred to a ferry and moved off in search of sun and sand. It was a sunny 30°C when we arrived in Poros and we spent the afternoon on the beach. It was a private, protected cove with still waters and as I lay on the golden sands the only sounds were seagulls, squabbling over empty tables at a nearby café.

After our last holiday attempt I was determined to have a good time. I wanted to eat until I couldn't walk, swim until my skin was wrinkled and lie on the sand until my skin became so brown I'd require a new passport photo. With fresh baklava, a Greek pastry filled with crushed nuts and covered in honey, readily available I felt I was in heaven. We still had plenty to learn from Christine and she was happy to teach us while we holidayed.

I didn't really want to learn at this point, preferring instead to make up for the previous French holiday and the recent English weather. By day we were tourists, by evening we were diners in the local restaurants and at night I wrote short stories about our lazy adventures.

Early one morning we boarded a boat for Spetzes and Hydra, two neighbouring islands. This was as I'd dreamed a holiday should be. Plenty of sunshine, open seas, space on the beach and plenty of empty tables at restaurants. I decided that if heaven is anything like the Greek islands, then I'm going. I wanted to simply play in the sun and forget about meditation. All such seriousness seemed out of place amidst life's simple pleasures.

Spetzes was interesting but not spectacular. Hydra was definitely familiar; I believe it's a place I've visited or lived on in a previous incarnation. The first glimpse of hundreds of tiny cottages crowded together up the hill against the wind, with whitewashed walls and window shutters of every conceivable colour, touched my heart. I felt as though I was coming home.

I walked all over the island, photographing almost every lane and cottage. We were surrounded by scenes of unpretentious lives with simple pleasures. It was almost too beautiful to be real, like a postcard, I thought while gazing out from the cliffs and then upwards to more solid little houses perched high on the cliff tops. There are no cars on the island and donkeys carry the provisions from the port up into the hills. The cobbled paths and rickety stone walls seem to set a scene of 100 years ago.

I found myself fighting back tears when the time came to board the boat to return to Poros and searched for reasons to stay. I stumbled across a small pastry shop which sold baklava and purchased three pieces. It had been freshly made and was still warm. As I took a bite the pastry shattered into a hundred tiny shards in my mouth and I knew I was in heaven. It was so delicious that I ate Amanda's and Christine's pieces before arriving back at the port. In a couple of hours I had grown to love the place and felt as though I had lived there all my life. When I located the girls at the port, Christine echoed my sentiments about the island.

The sea was very rough on the return journey and many passengers suffered seasickness. As we were in Greece I laughingly thought it only fair to offer prayers for our safety to Poseidon, the ancient Greek god of the sea, which seemed appropriate.

The next day it rained continuously all day. Dark stormy clouds and darker, stormier faces of fellow tourists filled my window panes whenever I glanced out. Christine and Amanda found some books to read and I was left talking to myself while trying to avoid even a cursory glance at the window. It rained solidly for two days and I was becoming stir-crazy from being inside so long. At the first glimpse of sunlight I caught a bus into town and hired a small motorbike. It was nothing elaborate and was not particularly roadworthy. Actually I paid 3000 drachma and forfeited my passport for the rusty remains of a Honda 50.

I volunteered to give Christine a riding lesson. Up and down the drive she went, in the innocently menacing way that only the unfamiliar have with machinery. To avoid complaints from the neighbours, I offered to take her somewhere less built up for practice. She jumped on the back and we headed off in search of a quiet strip of road. It didn't occur to me that I shouldn't be teaching Christine when Amanda was the motorcyclist in the family. I usually rode pillion.

I was surprised that Poros had such a steep mountain. We rode for 25 minutes in the cold and rain before viewing the ruins of a temple on top of the hill and then set out on our return. The wet winding road was dangerous and the motorbike's engine began cutting out intermittently. On rounding a sharp curve the motor faltered and the bike slid out from under us. We landed face first on the road.

Christine landed heavily on her knee and sustained an injury that required four stitches, while I lost skin and clothing. As she was unable to walk, I left her on the side of the road and steered the bike back to our apartment. Amanda caught a taxi to collect Christine and take her to the doctor. After that neither of us could walk very far, as we couldn't bend our legs. We were confined to bed. At first we read books but I soon tired of this. I wrote occasionally but only for 30 minutes at a time. Finally I meditated.

My guide gently questioned me. "What did you come here for?"

"For a holiday."

"Yes but why did you come away from home in the first place?"

"Oh, to learn," I said softly, realising that I was doing as much as possible to avoid learning.

"You have seven days left in Europe with Christine and then you return home. What do you want from these seven days?" I thought carefully but I wasn't really sure. Later, when we could hobble a little, we took the bus up to an old monastery. Stone steps loomed large before me and I knew that it was a reminder that I'd have been better off in bed in meditation.

At the top we found a delightful old building and while in the grounds Christine saw the spirit of a monk walking about. She mentioned this to us and briefly described him. Fifteen minutes later, when the next busload of tourists arrived, two middle-aged women stood behind us at the lookout balcony, ignoring the persistent wind that tore at their hair by the roots, discussing the brochure that included this particular monastery.

"It says here that a ghost haunts this monastery. Apparently it is the ghost of a monk who founded this place," said one to the other. Christine simply smiled and said "Thanks for the confirmation, spirit." It is important to seek verification of what you see or experience; to ensure that what you glimpse or sense is not merely your imagination. Corroboration can occur through physical reality or as a result of asking personal guides or master for proof. We returned to our apartment and Christine described a surreal occurrence.

"I'm seeing something strange in spirit. There are rings of spiritual masters appearing above me. They seem to be gathering for some particular purpose but I don't know what it is. There are many masters from different paths. I wonder what could be about to happen?"

This continued for days. When Christine spoke of masters being with her I simply accepted it. At first it seemed outrageous and I wondered about her state of mind but in time even unbelievable occurrences seem perfectly natural. After seeing cords of energy passing between people for the first time only recently, hearing about ascended masters gathering above in spirit wasn't too difficult to accept.

As the holiday progressed Christine was going higher and higher, as though in meditation but it was happening in the waking state. We could feel the energy radiating from her. It was strange, for she would walk into our bedroom while we lay there reading books (still cloudy outside) and complete a sentence or resume a conversation she had left unfinished three hours earlier.

I'd be halfway down a page only to hear Christine say "... and another thing. If you look closely at. . ." as she limped towards me. I learned to change focus between my thoughts and Christine's conversation very quickly in those two weeks. Towards the end of the second week it became difficult for Christine to venture outside. Her energy was expanding so that her auric or energy field extended more than two metres around her. She was more vulnerable to depletion of psychic energy from others who might, even unconsciously, need energy to get through the day.

She was reaching a high state of mental clarity and inner peace usually associated with meditation but she displayed these in the waking state during everyday activities. She was content to remain in the apartment or to take a daily stroll along the beach one hundred metres away.

One morning during the second week I meditated and met a Chinese guide. He was direct and to the point.

"You have only three days left now to achieve what you want."

"What can I achieve? What can I achieve in three days?"

"What do you want?"

"In the next three days or spiritually or out of life?"

"What do you want, Paul?" he asked again. I became excited at the prospect.

"Can I have whatever I ask?"

"With effort and sacrifice, yes."

"Anything?"

"What do you want, Paul?"

I thought for a few minutes. This was bizarre. I felt as though I must have done something right somewhere to be offered such a privilege. Or was it a test, or a trap? Would asking to be able to walk freely again be too simple? After all, in a few months my scar would heal naturally. In a cynical moment I had decided that perhaps the accident was to assist me in writing 'The Limper's Guide to Europe.'

I decided that this was an opportunity not to be wasted. Material objects did not enter my mind as I sorted through the possibilities. There was one thing I particularly wanted to experience but I knew that it was too much to ask for. As I discarded it from my mind, a statement I often used when counselling clients sprang to mind, 'If you can't ask for it, you can't have it.'

When I was young we were very poor and as a child I was taught not to even bother asking, because the answer would be 'no'. I learned that if I didn't ask I wasn't disappointed. I never did completely learn it, for I still ask for more and believe in the old saying that "to be all that you can be, you must dream of being more."

I looked closely at the guide. This was not going to be easy but if I didn't ask him; I'd probably regret it.

"I would like to go home," I said. "All the way home, you know; where I'll go when I die." He looked at me without smiling.

"Are you sure that is what you want?"

"Yes," I replied.

"I won't take this as final," he stated. "I want you to meet me again between 5.15 and 5.45 this evening. Tell me what you have decided you want. In the meantime, do not eat any meat or fish for the next three days."

I concluded my meditation and began worrying. Was there something better that I needed to ask for? Had I just been tested and my answer turned out to be inappropriate? Did I really want to go home? I was adamant. I wanted to go home, to see with my own eyes what is out there after I die. To feel with my own heart what home holds for me and to see my place of origin. I didn't want others telling me what was out there after this life without having any actual proof or direct experience. Faith was for other people. I wanted to see for myself.

I had heard conflicting stories about what occurred after death and this was an opportunity to see for myself what lay ahead in the greater journey beyond life. There were anxieties but my curiosity was stronger than my fear of what I might see.

4

The Journey Homeward

At 5.15 pm I was once again in meditation and confirmed my request to go home for a visit. The guide smiled and set me a task to complete before 9.10 pm, with instructions to be back in meditation between 9.10 pm and 9.30 pm. At 9.10 pm I was in meditation, my task complete. He welcomed me, quizzed me about my task and set me another task, before instructing me to be in meditation again between 11.10 and 11.25 pm.

The tasks, which involved emotional resolution of past situations with family and friends, were becoming more difficult, the time allowed for each task was less than for the previous task and the time at which to be back in meditation was becoming more and more precise. At first I was allocated 30 minutes, then 20 minutes, and now 15 minutes to return to meditation.

It was not my guide setting these tasks but one of Christine's guides whom, on advice from her master, she had lent to me so that he could assist me in my progress. After I had asked for that which I most wanted, I was given four hours to think it over. I discussed it with Christine, who seemed non-committal other than to say that she had been told that one of her guides would be helping me for a short period. Her energy channel itself was forming an offshoot to me to facilitate the transfer of the guide. I didn't notice anything different in the waking state but in meditation I could see and feel the difference in activity and preparations.

The guides I contacted in meditation seemed busy and preoccupied. It was more than simply Christine's guide helping me. He required a link right up through her master and out to the realms, which spiritualists describe as layers of heaven. When I meditated, my guide introduced me to Christine's guide, who set me tasks and communicated to me from that point onwards. In meditation I saw the offshoot from Christine's energy channel to mine. The bright white tunnel of energy temporarily joined mine just above my head.

At 11.10 pm I was again in meditation and another task was set for me. I was told to return to meditation between 11.50 and 12.00 midnight. At 11.55 I began meditating to be told that as I was about to sleep there would be no task set for me at this time but that between 3.10 and 3.15 am I was required back in meditation again.

I was sceptical about the precise times set for meditation but Christine reassured me by saying that she had been through a similar test previously and that I simply needed to trust her guide and follow his directives.

At 3.12 am I returned to meditation, thankful that my next due time to return to meditation for contact with the guide was between 8.30 and 8.35 am.

I slept until 9.15 am and awoke feeling terribly guilty. He did not scold me nor punish me but I wondered anxiously if it was quietly noted somewhere. He set me another small task and then set a time of 10.30 - 10.35 to return to meditation. I returned to meditation at 10.32 where finally the biggest challenge was given to me.

"I want you to find compassion in your heart to forgive all those whom you feel have hurt you and for you to find love within yourself for all living things," he said solemnly.

"What!" I exploded. "Do you seriously expect me to empty my heart of all of my hurts, pain, sorrow, sadness, disappointment and anger, to refill it with love and compassion for all living things within two days?" I was furious.

"Impossible!" I stated. He repeated this task and requested that I return to meditation at 8.00 pm sharp.

After the meditation concluded I cleared my head, reasoning that they would not set me a task that I was incapable of achieving, so I was determined to do exactly as he asked. I proceeded with two forgiveness meditations, designed to release others from past unresolved situations with me or my lack of forgiveness. Prior to the 8.00 pm meditation I tiptoed around, ensuring that I didn't tread on any flies or create any bad karma.

At 8.00 pm I was in meditation again, mentally shouting at Christine's guide that it was an impossible task to complete within 24 hours.

"It's 20 hours actually," he replied while I swallowed hard. He set me no more tasks and I agreed to meet him in meditation the following day, which was Sunday.

At this stage Christine described rings of masters set in place around her channel and she explained that all of her spirit bodies had moved up to be with them. Her spirit bodies were unable to return to her physical body until the purpose of the exercise was complete. Although Christine was at such a high level, she didn't sit cross-legged in meditation. Instead she hobbled about the place dragging her sore leg with her. She read out on the balcony, returning to the kitchen every few hours to prepare some food for herself.

I figured that the guide's reference to only 20 hours meant that my task was set for completion at 4.00 pm on Sunday and I had until then to develop love and compassion for all. I tried to complete what seemed like an impossible task. I sulked and fumed and choked myself with my own negativity and doubts. Upon reflection, his asking me to develop and expand my purest qualities seemed to manifest and focus all of my very worst characteristics.

I slept fitfully on Saturday night and awoke to my enormous burden on Sunday. I attempted a brief meditation but had no success. Whether my frame of mind inhibited me or not, I don't know. All day long I wanted to ask Christine for help with this task but I questioned whether she could help me. I doubted myself and began to have serious reservations about the whole experience. I started to question where reality left off and fantasy began.

I alienated myself from Amanda, Christine and from life and then blamed everyone for ignoring me. I was behaving like a spoilt child. I did exactly the opposite of what was asked of me by brewing an inner storm of anger and bitterness. It was amazing how much resentment, hatred and loathing I stirred up or created in such a short time. I wanted to ask for their help and advice but pride suggested that I could do it all by myself. Unfortunately my pride left very little room for humility or compassion.

"Forgive everybody? Huh! They're all bastards as far as I'm concerned!" I muttered. I became so wrapped up in myself that I was unaware whether it was a sunny day or if it rained. Amanda told me later that while she and Christine lay on the beach and I attempted to meditate back at the apartment, Christine told her that I wanted help but was holding back. She could sense that I was troubled but she also knew better than to simply step in uninvited and help.

It was 2.00 pm and I was tired. Suddenly it was not much of a holiday after all. When 3.00 pm arrived I attempted to meditate but with no success. I became aware that I had a great deal of energy invested in certain grudges that made simple forgiveness seem impossible.

I returned to meditation at 4.00 pm. Nothing happened. I tried again but to no avail. I became depressed and disappointed. Amanda and Christine were still at the beach as I lay there alone, feeling sorry for myself. 'If only he hadn't set such a difficult task for me to complete. He never tested me on any of my strong points, just the weaker areas.'

By 5.30 pm I had twice attempted to meditate but had no success. I gave up. Feeling bitter and cynical I sat and wrote the following:

'Here I sit, bitter with disappointment, wondering when exactly did my desire for knowledge and understanding of things I do not comprehend give way to gullibility? For a while there I believed all of the results my imagination conjured in its bid to fulfil my mind.

'I feel like a small child, alone, nursing a broken dream. I wanted so much to touch the divine, to find a goal so worthy of pursuit that merely to see it might heal myself of all past betrayals. But the ladder I built to span such heights was made of hopes and prayers and nothing strong enough to span from this world to that. In my imagination I was being tested, with the hope that I may be found worthy. The tests became more precise with time and soon I wondered if perhaps I controlled those testing me.

A question arose in my mind. If those who sought to help me seek the divine were subject to my will, then they were already subject to my limitations and therefore could no more help me than I could help myself. Perhaps divine beings only exist in imagination after all. It seems that my ladder from this world to that is built immediately, when I close my eyes. It doesn't require meditation for it's all imagination. The process was simpler than I had thought.'

At 6.00 pm Amanda and Christine returned home. I told Christine that she could have her channel and her guide back as nothing had happened and I was no longer interested. She asked me what I was so gloomy about and I told her about the test I had been set.

"They were all ridiculous tests if you ask me," I concluded aloud. "I may very easily have set them up in my imagination. Just some little thing to keep me busy or to help me to feel that I've earned the right to what I want."

"You're wrong if you think that you've mastered love and compassion," Amanda announced loudly. Christine followed. "I've not once seen you stop to pat or play with any of the cats and kittens around here."

"That's because they are wild and could have diseases," I responded. "We were told last week, they will all be poisoned in the coming months when the holiday season is over. So why waste love on them?"

"That's just it," Christine said. "Their lives are short but any love you give them in that time will make a difference. It may be enough to help them to evolve a little and have a better life next time."

They were both right. I believed that love had to be all or nothing until I realised that a little love is better than no love at all. Amanda asked me if I wanted to come into town with her for dinner. I wasn't hungry and so declined her offer. She left about ten minutes later. Christine limped into the kitchen and began to prepare her own dinner. I closed the door on the noise of the pots and pans and lay down in bed feeling emotionally bereft.

At first I was overwhelmed with self-pity and frustration but gradually I released these emotions and accepted that I had shown little compassion for others in the past. I didn't continually lack compassion for others but was guarded in showing my feelings outwardly. I believed that unless I was actually doing something practical about an unpleasant situation, feeling what others were going through was of no use to myself or to those in need.

I knew that I owed Christine's guide an apology, so I put my hopes aside and despite my exhaustion, returned to meditation. I met my guide who was to accompany me up my channel to Christine's guide. He was pacing back and forth.

"Where have you been?" he asked me, following with, "I've been waiting for you."

We moved swiftly upward and came to a stop where Christine's guide awaited me.

"Are you ready?" he asked with a smile.

"You mean I can do this?" I gasped. He moved to my side as my own guide stepped away from us and we took off up the channel to Christine's master. The light was very bright now and there were other beings around the master but I was unable to focus clearly on them. I greeted him and felt his powerful presence enveloping me. In that moment I became aware of his love and his compassion. His warmth enveloped me like a cheery burst of sunshine breaking through clouds on a winter's day.

He radiated an aura of inner peace. He was clearly a disciplined being on many levels but although I felt a deep respect for him I knew that he was not my master because I did not feel a deep connection to him.

Christine's guide stepped away from me and a female who seemed familiar stepped up behind me. I sensed her energy but didn't look to see who she was. She enfolded me in her arms and I felt myself protected by what seemed to be a shield of love. I felt like an excited child, looking all around me, trying not to miss anything. My vision soon became hazy and intermittent. It reminded me of the fade-out experienced when a radio gradually moves out of range.

We began to move off from the master now, gathering incredible momentum. I saw a flash of faces and scenes so briefly that I could not properly record them. Suddenly we came to a stop before a burly man with white hair and a long white beard. He resembled an ancient biblical character and to this day I've no idea who he was. He was eyeing me critically and talking loudly to a being or beings out of my field of vision.

"Who let you up here? You're not ready for this. How did you get here?" he demanded. His thunderous voice shocked me and I simply pointed to the being whose arms enfolded me. Although I did not hear her voice, I could feel that she was explaining the situation. The man's face relaxed into a smile every bit as intense as his previous frown and we progressed forward once again.

The scene fell away below me as we advanced higher and my vision was quite hazy until we came to a complete stop. There was a male figure in a huge white and golden field of energy. I immediately began to cry tears of joy, pain and release. He stepped out of the light (appearing to leave his auric energy field) towards me and I fell to my knees, sobbing uncontrollably. He extended his hands, palms upward open to me. I could feel his love and his compassion envelop me and I felt completely unworthy of his love. I became aware of all the times in my life when I had needed compassion and found none. His love was both painful and intensely fulfilling.

Taking his hands, I placed my face in them, all the while crying. My logical mind was concerned about how he felt about my tears all over his hands. He said something to me but I missed it with my sobbing. I felt a gentle tug from behind me and released this radiant being. With the female arms around me, we slowly began to move away. I felt that I recognised this radiant man's energy, especially as my emotional reaction was so immediate but I didn't know from where I knew him. Things around me became blurry as we moved off towards our destination.

I felt very peaceful and as stillness spread calmly through my body, my tears subsided. This serenity lasted about five or ten minutes and during this time I was unaware of what my traveller body was experiencing (the astral traveller body is the non-physical part of you that consciously travels the physical and spiritual worlds to teach you about the universe).

I began to wonder if it was time to return and thoughts of my physical body started the return journey. Once again I passed the being with the huge gold auric field, the burly bearded man and many others, to arrive at the master. I thanked the master for the opportunity I had been given and Christine's guide accompanied me back to my own guide in my own channel. He stayed close to my side until my own guide appeared and guided me gently back.

I had been on a journey with the help of Christine, through her channel and with the help of her guides. Without her assistance, doing what I had just done might have taken me years of hard work; others may have taken a lifetime to have had this experience. I felt wide awake and more aware and alert than I have ever been, yet somehow calm.

Whether a person experiences this is not a matter of how spiritually developed he or she is but rather whether it is right for that individual. I awoke from the meditation and lay still, dazed and strangely fulfilled. After 10 or 12 minutes I stood up and ventured into the kitchen to find Christine and tell her.

She was at the stove, trying to rescue a saucepan containing the charred remains of her dinner. When I entered meditation and began the journey up to Christine's master, Christine had 'lifted off' too, in the kitchen.

"Did you feel me behind you?" she asked.

"Oh, so that's who it was," I replied. "I didn't fully recognise you."

"Because it was my higher self—she doesn't look a lot like me."

"Did you see the master?" she asked excitedly. When I replied that I had, she continued with a list.

"Did you see the crowds around my master? Did you see Jesus or who I think was Jesus?"

"No, I must have missed that," I replied.

"You were crying and even on your knees at one stage. Whoever he was, you knew him all right." I realised from her description of events that the being in the bright aura might have been Jesus. I explained to her that my conscious awareness of what my spirit body experienced was limited or non-existent towards the end of the journey.

"You must ask that your eyes see what your traveller sees, your ears hear what your traveller hears and that you physically feel whatever your traveller feels. You request that as soon as you get into meditation."

"If only I'd known that before it all started," I moaned. Her response was immediate.

"Now that you know, go back and try again. Go now, while the link and the guides are still there." I couldn't believe my good luck. It was another chance and another journey. I returned to my bed and following the same procedures, I journeyed to her master. Christine's arms enveloped me again and we were off.

This time I saw much more clearly. We passed the burly man and suddenly a strange event happened. My spirit travelling body split into two right down the middle and fell away from me, revealing a lighter, brighter body. Christine later described this process as a splitting of light and dark atoms within, to enable the body entry to the higher realms. It felt as though every cell of my spirit body had split in two as though a cloak had been removed from my spirit body, revealing a whiter body composed of finer energy than before. I felt light, clean and more agile.

We stopped at the radiant figure once again and although I thought I was better prepared, I again fell to my knees sobbing. He extended his hands to me. A part of me still managed to keep alert mentally, despite the overwhelming emotions I was feeling at being immersed in such a pure love and compassion. It occurred to me to study the lines on the outstretched palms, as I had 13 years' experience as a palmist but this proved pointless as I was crying too much and unable to see clearly.

I noticed no nail marks or no unusual lines. At a glance they appeared to be palms as any other man might have. Somehow I expected a line-free palm or some brilliant sign or marking. At this point his hands were less important than the overwhelming atmosphere of love. It was difficult to concentrate as I wanted to be still to enjoy the inner bliss.

"There are no nail marks," I said, examining the palms closely. He simply smiled and said, "There were never any nails." Whoever this being was, I recognised him and felt overcome with emotion at meeting him.

Remembering the purpose of my journey, I reluctantly bade him goodbye as we moved onward. Soon afterwards the cells of my body split into two again, revealing an even finer, more transparent body. We passed across a scene which from above appeared to be a herd of winged white horses galloping across huge open fields.

We entered another place through what appeared to be an enormous porthole. There we stood motionless and apprehensive. Nothing happened.

"Where are we?" I asked in my mind.

"At the first," my mind responded. The first realm I reasoned.

"It's not as I expected," I stated to myself.

"What did you expect?" came the question.

"Well, love. Lots of love."

"And what do you experience?"

"Stillness. A great stillness."

"Do you have any needs?"

"No," I replied

"Are you at one with yourself?"

"Yes. Yes I am."

"Then is this not love, if you have no needs?"

"Yes. I guess it is."

"Is it your expectation that disturbs you?" We began to move on further and I missed some of what was going on around me because my physical body was uncomfortable. My back ached slightly from the old mattress beneath me.

Having found a more comfortable position on the bed I returned to focusing on my traveller body. We passed through what resembled a giant vertical wheel, roughly a kilometre across. On the inside rim of this wheel, which was slowly turning anti-clockwise, I saw many capsules. Some were occupied and many were empty; perhaps awaiting an occupant. I found one awaiting me. It did not have my name on it but I recognised it and knew that for a period of time I would fill it. I had no idea of its purpose. I don't even have a theory about it. It seemed like pure science fiction and I was merely an ignorant observer.

We moved through this wheel and on to another realm, although I had difficulty recalling what I saw there. I consciously saw three realms in total, before turning back for my physical body. I know that there are more than three realms but I only consciously managed three.

When I questioned Christine later she explained that to reach the realms means that you're at the start of the journey home. As a person evolves spiritually, he or she progresses up the realms (there are eight realms) during time spent between physical lives. Ordinarily a person would not be able to see deceased masters before the second realm. I was able to because Christine was guiding me and operating from the second or perhaps the third realm.

When I returned to the room and to my physical body I was overjoyed. In the kitchen Christine and I discussed each part of the trip in detail. It amazed me that she remembered much more than I could. She had again travelled the journey with me.

"That's what your channel is for," she explained. "Your channel is your path home when you pass over into spirit. Think what happens to those people who have wasted their spiritual energy on material things or been pulled out of their channel through giving psychic readings to others. Or what about those who simply were not conscious of its existence in the first place? What chance do they have of passing all the way home successfully?"

"What happens to them?" I asked.

"Well, they move away from the earth plane but sometimes they get stuck out there along the way and more of them are getting stuck out there than ever before.

"If you're serious about your spiritual welfare," she continued, "it is important to work to clear your spiritual energy channel all the way back home. You must strengthen it where it is weak and follow your spiritual path. It's essential to live a spiritual life. Once you open the door to those in spirit they are going to walk in. When you do open up to them they will test you, help you or thwart you when you're attempting something that is against your spiritual development, against others or contrary to your path in life. When starting out with tarot cards, psychic development or a channelling course, it is important to be aware of where it may lead you. In time it might be difficult to exercise your free will when those in spirit have other plans for you.

"You're very lucky, you know," Christine said to me, "You have been back consciously and you now know what it's like and what you are striving towards. I pity those people who sacrifice and strive to live a spiritual life and have no conscious recollection of where they're heading to eventually. It must be so much harder for them. They must possess so much more faith and perseverance than you and I. We know what awaits us out there and we know that it is worth the effort. They have to believe it, without the proof."

"What about all my destructive attitudes and moods this weekend? How did I manage to complete the journey with such a negative state of mind?" I asked her.

"You must remember that immediately preceding or following a great meditation, particularly one where you experience great light, darkness is also present. Darkness seeks the light, not to conquer it as some people suggest but to join with it to balance itself out. You experienced great light and it was preceded by darkness, which consumed your faith and hope. It is similar to people who telephone us the moment we begin to meditate, because on some level they sense changes in our energy.

To understand this more fully, it helps to realise that the soul is joined to the mind. The mind is also chained to the senses and is regularly pulled out and down, to the physical body. The mind sends the senses out to others or to the past, which weakens spiritual resolve.

Meditation frees the mind from the senses and in turn the mind becomes more positive, being directed towards spiritual instead of physical or material pursuits. Regular meditation liberates the mind from the senses directing it toward spirituality.

Now that the meditation is complete you still have a strong connection there, which will probably last up to three days. Darkness will still be drawn to the light that presently surrounds you but it will be temporarily deflected from you by that light. Through this period, your partner or anyone living or working closely with you can feel the excess light you cannot cope with as it is deflected from you. Regular meditation helps you cope with more of this light and deflect less of it to others. People close to you may experience illness or general heaviness or negativity while you have this strong connection because they usually cannot cope with this unnecessary amount of light."

"Does this happen with disciples of masters?" I asked, remembering some of the masters I had seen speaking to their disciples in ashrams and at public seminars. "Do they feel the backlash of negativity that comes when the master channels great light?"

"Masters do not reflect the light in the same way, as their minds are attuned to spirit. They are able to direct smaller amounts of light to others, usually in quantities that others can cope with. It depends on the particular master and the situation."

"How does a master get up high in the first place, when often they are corded by so many people less experienced than themselves?"

"It's important to understand that just because someone doesn't know where their Astral traveller body or senses are, doesn't mean that they are less developed. It simply means that they are less conscious of what is occurring spiritually."

"Amanda experiences this," Christine explained. "She gets very high in meditation and during sleep at night. Her traveller body often comes out with me on journeys, yet she is not conscious of this. She doesn't have a continual conscious connection with all of her bodies."

The senses (also described as spirit bodies because they can resemble the physical body) travel from the physical person during daily life. When the causes of departure from the physical self are not resolved, spirit bodies can remain out of the physical body for long periods of time. Months or years may pass before they return or are reunited with the physical self. In some instances these spirit bodies can remain trapped out of the physical body. When retrieving personal senses expect to feel strong emotions, as these energetic parts have been away from you for months or years.

Regular meditation bring senses back to the physical body, increasing the likelihood that they will remain permanently (see Chapter 28, The Senses).

Retrieval of a sense or a spirit body that has been away from the main spirit for a lifetime occurred with Amanda. With Christine's help she traced a cord of energy from herself outwards to a past life, where she was travelling in a carriage. In that situation she was despondent because she had been let down by a partner. As a result a spirit body had left her physical body (and the main core of her spiritual being) in search of fulfillment that it was unable to find in her life. Her spirit form needed encouragement before it was prepared to commit to returning to her present physical body.

In the process of returning her long departed spirit form to her present-day physical self, she was able to reclaim more of her spiritual energy and focus in the present. She explained that she felt more whole and less of the enduring emptiness she had previously experienced. As she reclaims other part of herself that are currently out of her physical body, she'll amass more energy and focus for spiritual development.

Senses or spirit bodies that have been trapped in very dark places can sometimes appear as demons. It is unnecessary to be afraid because these sometimes grotesque forms are the result of collecting gross energy over the months or years that they have been away from your physical body, which is their natural source of spiritual replenishment. It's possible to cleanse these bodies before they are successfully returned to your present physical self.

A guru is able to tap into his or her disciples' channels above their crown chakra and access some energy without the disciple even realising. It is important to remember that gurus are not necessarily masters. Spiritual masters have traversed the path up the mountain and are prepared to act as guides, whereas gurus have not necessarily travelled the path completely. They too are on a journey somewhere.

A guru can act as a guide for a person's spiritual journey up the mountain but it's possible to climb the mountain without a guide. Guru-resistant people can ascend to great heights without a map but it may take longer. Once reaching your inner summit, others may want you to guide them. You can offer them the map you've made through your own journey or simply advise them to make their own plans as they discover unique paths to the summit.

There are countless spiritual paths up many different mountains. While some of us prefer to share the route with like-minded people who can support us when the gradient becomes challenging, others favour solo expeditions. Some people share parts of the path and then proceed alone when an individual approach is required. The important objective is to reach your inner summit and the easiest way to do this is to summon all of the different parts of yourself (physical, emotional, mental and spiritual parts) to help with the journey.

As each map is unique, even gurus or masters cannot give you an exact chart to your spiritual goals. They might provide you details about turning points, the consequences of decisions or encouragement when you feel overwhelmed but the finer points of creating an accurate chart to your spiritual goals is your personal responsibility, as you proceed or at the conclusion of your journey.

5
Spirituality and Religion

To understand the difference between spirituality and religion it is necessary to define them. Spirit energy exists in everything living and non-living. It is an essence. Some people believe it is a residual energy left by the creator of all life. This is similar to a painter leaving some of his or her essence or energy in each work completed.

Each person has specific energy by which they can be recognised, aside from physical attributes such as their voice, appearance or scent. When seeking a particular person through astral travelling or in dreams, it's easy to locate them anywhere by homing in on their essence or energy blueprint. Friends can be located through the memory of their spirit energy. DNA is the closest that science has come to an individual human blueprint but the personal memory of a close friend's essence or spiritual energy is an even more precise method of recognising that person.

Religion is person's way of maintaining the accuracy of particular paths back to God, or the source of spirit. There are many paths home and this book offers one. Each religion offers a specific path and diverse paths suit different people. Spirituality is contained within most religions but religions are not necessarily connected with spirituality. It is possible to be spiritual without being religious and religious without being spiritual. They can co-exist but they are independent of each other.

Throughout history people have sought to replenish themselves spiritually. Some of the more accessible sources of spiritual energy include the sea, forests, mountain tops, sunrise, sunset, meditation, prayer and harmonious group activities such as singing, storytelling or group meditation. Although these activities can replenish spiritual reserves of energy, they do not necessarily offer a glimpse of the path back home to God or to the source of spiritual energy. Perhaps meditation is the exception. Through specific meditations it is possible to locate an individual path home. To ensure a good clear meditation and a sound connection with spirit, balance within the physical and emotional bodies is vital before commencing meditation.

Some tools that may assist re-harmonising physical, emotional, mental and spiritual bodies include pure, clean sounds. Simple tuneful music or an unaccompanied voice can encourage the required stillness within. While repeatedly using the same sounds to re-harmonise yourself, these become an anchor, reinforcing a balanced state each time you hear them.

Years ago I made a hypnosis tape for Amanda which included some positive suggestions and simple background music. She listened to the tape regularly and the music soon became an anchor for the hypnotic state. I noticed this because one evening as I was working, I put on a tape of the same background music. Amanda was sitting reading a book in the room and within ten minutes she was in a hypnotic state as the music acted as a trigger for her. With any positive habit a person wants to establish, such as meditation, repetition is important for success.

Not all meditation attempts are successful but often those in spirit meet you halfway. Personal guides want to connect as much as you want to connect with them. To facilitate a good clear connection it is important to avoid tension, loud discordant music or arguments prior to meditation, as the residual tension can interrupt a calm meditation.

Resolve any immediate issues before meditating, as a peaceful state encourages a clear connection with spirit. If you have issues with others who are not prepared or able to resolve them, it is important to find some resolution within, regardless of what goes on between yourself and others.

Melissa experienced difficulties almost every time she attempted to meditate, because of unresolved issues with her family. During her childhood, Melissa's parents seemed unable to love or value her and each time she tried to meditate she felt anger and resentment regarding her loveless childhood. As soon as she sat down to meditate, resentment descended over her like a heavy blanket, darkening her mood and taking her further away from the inner peace she needed for a clear, effective meditation.

"It's not enough for them to restrict my childhood and flatten my dreams but now they are ruining my meditations. It never stops," she stated bitterly. When she was reminded that she had moved away from her family and was now responsible for how she lived her life and nurtured herself emotionally and spiritually, Melissa resolved to lessen their influence over her.

Before each meditation, she stated aloud that it was okay for her parents not to value her as long as she valued herself. Each time she meditated she reaffirmed her love for herself, which eventually became an anchor for her. With repeated use of this technique, meditation triggered self love and respect. The more she meditated, the more she nurtured herself, gradually unravelling the knots she had tied herself into when attempting to be loved by her parents.

6

Giving Psychic Readings

Continuing to work as a psychic gradually required more discipline than before to do the job. I felt a sense of conflict within, wanting to explore other dimensions while my clients were paying me for information on career prospects or a new car. Throughout personal readings the recorder ran almost continuously, making me conscious of silent periods which might make frustrating listening for the client later on.

'Performance under pressure' is the way I view readings. Readings have their place and purpose but during the two years which followed my meeting with Christine, almost every time I ventured into meditation it was for someone else. These days I prefer to meditate more for personal benefit.

I have observed that the more I meditate the greater my desire to meditate and the less I meditate the more excuses I find to avoid it. The slovenly and undisciplined part of me waits for life to remind me, 'Okay, don't meditate, it's your soul!'

The evolved part of me understands that discipline is required and this part treasures the results, while the lazy part wants to be coaxed into meditating. Connection is important to me. If I meditate without gaining a spiritual connection my concentration is poor, I fidget, my mind wanders and I am more easily distracted by sounds around me.

When I do connect spiritually, I feel inspired, fulfilled and humbled. This is not simply meditation for relaxation. It is a purposeful sojourn into the realms of spirit guides, to avail myself of their knowledge and assistance. It is uplifting. Accompanying clear meditations are calm feelings of peace, completion and stillness which is both unearthly and spiritually familiar.

It's all very well being able to channel the spirit of the late Aunt Mary and Uncle Boverly but if she was a simple farmhand and he was a plasterer during their respective lives, being dead doesn't necessarily enlighten them. She'll still be interested in your garden and he'll more than likely want to discuss your hopeless attempts at plastering your home extensions. If insight is your purpose, then spirit guides may help despite their own imperfections.

Everyone has guides or helpers in spirit and because we don't contact them doesn't mean that they don't exist. On one end of the spectrum is the belief 'If I can't see it and touch it, it doesn't exist' while the other end is a blind faith in 'messages from the other side'.

Seeing is believing but even though I have seen them, I've had my doubts. Ensuring a clear connection before accessing information is essential. I've seen more people in trouble because of taking every 'message' they receive literally, than I've seen people with open minds and level-headed approaches to spirit guides. Sometimes displays of spontaneous clairvoyance have thinly veiled motives, including obvious attempts at scaling the spiritual stepladder in the eyes of others. There is a need to be conscious of ego gratification in these circumstances.

We all have spirit guides but don't take my word for it, prove it for yourself. When you locate them, test them because they'll test you. An example of my testing guides occurred this way.

I was contacting guides on behalf of my partner one evening, as she was having difficulty getting through to her guides. I asked her guides a series of questions on her behalf and although she was content with the answers, I wanted proof that they were indeed her guides, or even guides at all. I could have been imagining the whole thing, for all I knew.

I had explained to her that I wanted to test them and she hadn't objected. As a test I asked them for some information. I sought clear, accurate information regarding her, information which I could not possibly know, about events which occurred prior to our meeting each other, that she had not related to me and that she would remember.

They gave me some information about a boyfriend she had when she was 14 years of age which I relayed to her. I thanked the guides and then concluded my meditation. When I opened my eyes, she was red-faced with embarrassment, saying "I would have told you but it must have slipped my mind." I laughed, knowing that I had proof.

Although it sounds easy, it can be very difficult at times. I can recall many scrappy meditations complete with restlessness, poor reception, zero concentration and nonsensical answers to questions. When this occurs, try again. Spend a few minutes exercising to relax your physical body before trying another meditation or meditate again the following day.

7

Your Spiritual Energy Channel

One way to improve meditation quality is to meditate in the same place. A place that is private and not used by others is perfect. Continuous repetitive meditation in the same spot in your home or garden builds a channel of energy in that spot. A channel is simply a tunnel of light or energy which, through repetitive use, enables a clearer connection with your source or guides. A channel is a corridor of energy surrounding the physical body and running through you from head to toes and beyond. This energy channel connects you to the earth and to the universe and it must be private.

Allowing others to sit in your channel interrupts the flow and also allows that person to tap into your source of energy. This will not help them, as they can only develop spiritually and fulfil their life purpose through tapping the supply of energy in their own channel. Allowing others to siphon off personal spiritual energy may make them dependent upon you and can restrict you from fulfilling your destiny. It is similar to allowing someone else to drive your car while you walk everywhere. You will probably reach your destination but more slowly.

It can upset the flow of the channel if others 'dump' energy into your channel. Dumping is an unconscious releasing of negative energies, emotions or spiritual entities collected. People who are new to spiritual and especially psychic development quickly learn how to 'open up'. This opening of their chakras or energy centres, is positive but it is important to close these energy centres after each meditation. While these energy centres are wide open, they act as a beacon for negativity.

Chakras that are wide open can draw negativity to the individual. This person must then contend with the energies collected, pass them over to spirit or dump them somewhere. Psychic development centres, consulting rooms of counsellors or clairvoyants and churches are some of the most common dumping grounds.

In Thailand and in most of the East, churches or temples often burn incense in great quantities to clear away all the dumped energy. This energy can take the form of grief, desire, hatred, guilt or simple negativity which people collect daily. It may only be a small amount of energy but with many visitors to a temple all bringing small amounts of energy, it soon adds up.

A strong channel is not created instantly but forms gradually over a period of time with regular meditation. It doesn't have to be formed through meditation, for if you work at a desk all day, chances increase that you'll develop a channel where you sit. Channels of light or energy vary in width and intensity. We've recently moved house and I have an office at one end of the house. It's a large room with privacy and yet I prefer to complete my writing here in the living room and I'm building a channel here. Also, I feel that the room I use as an office was previously used as a bedroom and a strong channel is created where a person sleeps at night. This means that a channel created by the previous occupants is still dissolving.

An energy channel can take days or weeks to dissolve. As I don't particularly like the feel of the energy presently in my office, I'm burning incense daily to dissolve this energy. The ambience in the office is gradually improving.

Other methods for cleansing a room of negative energy include the placement of a bowl of water, which is changed daily, in the room to absorb any stagnant energy. As water absorbs negative energy, be careful not to place a fish tank in a room filled with stagnant or negative energy. Try the bowl of water method for a week or two and notice the difference. Keeping a lighted candle in the room helps, as does opening all the windows (weather permitting). Fresh air also clears away the psychic cobwebs.

In situations where negativity has been built up over many years, a solution of cloudy ammonia and warm water can be used in washing the walls, windows and all the surfaces. One or two cups in a bucket of warm water is perfect. Wear rubber gloves if using a sponge to wipe down window ledges, glass or floor tiles to avoid skin irritation. Cloudy ammonia is available in the laundry section of most supermarkets and can be used regularly to ensure that the home or office are energetically clean. If you are out of the house for the day, a radio left playing classical music can assist in breaking up existing stagnant energy in the house.

Building and maintaining a channel is an important process, for a channel can be a sanctuary when life becomes too difficult. Sometimes, when I have been drained by a client or uncentred by life, I return to my channel and restore myself through meditation. Meditation enables me to return to my physical and emotional spiritual centre. I know I am centred when I feel still and calm within. It is similar to recharging emotional and mental reserves by immersing yourself in nature, wading into the ocean or bush walking.

Whenever required to spend time amongst people you would rather not associate with or you find someone dumping negativity your way (through abuse, arguments or even in a casual conversation), you can return to the energy channel and restore personal vitality again. The simple act of meditating in an established channel of energy is like a spiritual tonic.

If a negative situation persists, other measures may be taken to ensure inner peace, so that you are not developing the habit of using this channel as a bandage. Also, when travelling, a temporary channel can be created. Temporary channels are not as powerful as a permanent one but they serve a purpose.

Meditating in your car (i.e. in a shopping centre car park) can have unintended after-effects, as a clear channel tends to lift you to higher spiritual planes which often results in diminished focus in the physical world. This may result in poor concentration when driving, increasing the likelihood of an accident. Even a passenger meditating can affect the driver. An example of this occurred during a 5.00 am drive to the airport with Christine, who decided to enjoy a few minutes meditation. We were nearly killed when Amanda, who was driving and I drifted off with her. We found it necessary to involve both the driver and passengers in conversation to keep everyone focused.

When making a good connection in meditation, i.e. when connecting with a higher guide or a spiritual master, it is usual to keep this strong connection for three days, even out of the meditative state. The result of such a connection is an intense feeling of being centred and an inner calm. Decisions made in this state are easier, thinking is clearer and you are likely to feel more emotionally and spiritually nourished.

Some people who meditate every day maintain a connection with high guides and masters for a week or longer but invariably someone or something in the physical realm breaks that connection. Desires, fears and worry all disrupt the peaceful flow received when forming a strong connection with spirit in meditation.

Attending to personal spiritual needs is like eating one hour before going out to a restaurant. The person who is ravenous is more likely to order hastily and carelessly than the person who is not very hungry. Anyone who is famished and watches a fellow diner question the waiter as to the exact contents of each sauce on the menu can attest to how hunger reduces one's personal standards.

8
Fear and Desire

Fear and desire are two of the greatest stumbling blocks to peaceful spiritual development. Imagine this scenario. You have set aside two hours for a long, restful, rejuvenating meditation. You've drawn the curtains, the telephone answering machine is on and you are not hungry, thirsty nor overly active.

You sit comfortably in your channel or lie down if that is your preferred position and close your eyes. You take a few deep breaths, releasing each breath slowly to relax your physical body in preparation for meditation once again.

Assume that you have taken care of all the physical or practical concerns which might disturb you. All that is left to balance are the mental and emotional issues. At this point you're hoping that the mental or emotional factors will not distract or disturb you. You might anticipate that once you have connected clearly, these concerns will fade away, appearing foolish or diminished.

Perhaps you are not so fortunate today. You take three deep breaths, ask for protection on all levels (physical, mental and spiritual) three times, and gently slip away as you feel the light entering the top of your head and filling your entire body. Each and every cell, every molecule is tingling with life as a result of this connection with spirit. "The mortgage," you think, "Is it due tomorrow or next Thursday? Now let's see. When did I pay it last? Yes, it is due tomorrow if my calculations are correct. Where will I get that much money from anyway?" This thought can trigger fear about not having enough.

"How much money would actually be enough?" you find yourself thinking. At the very least I require a leather chesterfield lounge, a new bookcase, a trip to Canada to a native Indian reservation, to feel that I have enough to be satisfied. Oh, and a new car, house, job, haircut and suntan.

Where is that spiritual connection now? Fears about not forming a solid connection, not progressing quickly spiritually, wasting your time with this 'spiritual stuff' while there are places to see and money to be made and weight to lose, take you away from the present into the past and the future.

It is possible to prevent this from happening. You might fulfil all of your desires and resolve your fears by earning enough money to have everything you desire. You might resolve fears through understanding them, facing them or ignoring them but doing this is likely to cost you most of your remaining years, when all you set out to do was to meditate for an hour.

Fears and desires have a habit of sneaking up on you, until realising that 25 minutes have elapsed and you are still thinking about financial matters instead of meditating. A relaxing meditation? You'll probably need a rest after that

Fig 1. The Energy Channel (a path of spiritual energy which flows through us all).

one and all the while you've been filling your channel with your fears and desires so that next time you sit there, you may take over where you left off. Good meditations are the result of discipline, technique and familiarity.

Without being paranoid about thoughts while in your meditation space, an individual is free to indulge personal fears and worries anywhere and at any time. It is not necessary to use this time and place for them.

A simple technique to deal with worrying thoughts requires a small box, some note paper, a pen and a little discipline. This technique is suggested by Robert A. Monroe in his book Journeys Out of the Body. Select a box that can be closed completely. A hat box, shoe box or even a cereal box will suffice. If feeling creative, cover it in wrapping or plain paper.

A few minutes before sitting in your channel for meditation, reflect and ask yourself the following: "Do I presently have any fears or desires that must be dealt with immediately?" If so, deal with them if possible. The energy spent in worrying about them can be better spent in creative or spiritual pursuits when resolving these issues.

Then ask yourself, "Do I have any desires, fears or worries that I can safely put aside until after my meditation?" If this is so, write these things down on a piece of notepaper, reminding yourself as you do this that worry solves no problem. Now fold the notepaper and place it inside the box. Once you have done this, dismiss all thoughts of the list.

If thoughts of those issues arise, cancel them (visualise a red 'Cancelled' stamp mark across the issue of concern) until a more appropriate time, after the meditation. Upon completion of the meditation, open your box and retrieve the list. Re-read it and you may be surprised to notice that some issues on the list will no longer concern you. The list can be shredded or burned to ensure privacy.

This box can be used for occasions other than meditation and when well versed with this technique, you can create a box in your mind and mentally complete the technique. It's best to complete this box technique physically for the first ten times, as re-reading fears and worries can have the effect of clarifying actual concerns.

I am presently writing this on a sandy beach, with 50 or 60 surfers in view. They are enthusiastically pursuing almost every wave and I am inspired to want to join them. Another part of me, however, has been saying 'You should be at home. Working hard and earning money.' As my inner voice is getting in the way of my writing, I've put the 'shoulds' in a box in my mind so that I can get on with writing.

To take the box idea a little further, it's possible to place worries, fears and desires into it all day and retrieve them at night, not just prior to going to sleep, as this can result in sleepless nights. This is not a recipe for avoidance or denial. It is about disciplining the mind and realising that fears, desires and worries need not control you. You can control them. If you are still uneasy after having written the list and placed it into the box, remove the list and re-read it. Has something been omitted from the list? If so, add it.

When satisfied that the list is complete, ask yourself this question: 'When I die and leave this life behind me; when I step into spirit and undertake different challenges, will these current concerns make any difference then?'

It is necessary occasionally to re-glimpse the big picture. Put into daily terms, this is one day in around 7,300 if you live 20 years.

One day in over 10,950 if you live 30 years.

In over 18,250 if you live 50 years.

In over 23,725 if you live 65 years.

In over 29,200 if you live 80 years.

How many of these days have been spent worrying about exactly the same things you choose to worry about today? How many more days will you worry about these and other issues? This is one day, in one week, in one month, in one year, in one lifetime. With this in mind, is it so important if you miss one car payment, put off some chores, or fail to live up to somebody's expectations?

This isn't to deny the importance of life in the moment but suggesting that the knowledge you take with you is more important than becoming bogged down in the material world. It is like the surfers before me in the water. If they miss a wave they wait and prepare for the next one.

The box technique is simply the beginning. When meditating regularly and enjoying a good connection with spirit, fears subside and desires diminish with the realisation that the only lasting fulfilment is not physical but spiritual. Desiring the transient experiences of the physical usually only brings temporary fulfilment.

Sometimes anxiety is the result of comparison, e.g. I work harder than she does, yet she earns more than I earn. Sometimes, instead of resentment, comparisons trigger feelings of guilt. I sit on the beach writing, while others work 9-5 somewhere. Comparisons don't work. There is always someone better or worse off than you are presently.

It's possible that fear is the single greatest barrier to all growth and learning for human beings. Can you recall a time when you attempted to do or to learn something when you were filled with fear? Fear can shrink confidence and abilities.

The opposite to love is not hatred, it is fear. Fear is the basis of many crimes or huge military budgets and is often present as a barrier to intimacy. Fear can stop us from doing what is truly in our hearts. When the time comes to step away from life and our present physical bodies, will there be any regrets regarding things we did not do?

If we do have regrets, will they be for what we did or for what we failed to do? If you had attempted everything you desired—who would you be now? Where would you be now? Who might be beside you now?

When Jackson was 12 years of age he was given the opportunity to spend 14 days in Fiji with a school group. With one year to save for the trip he set out working hard for the money required. Jackson earned $1.50 each week for washing the clothes for the family of eight, and saved slowly. An aunt generously agreed to make up any shortfall in costs if he saved up until the departure date.

As the month of departure drew closer Jackson began to fear the trip. He'd never been out of his home town before and this trip was to a foreign country. Every time he thought about it, Jackson felt sick. With regular work and odd jobs he had managed to save around $285. The weeks were closing in on the final departure date and he was becoming paralysed with fear. His family repeatedly pointed out the pitfalls of other countries and travel in general, proving themselves to be excellent fear builders.

Jackson was afraid to go. In fact, staying at home in familiar surroundings was becoming more and more appealing. Instead of exploring these fears (he was only 13 years old) and dealing with them, Jackson gave into these fears and sabotaged his trip.

Two weeks before he had to pay for the travel he ventured out and spent all of his savings on an exquisite reclining chair. His friends and family couldn't believe it. It was a bizarre act to them but to Jackson it was reassurance that he didn't have to go anywhere. It was possible to sit still and not have to face his fears. In fact, he could sit still in the comfort of his new chair and not have to go forward into his life. All of us have limits, small and large. Many of these limits are set by the fear of what might lie beyond them. Fear has its uses though— most people wouldn't dive from a 30-metre cliff into a raging sea if they can't swim. However, breaking into a sweat, fearing for survival and wanting to be physically sick upon entering your supervisor's office may indicate that fear is crippling you.

Fear is a necessary part of excitement. All adventure requires an element of fear. I recall my first parachute jump. I was sick with fear on the flight up and the ten-minute journey seemed like three weeks. The only consolation was that the same expression appeared on the faces of my three fellow first-timers.

The rush of the wind, the sudden silence on the fall earthward and my decision that if I was about to die I might as well have a good view of the scene of my demise, stays with me clearly to this day. I was terrified but I have to admit that it was also an exhilarating experience. Had I seen the same view from an armchair I may have missed some of the excitement because of not experiencing the fear.

Desire is a part of life and outer desires can usually be traced to deeper, more fundamental desires. During a course exercise to identify the fundamental desire behind the outer desire, the process is centred around a fundamental question "And what would you get from having that?"

Leo volunteered to complete the exercise in front of the group. I asked him the question repeatedly and It went something like this:

Paul: What is it that you desire?

Leo: Money. Lots of money.

P: What would you get from having that?

L: Control of my life.

P: Control. And when you have control, what would you get from having that?

L: Independence.

P: And what would you get from having independence?

L: I could be free from others' demands.

P: And what would you get from that freedom?

L: Time to pursue my studies.

P: And what would you get from pursuing your studies?

L: Knowledge.

P: And what would you get from having knowledge?

L: Spiritual understanding.

P: And what would you gain from spiritual understanding?

L: Stillness.

P: And what would you gain from that stillness?

L: Inner peace.

P: So inner peace is your real need and making a great deal of money is the path you have chosen to gain inner peace.

L: Yes, I guess it is.

P: Is making money the only path to inner peace?

L: No.

P: Can you suggest one or more other possible paths you could take to inner peace?

L: Meditation. Restructuring my time to read and study more.

Leo's surface desire was for money, yet when delving deeper, we discovered that his deeper desire was actually for inner peace.

When this exercise was completed I asked Jacinta if wealth had brought her inner peace and she shook her head, saying "I have a big house and gardens and a boatshed but it all requires maintenance and it all costs money. You wouldn't believe the land tax I paid last week."

To emphasise the point, I asked Jacinta how long it took to clean her enormous house.

"It takes two cleaners eight hours each week to keep it clean. That's 16 hours of cleaning each week."

Instead of underlining the costs of maintenance, it seemed to arouse curiosity in some of the students. They wanted to see a house which took 16 hours to clean. I suggested that perhaps the people who most enjoyed Jacinta's house were her guests. She agreed. She then explained that she was looking forward to selling the house and moving somewhere smaller. I proposed that she exchange houses with Leo. He was immediately enthusiastic with the prospect.

9
Karma

I received a phone call from a friend tonight, confirming a tarot reading I had given to a friend of hers several years ago. In the reading the woman asked me if she might see her son again. He had left home and cut off contact with her, preferring to live with his father. Apparently I had told her that the boy would return of his own accord in three years. Now, at 17 years of age, he has just returned to her. I felt good that I might have given her some hope in her time of need.

Later I returned a call from a man who had left a message on my answering machine. He said that he'd heard me on radio being interviewed about locating the body of a murdered woman. I assured him that it was not me, as I avoid locating bodies. He went on to explain that his 16-year-old son had been missing for three days, disappearing after separating from his girlfriend. My stomach tightened while he spoke, as I felt his link into my navel chakra immediately. I explained to him that I didn't give readings about missing persons because those asking are often filled with desire for one result, reunion and as emotion increases, accuracy decreases. "Oh, my wife and I are over the worst of it now," he explained but I was unconvinced. "I have a son, and if he was missing, I couldn't give up hoping that he would be found," I said, without judgement.

I gave him the name of a spiritual medium with a good reputation and told him that I would contact him if I had any news of the boy. Afterwards I experienced a nagging fear for the boy and guilt that I had not helped the man in his desperate time. I walked to my office and shuffled my tarot cards. I asked question after question to find something positive to tell the boy's father but the outlook only became more gloomy. 'Will that man see his son again by Tuesday?' No. 'Will that man see his son again by Thursday?' No. 'Friday?' No. 'Will that man see his son alive again?' No. 'Is the boy in question still alive?' Yes but only just.

At this point I felt ill. Awful thoughts ran through my mind. Was the boy in hospital? In a drug-induced state, or lying in a park somewhere? Was the boy held against his will by a person or persons unknown? How could I not tell the boy's father? I didn't want to tell him anything, as I was becoming increasingly emotional and accuracy was decreasing accordingly.

'What is the lesson for me in this?' I asked the cards. To meditate, came the reply. After several minutes spent debating whether to phone several people for some support around this, I sat still and began to meditate. The news wasn't good. Through spirit guides I was told that the boy was still alive but that he'd die soon and that the parents would never see the body.

When I asked if I should alert the parents and help them to trace the boy, I was told that I would be too late. I was also told that I'd only be exposed to energies and situations which would not benefit me in the long term.

I argued that it was right to do whatever possible to help them because if I didn't, my own boy might one day disappear without trace, as a lesson to me that I should have helped them. They explained that it was not my place to interfere and that by doing so the outcome would not change and the spiritual progress of the parents and myself would be hindered.

After the meditation I still couldn't sit comfortably with this, so I phoned Christine in London. I explained the situation to her and she confirmed what I had been told. She explained that a similar situation had been the reason she gave up reading for others. She told me about a small boy called Peter, who had been murdered several years ago. Peter's spirit appeared to her asking if she would guide the authorities to where he had been buried on a moor.

The killer, who was already serving a term for other murders, was released to assist the police trace three undiscovered bodies. It was to no avail. Apparently the moors had grown and changed since the deed and the search party was unable to locate the bodies.

I asked Christine if she assisted with the search. "No. The spirit of that boy wanted me to end the suffering of his parents but I knew that I would also be ending their opportunity to grow spiritually through the suffering."

"So where do you draw the line?" I asked.

"The more you work with spirit, the less you seek to interfere with the soul's journeys of others," she replied.

I felt unnerved. I have great respect for Christine, yet still have a fear that perhaps I could have stopped the destruction of a 16-year-old boy's life. Instead, I sit here typing away my guilt and searching for a rationalisation to quieten my mind.

To be awaiting a premature death but hoping that your parents might find you is natural. To think that it was not your karma to be saved, despite some person somewhere knowing of your whereabouts, means that you would face death with your trust in the human race ruined. I didn't know where the boy actually was or how to find him but still felt helpless at not being able to assist.

My question is "How can I live with myself if I sit by and do nothing?" My rational mind tells me that I have given the boy's father the name of a reliable medium, who may help him, if help is to be given.

It's an old dilemma. I love the temptation of working with spirit and evolving spiritually but I occasionally forget the price that is extracted in return. I forget all the experiences and habits I'll need to rescind to progress.

These include simple joys I have grown to enjoy over the years, such as a glass of champagne at sunset when on holidays or a few glasses of cider by a log fire in a pub during a cold winter's weekend. In time the price increases to include being confronted with my own inadequacies soon after I notice them in others.

The desire for possessions also brings its own responsibilities. The more possessions a person has, the more there is to maintain. Each individual has a list of personal effects that are essential. Having spent six months living in London without many of the comforts we believed were essential, we developed a policy when it came to household effects: "We are not here for long, so if you can't see it around the house, we don't need it."

I lived in the same clothes almost every day and didn't care what others thought of me. I reasoned that I was only passing through. When I returned home to Australia and all my other clothes, I still preferred living with a limited choice of outfits. Having returned, I began to develop more awareness of what others thought of me. When I felt that I was becoming too concerned about the opinions of others I reminded myself that, in spiritual terms, I am only passing through. My soul has this body for this incarnation and although I am attached to it, I am only passing through and eventually my soul will leave my body behind.

It occurred to me one day that if I have a desire that is so entrenched that I cannot release it, such as the desire for achievement, I will have to go out and fulfil it. It will be essential to go out and have or become what I desire, before releasing it. If I don't do so, all the un-faced fears and unfulfilled desires will only call me back onto this earthly plane again. Earth is a place to work out personal desires and then to release them. Fears and desires prevent people from visiting the realms in meditation and after physical death these unresolved fears and desires require more physical lifetimes to be resolved.

Buddha is an example of someone who worked out his desires, particularly lust, in his early years. It was only after tiring of the physical pleasures and the impermanence of physical satisfaction that Buddha released those desires which enslaved him.

"But what would become of the world if everyone went out and did exactly what they wanted to do?" a friend asked me one day. It is a highly unlikely prospect, for there are plenty of people who vehemently deny their desires.

Some traditional philosophies believe that thinking about a 'wrong action' is almost as bad as doing the deed. This is perhaps partly correct, because thoughts set up energy patterns. Every thought has a subtle effect.

To prove how the thoughts of one person can affect another, there is a simple experiment. Next time you are sitting in a train or on a bus among strangers, direct your thoughts toward someone and mentally say to them 'Scratch your nose. It's very itchy. It would feel very good to scraaaatch your nose.'

If you receive no response, try again in a minute or so. Become aware of others around you as, although the person you have directed your thoughts to does not respond, sometimes someone else will. When you have a response, suggest that they scratch an ear or an eyebrow. When you have proved that this works, thank them silently and withdraw.

This exercise involves trespassing upon the aura or energy field of another person, so once you have proven that this can be done, leave it alone. If you persist, you have no right to feel violated or unfairly treated when others trespass upon you and your energy field.

This technique doesn't require special power of force. Simple instructions, clearly and silently given, repeated several times if necessary, are all that are required. This demonstrates how the thoughts of one person affect another. Thoughts have effects, however subtle. If your thoughts can affect someone you have never spoken to, think about they are affecting you every minute of every day of your life. What we repeatedly think, we eventually become.

It's possible to gradually change personal attitudes, from negative or fearful thoughts to serene or more positive contemplations by catching yourself when your mind is focussed on negativity. Instead of criticising yourself, simply steer your thinking away from angry or fearful thoughts towards more positive possibilities. Worry can become a negative habit that you can train yourself out of with regular practice and vigilance. To do this effectively, it is necessary to catch yourself when engaging in negative thoughts or worry and redirect your thoughts.

If you are repetitively worrying about money without doing anything to change your circumstances, you might benefit from noticing each time thoughts turn to personal finances and redirecting your thoughts towards more positive areas of your life. If each time you think about personal finances your body becomes tense, then positive thoughts about your garden, a creative project or a good friend may help you to avoid this physical stress.

For more than a year Angela spent five to ten minutes at the end of each day being grateful for all that she had received that day. She took time to notice how often life supported her in a range of smaller ways, such as an email from a friend, a note on the fridge from her son or a sunny afternoon outside the window.

Gradually this habit reduced the effects of worrying about possible impending disasters and her stress levels subsided. She began to see opportunities where she had once only perceived threats. She didn't take every opportunity around her but felt more support by life for having these choices. When a more senior position was advertised in her company Angela applied for it and was offered the job. Previously she had talked herself out of applying for better positions and felt frustrated at remaining on her limited income.

10
Psychic Energy Cords

Invisible cords of psychic energy pass between friends, family and work colleagues every day. These cords are conduits for communication. Cords can also be used for information retrieval. During a radio interview recently I was giving a clairvoyant reading to a caller. I had about two minutes to retrieve accurate information, which she could confirm to demonstrate the reading process. I sent a psychic cord down the line and retrieved information about her husband.

"I have a tall, red-headed man in my mind. He's thin, with curly hair and he works with computers. Not personal computers but the old mainframe type. I didn't know mainframes still existed," I said.

"Yes, that's my husband you're describing," she replied and within seconds the telephone switchboard lit up with callers trying to get through. After the interview I cut the cords to each caller. A cord cutting procedure is outlined in chapter 19.

A simpler example is when visiting a friend who is ill or depressed. You walk away exhausted, although not having done anything to obviously deplete your energy. If people around you want a little (or a lot) of the stillness and peace you've found through meditation, they'll cord you unconsciously. This is done by sending out a cord or cords of energy to you, usually via one of your chakras and form a link to you. Through these cords they can siphon off some of your light or energy, leaving you depleted in that area of your body.

Before rushing out and pointing a finger at people, remember that they are probably unaware of what they are doing. Their spiritual energy is only responding to their desires. Before casting the first stone, it is possible that you have corded others through your own desires.

The sort of occasions that set up the desire for cords to be sent out include many daily situations. Those times when you think to yourself 'I wish he'd telephone me!' you send a cord out to him. Whether he responds to your cord usually depends upon how sensitive he is to you or what is going on with him at that time.

A man sees an attractive woman at the beach. He runs his eyes over her and feels a trace of desire. He cords her. This cord remains in place for a few days then fades away if the desire is not acted upon. A driver appears out of a side street and pushes into traffic in front of you in a dangerous manner. You become angry and shout something aloud to him. Although your windows are closed and you cannot be heard by the driver, you cord him through personal intentions.

A friend telephones for some advice regarding a personal problem. She desires your input to restore her to balance and in doing so she cords you. People involved in careers such as counselling, social work or clairvoyance, where psychic cords are unceasingly likely to be formed, need to take measures to cut existing cords regularly. Simple steps to break cords include swimming or immersing yourself in water such as the sea a river or a salt water swimming pool. Even taking a bath severs minor cords.

With all the cords you've collected or made in the past month, how high can you expect to soar in meditation? How can you clearly communicate with your spirit guides if you are choked up with cords? Spiritual energy works along similar lines to electrical energy. If there are too many psychic cords to others, you quickly lose vitality.

In extreme situations, people depleted by too many psychic cords become overloaded and collapse, physically or emotionally. It is akin to plugging too many appliances into one power point. It's not surprising that the burn-out rate for individuals in the counselling professions is high. There are a few alternatives for those long-term helpers, if they wish to reduce their number of psychic cords.

They can:

- Deal with their cords regularly through daily meditation (see Chapter 19, Cutting Cords).
- Swim each day.
- Distance themselves from their clients and their clients' needs.
- Teach clients how to become more self-sufficient.
- Give up and pursue a profession that involves less needy clients.

Clairvoyants actively cord clients for information. Cords are usually like a two way street. Although a psychic may send out a cord to a client for details about that person's life, there is nothing to stop the client's desires draining the psychic during and after the reading takes place.

Clairvoyants may cord clients to gain information about friends and loved ones. People who regularly consult clairvoyants may have experienced a reading where the clairvoyant focussed on a friend or a partner more than the client. This occurs when the clairvoyant linked in psychically. He or she didn't link into the client but into a cord connecting the client with their friend or partner. Effectively the clairvoyant was linking into a cord to the client's friend.

This sometimes demonstrates that the clairvoyant is not precise enough in differentiating between links. When consulting a clairvoyant, you are giving permission to link into you for the information you desire. Problems may arise when you leave, if the clairvoyant does not dissolve the cord to you. Most clairvoyants cut cords at the end of each working day or once a week. Some clairvoyants do not consciously know what they're doing in this regard and may consider their abilities a 'gift' and not a skill that needs discipline like any other ability. It's no different from a medical practitioner washing her hands and cleansing her tools between patients.

To understand energy cords, assume for a moment that the physical body is composed of energy in various forms and vibrating at different frequencies. The human body has physical limits and boundaries that are clearly visible. Surrounding the physical body is an emotional body that resembles the physical body but this body expands or contracts according to the emotions experienced at the time. Then there is a mental body, composed of even finer, invisible energy. While the emotional and mental bodies surrounding the physical body do not correspond to the limitations of the physical body, they do have their own limitations.

Some people exercise great discipline with their physical bodies: tanning, exercising, training and tuning them. Others display a complete lack of discipline with their bodies. Both overweight and underweight bodies can be undisciplined.

As we vary in our physical bodies, it is natural to expect that we vary in our emotional and mental bodies. However, it is not necessarily accurate to assume that someone who has an unbalanced physical body has an unhealthy emotional, mental or spiritual body. Some people work hard to achieve a healthy physical body while ignoring their emotional and mental needs. Conversely, some spiritual teachers and students are not as disciplined with their emotional, mental and physical bodies as they are with their spiritual forms.

We each have a physical, emotional, mental and spiritual body to maintain. The energies of these bodies are continuously interacting with each other. The doorways to these finer energies are through the seven chakras of the physical body. The senses or spiritual awareness escapes through these chakras (see Fig 3), e.g. if a man feels a sexual attraction for a woman, his sense escapes through his base chakra or navel, forming a cord to that woman.

Maintaining the physical body requires good food, clean water or liquids, oxygen, sunshine, regular exercise and sleep. Maintaining emotional balance requires that we replenish ourselves emotionally with uplifting emotional input, such as music, laughter, the scent of fresh flowers or whatever is personally emotionally fulfilling. It also involves avoiding stress or trauma, so that the sadness, loss, grief, worry or fear are balanced with joy, excitement, peace, stillness, laughter and love.

With careful reflection and planning it's possible to gradually balance stress with inner peace, feelings of loss with acceptance, grief with joy, worry with anticipation, fear with confidence, sadness with laughter, bitterness with compassion and anger with goodwill.

Psychic cords from others can uncentre a person. When James ended a relationship with Annette he could not get her out of his mind. Each time he thought of Annette, James experienced a sense of loss and confusion common to many who have recently separated.

In energetic terms, each time James thought of Annette he felt empty because he had left many parts of himself behind with Annette. Resolution of issues with her, led to the recovery of some of those parts of himself and meditation helped him recover the rest.

It can be difficult for people who leave relationships without any intention of resolving outstanding issues, as the energetic parts of themselves they leave behind are not present in their next relationships. If James was to have several deep relationships without any resolution or reconnection to those lost parts of himself, he might eventually be referred to as the man formerly known as James. Perhaps for this reason poets are right when they suggest that there is nothing quite like the first love.

Learning to recognise the symptoms of being uncentred is the first step to remaining centred for most of the day. Shelley was addicted to chocolate when she felt emotionally empty. Several times each week she noticed a half-eaten Toblerone in her hand with no recollection of buying it. Shelley entered an altered state, where she needed to purchase a chocolate bar and eat half of it before feeling good enough to regain awareness of her physical body and her surroundings.

After a day of clairvoyant readings I sometimes feel empty in my belly and if I don't consciously sit for a while out in the garden or meditate and fill the second chakra with light, I end up ravenously devouring sweet food. This is an attempt to restore the balance of energy but it is not the most effective method. The quickest method is to meditate.

To ensure long-term balance I need to regularly cleanse myself and the environment deeply, reduce the number of clairvoyant readings I give or cease giving personal readings to clients. Maintaining mental balance requires nourishing the mind with new ideas and concepts, fresh challenges or tasks, and information. Adding space for the mind to rest and to be at peace allows the mind can process what it has received.

Maintaining the spirit requires a respectful treatment of each level. This means physical, emotional and mental nourishment is needed to maintain a spiritually positive outlook. Regular exercise balances the physical body while positive social and emotional input from others improves emotional balance. Fresh concepts and ideas help maintain mental balance while meditation, reflection or prayer upon spiritual purpose maybe necessary for spiritual balance.

The spirit is not usually enamoured with life on the physical plane because the energies of everyday life are too heavy and restrictive. These limitations include time, gravity and temperature. The spirit also feels restricted by turbulent emotions and emotional and physical desires. Residing in a healthy, balanced body enables the spirit to embrace its lesson this lifetime. When polluting the spirit, you are depleting yourself spiritually. If continuing to pollute or destroy your physical, emotional or mental needs, your spirit will exit, in search of nourishment. Traces of yourself can remain with friends, family members, past partners or in environments which serve as sanctuaries for your spiritual energy if it is not being nourished where it belongs – with you.

Continuous inner hunger resulting from spiritual emptiness or a lack of spiritual purpose can be a sign that part of the spirit has left the physical body. Feeling empty despite having personal needs met on other levels can suggest spiritual deprivation. Sometimes, to compensate for spiritual hunger there is a tendency to become addictive or compulsive on the other levels. Emotional obsession, addiction to drugs and alcohol and food or a compulsion to make intellectual sense of life, can be the result of spiritual depletion or spiritual departure. In simple terms, you are your own jailer but you have the key to set yourself spiritually free.

Allowing emotional and mental energies to resemble a jumble sale discourages peaceful spiritual cohabitation. Accidents or severe illnesses may also trigger a flight of the senses. This occurred with a colleague of mine many years ago, who several years before had lost some of his physical, emotional and mental awareness due to an accident.

When I met William he struck me as being an absent-minded professor. A brilliant man and a well-respected healer but he was somehow not quite present in his physical body or in his day-to-day life. It was as though a part of William had walked away. I dismissed it as being his way, until he asked to trade a reading for a healing session. It was during the reading that the problem emerged. I entered meditation for the latter part of the reading, immediately becoming aware of the spirit of a drunken Scotsman standing behind me. This man in spirit was shouting, as though he was watching a horserace.

"Tell 'im to go back, for Christ's sake."

"Back where?" I asked.

"Back to Cornwall, o' course!"

"Why Cornwall?"

"Cause he's left some'ing behind."

I hesitated to say anything to William, as I'd never before been told anything by someone in spirit who was obviously drunk.

"Just tell 'im for Christ's sake. 'e'll know," the man in spirit finished. I concluded the meditation after answering some of William's career questions and in passing, I asked if he had ever lived in Cornwall.

"No. Why do you ask?"

"Well it's probably nothing but I had this drunken Scotsman behind me, yelling and shouting about you having to go back to Cornwall, to collect something you've left behind."

"Well, it's a strange story," he began. "I stayed down there on holiday about seven or eight years ago. Late one night, after the village pub closed, I was walking along a lane when I was hit by a passing truck and knocked unconscious. I lay in the road all night, and was discovered the following morning and rushed to hospital for treatment."

I wondered to myself what on earth he could have left behind but soon I was swept up into my other clients for the day. A conversation with Christine a few days later answered the question. We were discussing spirit bodies and I mentioned this colleague and his story. Christine 'linked in', sent out a psychic cord via me to William for the purpose of gathering information and confirmed that he had left several spirit bodies behind in Cornwall due to the shock and trauma of the incident.

It was two weeks before we shared a shift at the healing centre and I explained to him what Christine had told me and he nodded excitedly. A week after his reading he had left London and returned to Cornwall to the

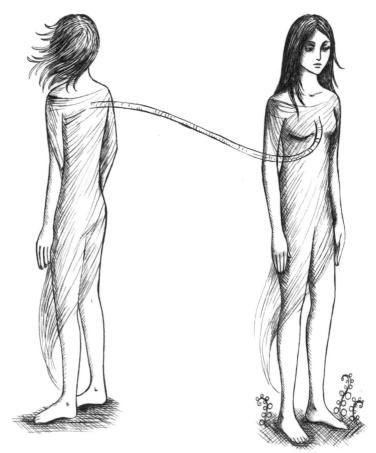

*Fig 2. Psychic
Energy Cords*

scene of the accident. He spent about an hour there in silence, gathering himself and his thoughts.

He said that since that day he had felt somehow more complete. I observed him closely throughout our conversation and noticed that he was much more present with me that I had ever seen him before. Gone was the absent-minded professor; this man was fully present in his physical body and connected to his environment. When people are fully present they are described as having presence.

Shock, illness, or a continual lack of nourishment on a spiritual plane can place added stress upon the senses, which makes it more difficult for personal awareness to remain in the physical body. Awareness naturally leaves the physical body occasionally but it can become reluctant to return for many reasons, including a lack of spiritual nourishment.

An indication of lack of presence or inner awareness is a vacant look in the eyes of the person, along with a lack of presence in the physical body. This individual seems less alive somehow. This is distinct from a temporary lack of presence when a person is day-dreaming. People experiencing prolonged spiritual depletion never seem quite present when in conversation, even when discussing passionate subjects.

Generally several meetings or conversations are required to establish this with any degree of certainty. There are some people who, although surviving adequately, are walking about incomplete. It is their own responsibility and no one is obliged to make them whole. They may perceive this help as interference.

There are karmic implications involved in helping others see that they are not whole. Perhaps the biblical story of Adam and Eve illustrates this. There is a version of events that suggests that Eve opened Adam's eyes to his spiritual purpose. Eve enlightened Adam about his incompleteness and neither Adam nor history has thanked her for it. The safety net for trying to help others by explaining the concepts in this book is that those who are not whole may regard these concepts as pure fantasy.

Awareness of spirit bodies or senses, allows the choice of being responsible for them and it is possible to nourish the senses and encourage

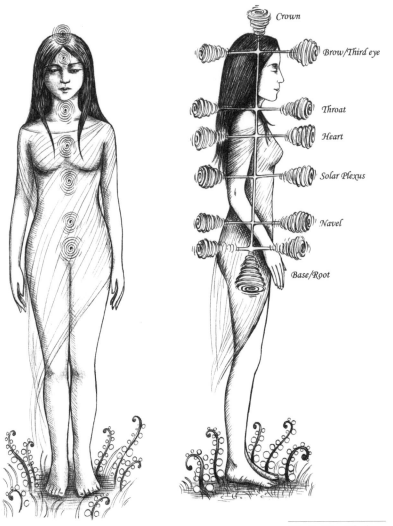

Crown

Brow/Third eye

Throat

Heart

Solar Plexus

Navel

Base/Root

Fig 3. The Chakras

them to stay. Reclaiming the senses is as important as maintaining them and re-balancing them regularly. Regular meditation helps to re-balance and realign emotional, mental and spiritual bodies.

Having reclaimed personal senses through meditation, it is possible to proceed to the next step, of reclaiming spiritual vision. There is a saying attributed to Jesus that states 'When your eye is single, your whole body will be full of light,' which means that when operating from the third eye or brow chakra, you will be full of spiritual light. This is what spiritual masters do. Clarity is possible because of being centred and not distracted by cords or desires.

This spiritual vision is sometimes referred to as 'second sight' or psychic vision. Reclaiming spiritual vision is another powerful step towards spiritual balance and growth. Accompanying this second sight are responsibilities but this sight enables each individual to rise above obstacles and avoid actions that may be harmful long term.

Spiritual vision or the ability to see spirit bodies and psychic energy cords, also allows one to rise above ignorance and superstition. It is possible to enhance spiritual development by regular meditation that channels universal light and love, replenishing the spirit. This is partly what sleep does. While the physical body is asleep, the spirit has an opportunity to step out and to enjoy temporary freedom from the constraints imposed by the physical body. These restraints include gravity, temperature, time, etc. During sleep the spirit replenishes itself before another day of physical reality.

Without regular meditation or replenishment of the spirit, what level of inner peace and fulfillment can one expect? What use is physical, emotional and mental wealth if you are spiritually impoverished? At first, meditation often requires great discipline. Many initial attempts are marked by fidgeting, restlessness and mental distractions. Focusing upon a lighted candle may counteract the mind's tendency to wander and helps still the body.

Some beginners experience many days of poor or average meditations before feeling a spiritual connection during the process. When this spiritual connection is finally experienced, it feels like a rush of light or energy throughout the body. Sometimes the excitement weakens or severs this delicate connection. The act of repeatedly sitting and meditating is a signal of personal commitment to spiritual development and those in spirit may encourage you with signs or assistance, through dreams or during meditations. Eventually your emotional and mental energies align with your spirit, even if only temporarily and you become centered, peaceful and at one with yourself.

The energy is often so pure that you may laugh or cry with joy. It is possible to experience a flood of energy after centering yourself, that is worth the effort. Once achieving this centeredness, it is relatively easy to find it again in subsequent meditations because you have a memory of what it feels like. You are aligning yourself to better channel your rightful spiritual energy. Using a river as a metaphor for spiritual energy, the following story illustrates the alignment procedure.

A small boy grew up beside a wide, swiftly flowing river. His family used the river to wash, to irrigate their crops and to provide them with fish. When he became a man he ventured away from the river, inland. The further he went, the drier and more barren the land became.

Eventually he reached a point where very little grew on the dry, dusty earth and he became weak with hunger and thirst. He stumbled for days across the desolated terrain, confused and exhausted. Eventually he collapsed and awoke beside a campfire.

The people who found him explained that he could accompany them to the next river, and then it was possible for him to make his way around the country by following the water course. After several weeks the group arrived at the river, where they bade him goodbye. This time he stayed close to the water's edge and soon his health was completely restored. As he travelled, he became strong and knowledgeable. He travelled slowly, often spending days or weeks in small villages along the river's edge.

One day, after months of slow progress through the thick jungles that crowded along the water's edge, he came upon a tiny cluster of simple houses that looked familiar. He had come home to his birthplace, having discovered that the river is truly the source of life. Sinking into the arms of family and friends, he was overjoyed at the prospect of living in his birthplace again.

11

Psychic Cords to the Chakras

To understand energy cords it is important to become familiar with the chakras, or energy centres of the body. Chakra is an ancient Sanskrit word meaning wheel or disc. The chakras of the body are energy centres where the spirit body connects with the physical body.

There are seven main chakras in the human body, aligned up the spine from the base to just above the head (see Fig 3). There are also smaller chakras in the hands and feet, but they are less significant for our purposes.

The first or base chakra is at the base of the spine in men and between the ovaries in women. This is the only chakra which differs in placement according to gender. The second or navel chakra is just below the navel. The third or power centre chakra is located at the solar plexus. The fourth or heart chakra is located at the centre of the chest at the level of the heart.

The fifth or throat chakra is located in the centre of the throat and the sixth or third eye chakra is located in the centre of the forehead, between the eyebrows. The seventh or crown chakra is found at the top of the head and extends a little above the head.

These chakras correspond with physical glands in the body and the seven colours of the rainbow are ascribed to them, with red for the base chakra, orange for the navel chakra, yellow for the power centre, green for the heart chakra, blue for the throat chakra, indigo for the brow or third eye chakra and violet for the crown chakra.

When the chakras are balanced, which requires vigilance, then comes the second part of the challenge. When an individual regularly meditates, connecting with and recharging the inner spirit, this person becomes a light, a beacon in the darkness. Other people, particularly those who are striving to develop spiritually may want some of this energy. It is not necessarily a conscious wanting but it is a desire. They send cords to sample some of this newfound energy. Most people are unconscious of the cords they send to others.

Psychic cords vary in strength and intensity, according to the amount of desire that created them in the first place. A momentary desire for someone sets up a psychic cord between you and that person, which dissipates or fades away in three days if it is not reinforced. A psychic cord between two relationship partners who have been together for several years is likely to take a long time to be broken, if it can be broken at all in this lifetime. If the two partners have created some karma requiring resolution, they may have cords between them for the rest of their lives.

When we die, it is these psychic cords we have with others, that prevents us being able to return home, to our place of spiritual origin. If we have resolved all of our karma, and we have no psychic cords to others when we die, we are free to travel home with the assistance of our masters in spirit.

It is no accident that a person feels better when resolving an outstanding problem with another person. This allows more energy to devote to true purpose or simply to day-to-day plans. As most people are unlikely to resolve all personal karma this lifetime, it is important to limit the number of new cords created and resolve some of the current cords.

Some clairvoyants are unaware that they are cording a client to retrieve information. These cords usually don't last very long (a few days to a few weeks) but occasionally the clairvoyant releases negative energy into a client's energy field when sending out a cord to an individual. This can leave the recipient feeling flat or exhausted for a period of time. The feeling of being corded varies from person to person but there are a few signs of possible cords to others.

A cord to the base chakra can deplete physical and sexual vitality. You may find that you're not as grounded as usual. Clumsiness or tripping over your own feet can result from being un-grounded.

A cord to the second or navel chakra can cause a lack of enthusiasm or even suffering temporary bloating of the abdomen and lower intestines. Back pain in this area can also occur. A cord to the third or power-centre chakra often results in exhaustion or feelings of powerlessness. A tightening of the muscles around the solar plexus area or in the spine at that chakra can result. Excessive power struggles with others may occur.

A cord into the heart chakra can be emotionally draining. Breathing difficulties or asthma-type symptoms and a tightness in the back at that chakra can also occur. When corded into the fifth or throat chakra a continual sore throat, tightness in the throat or in the neck are common symptoms.

When corded in the throat, I feel as though I have swallowed a cheese grater. Sometimes there is a sensation of my throat closing up when corded here. Cords to the sixth or brow (third eye) chakra may cause hazy, indecisive or confused thinking. Headaches can sometimes result. Constant thoughts coming out of the blue about a particular person, usually the person cording you, may be a sign of a cord here.

Cords into the seventh or crown chakra are rare, for someone must be well developed spiritually to be able to do this. In most instances someone so developed is aware of their desires and unlikely to cord another person. Cords here can result in a feeling unable to reach great heights in meditation and a lack of inspiration.

Cords to the crown chakra can happen when someone gives you spiritual healing or when a chiropractor or an osteopath works on your head area. I recall feeling very lightheaded after a haircut one day, to be told by the hairdresser that she was mentally drawing energy out of my head as she worked, as she was having a bad day. It was my last haircut with her. I left the salon feeling fuzzy in my thinking and slightly dizzy.

Crown chakra cords are common in a guru-disciple relationship. The guru may sometimes take the disciple's energy to further increase his or her power. In return, the guru passes on to the disciple some information which has been learned. Unfortunately this is not always the process, as occasionally the guru can decide not to pass on what he or she has learned.

In this way a guru has access to the spiritual power of many disciples and can use this power for personal journeys out into the cosmos, into other realms and spheres. While the disciple receives love, security or nourishment on some level, he or she does not directly experience any of what is out there in the cosmos. The disciples' risks are diminished but so too is their growth. Cords not only deplete people and interfere with spiritual, emotional and mental make-up, they also take us away from who we are. This is evident when you arrive at a location feeling balanced and content and soon you're feeling empty, competitive or fuzzy headed. If a friend cords you because he feels that you have something he doesn't, such as contentment or a better lifestyle, you may gradually lose this sense of contentment as the cord pulls you away from yourself.

Cords are often created by desire or a perceived need:

Crown	I need you to help me to locate my spiritual path.
Brow	I need you to think for me or to clarify my issues.
Throat	I need you to listen to me or to talk on my behalf.
Heart	I need you to love me.
Solar Plexus	I need you to empower me.
Navel	I need you to enthuse me.
Base	I need you to support me.

When meditating, the purpose is to have spiritual sight. This is simply the ability to see beyond the physical plane to emotional and spiritual energies. Most people can learn to see beyond the physical. Some people perceived these energies as small children. Children often lose these clairvoyant abilities as their logical minds develop and they seek to master the physical world. Like most skills, developing and maintaining second sight requires practice.

When entering meditation, practise looking for cords into the body or ask your spirit guides to do this for you. Notice which area is corded most often, as this gives clues as to the weaker chakra areas or weaknesses in the energy field. Wherever there is a weakness is where others can cord you more easily. It is necessary for balance and harmony to work on these weaker areas, to strengthen yourself and your aura. This ensures good health physically, emotionally, mentally and spiritually.

It's not possible to prevent others from cording you but learning to recognise the signs of being corded, helps you deal with the cords. The sooner the cords are removed, the sooner you can return to a balanced, stable state. Gradually you'll recognise the people around you who cord you most frequently and can be better prepared when with them. Sometimes, in the process of tracing a cord back to the person who sent it, you might come face to face with an unknown person.

If you need to know why that person has corded you, your guides can tell you. It is important to know why you have been corded to change behaviour patterns that might encourage cords. Meditating in public can open the chakras, making you vulnerable to psychic cords. Cords can also be encouraged by regularly over indulging in drugs or alcohol or, in extreme cases, even your work. In jobs that deal with needy people more cords are likely to be formed. Nurses, counsellors, teachers, night club workers and bar tenders need to be more disciplined about cuttings cords as these work environments are usually populated with needy people.

Carmel consulted me for hypnosis to increase her confidence. Each week she arrived for her session exhausted and completely uncentred. When I questioned her as to what might be keeping her in this state she mentioned her part-time job. She was an exotic dancer in a club three nights a week.

When she first explained, I thought that she might have trained in traditional Thai dancing or some of the ancient traditional dances. She told me that each night almost a dozen men slipped banknotes into her garter while she danced almost naked around their tables. Her dancing triggered desire in the patrons, which produced cords and these psychic cords kept Carmel uncentred. This was confirmed as the cause when Carmel arrived for her session one week and I noticed that she was reasonably balanced. She hadn't worked as a dancer in the previous week.

In the early stages of detecting and tracing cords it is wise to check with a guide as to who has corded whom. You may have corded another person, therefore it is your responsibility to apologise mentally and dissolve the cord. If you do not know why you have corded another person, ask your guides.

When someone cords you psychically they may not do it directly. They can even work through an animal or a pet. If you love your dog or cat, it will openly receive your energies, while loving it in an unguarded fashion. This is natural.

If your partner wants you to love him unconditionally as you love your pet, he may unknowingly link into your pet and indirectly to you. I met a couple on a recent trip to Europe who have a difficult relationship. Edward is possessive and domineering and Jodie is weary from fighting back. She has retreated into herself and opens her heart mostly to her dog. As Edward cannot get the love he wants from Jodie by any other method, his spirit has sent a link through her dog to her heart. Now each time Jodie hugs and loves her dog, Edward's spirit is receiving some of this energy or love although he is not consciously aware of this.

To break a link like this Jodie needs to break the link between herself and her dog and then sever the link between her dog and her husband. Having done this, Jodie may then set up another link between her dog and herself.

Some cords re-form quickly no matter how often they are broken and there are several reasons for this. Firstly, they may be karmic cords. These cords return and remain until the karma or lesson between the people involved is complete.

When cutting long-term cords it may feel to others as though you have gone away. They may try to reconnect to re-establish the cord to you. During a psychic development course, Jacinta described an example of this. After cutting her cords one night, her ex-husband telephoned to speak with her. She did not hear the call and he left a message on her answering machine.

He telephoned three times over the next five days, reaching her at 1:00 am a week later. This is a man who usually called once or twice a month. He did not call with any urgent purpose; at least not one that he was aware of consciously.

When cutting cords to others, those cords that are karmic are likely to be re-established within days. One night recently I cut many cords when in meditation and then fell asleep. I was awoken at 7.25 the following morning by a telephone call from my five-year-old son. I had inadvertently cut the cord linking us and he was re-establishing it. He had awoken thinking about me and I sensed that he felt that I was going away from him energetically. He telephoned for reassurance that I was still alive and part of his life.

Since then my practice is to cut all cords and then, before completing my meditation, I think of him and a cord is re-established. It's a pleasant way to complete a meditation and it allows me to sleep in the next day.

Assuming that a cord is karmic simply because it continues to be re-formed each time you remove it is sometimes incorrect. It may be the result of persistence from the other person. Check with your guides as to the existence of any karmic cords. If it is merely persistence, trace the cord to its originator and explain clearly that you don't want his or her cords. Even if the physical person is unaware of cords being sent to you, the spirit of that person usually responds by ensuring no further cords reach you.

Rupert, a friend of mine, left his girlfriend, Julia and moved overseas. Julia was devastated but kept up a brave face and soon commenced another relationship. Several years later Rupert returned to his home town and re-established a friendship with Julia. Rupert was married and Julia was in a relationship but every day that Rupert lived in that town he was corded by Julia, whose spirit responded to her desire to have Rupert back. Rupert regularly cut her cords to him and in meditation occasionally saw her spirit appear hysterical when he did this. This visual insight in meditation comes with practice.

Not long after each cord-cutting session, Rupert came face to face with Julia or she'd telephone him and the cords reformed. Julia only had to think of him for her desires to be triggered, resulting in her spirit sending out a cord to his spirit. Rupert suffered severe headaches, sometimes lasting two or three days, along with pains in the throat and the spine due to Julia's cords. Some people persistently cord others psychically. If cords are repeatedly cut and there is no contact between the people concerned, it's likely that the person being corded gradually fades from the conscious mind of the person sending cords. Over a period or weeks or months more time elapses between a cord being cut and another being formed. Eventually when cords are cut they are not replaced by new cords as the person sending the cords has moved forward with his or her life.

A simple exercise to improve visualisation skills (the ability to see in meditation) is to close your eyes and spend ten minutes recalling a house where you have lived in the past and remember each room in that house, including all the furnishings and the colours of the walls. When you can do this easily, move on to the homes of friends, recalling in careful detail where things are in those homes. To improve these abilities study a bookshelf lined with books for two minutes before turning away from it and listing all the book titles you can remember seeing on that shelf.

Some people find that visualisation comes easily to them, whereas others need practice to improve their skills. When dealing with a person who persistently cords you it's wise to reason with them. Ask your accompanying guide what you need to do to reach a solution which benefits both of you. Ask, too, if you are doing anything to encourage the cords.

Sometimes a face-to-face meeting may be necessary to resolve an issue or to make amends or to apologise. In some situations a letter or a phone call will suffice. Usually the process of stating your position or seeking forgiveness in meditation, is enough. In rare instances a great distance must be put between you and the person cording you. This helps because it is more difficult to cord someone far away, especially when an ocean divides you.

In very rare situations someone practising negative magic may cord another person for power. If this occurs, you are ill-advised to battle it out. The safer option is to ensure that you are adequately protected (see Chapter 20, Psychic Protection). This is very rare, and most people go through a lifetime without any such interference.

Cords sent out by people practising negative magic are usually difficult to break, as their senders know what they are doing and sometimes use a number of tricks to cord a person. These can include cording a close friend of yours and then sending the cord on to you. In this way, when you trace the cord back, you arrive at your friend and mistakenly think that he or she has corded you. Sometimes you'll leave that cord alone, being happy to be corded by a close friend. This provides the magician with a shield but there is a way around it. In meditation, draw down as much energy as possible into your body. Then with an outward breath, release this energy in one burst while visualising it burning the cord back to the person who sent it. Ensure that any residual energy of your own is collected when returning your awareness to your physical body.

If an individual is in this position it requires powerful energy and determination to shake off such an intruder. This power is available through the channel, which is why it is important to protect and maintain it. Disturbance from everyday stresses of life may deplete this channel. Without regular meditation to replenish yourself, it can leave insufficient energy to ward off such a nuisance.

A friend of mine, Alice is a powerful channel and consequently encounters more than her fair share of intruders. Magicians are drawn to her power because it is easier for them to siphon off some energy from another person than it is to channel their own energy. Sometimes people who study magic seek short cuts to enlightenment, when in reality, there is no short cut. The path of magic is fraught with dangers, both real and imagined but the desire for power can be very tempting.

When Alice finds any intruders she usually meditates, building up an incredible reserve of power, which she releases instantaneously. This sudden release of energy burns all the cords from her body at once, resulting in a burn-back effect to each person who has a cord to her at that time. At that point those who have been connected to Alice feel sick or suffer sudden pains. It is a very effective technique but so far Alice is the only person I know who can use this technique effectively.

Sometimes people receiving a magician's cords turn out to be as sneaky as the sender. In one instance a person receiving an unwanted cord, extended the cord around her body and turned it back to the sender, so that, in effect, the sender was plugged into himself. Most people are unlikely to be corded by a magician until there is a strong connection with spirit and can easily channel a powerful force. At this time it is possible to pass almost any test set by people who may deliberately send out cords.

It is wise to guard against justifying the actions of others by thinking 'It's only a little energy and poor Marge really does need it as she's in such a state.' If Marge is learning a lesson or if she has wandered away from her spiritual path in life, it is not going to assist her development if you also become lost.

If there is something constructive you can do that Marge can benefit from, without impeding her spiritual growth, do it. Be careful that the need to assist is not coming from your ego. If helping her requires that you remain corded or become entangled in a drama from which you eventually require help, then perhaps it's better to reconsider the consequences before proceeding.

Traditionally, in parts of China, to reduce the

Fig 4 Psychic Cords to the Chakras

'negative luck' associated with desire, a host offered his guest anything that the guest admired aloud. This tradition is based upon the understanding that the guest's desire forms a cord to the object which disturbs the energy of the home. The guest desiring something in his host's home causes the guest to envy the host, which may disturb the host's 'luck' or his ability to live in peace.

It is sometimes easier for the host to give the guest the object rather than to experience the bad luck that may result from his guest's desire or envy. Vacuums don't exist for long in the universe, so if it was not his karma that he give the object to the guest and he does so, it is usually replaced in some form.

An example of karma is Ellie, a student in a recent course who could not cut a stubborn cord linking her to her deceased grandfather, as she had not resolved the conflict which created the cord. It was the result of a painful incident in her childhood. In time she may be ready to lay it to rest, if only to retain more of her energy within herself.

It is possible that the pain Ellie suffered as a result of this incident was her karma for an incident in a previous lifetime. Regular meditation may offer her a glimpse of the purpose of such an incident. Alternatively, counselling may help her to resolve her outstanding feelings regarding the incident, allowing her to cut the cord and move on with her life.

For karmic cords to be effectively cut, the karma between both parties needs to be completed. An effective way to identify the karma or the underlying lesson in an incident or a situation is to ask personal guides when in meditation. Usually they'll explain the underlying spiritual lesson. Once the lesson is learned it becomes easier to cut a longstanding cord to that person. Although it sounds straightforward, it may be necessary to forgive someone or to ask for forgiveness, which can be done in meditation. If forgiveness isn't possible at this time, the cord cannot be cut until you are prepared to release both of you from the incident or experience.

12

Becoming Centred Before Meditation

To encourage calm, balanced meditation it is important to ensure that you have not been drawn away from your centre by desires, either your own or those of others. There are three simple techniques for determining whether you are centred before proceeding to meditate which apply to visual, auditory and kinesthetic types of people.

If you are a visual person, when you are positioned for meditation, ask for protection and ask to see your energy channel. If it is not aligned with your physical body (see t), then look for psychic cords that may be contributing to its displacement.

An auditory person can ask guides to tell them if the channel is centered. Alternatively, ask where cords exist that require cutting to ensure that the energy channel is rebalanced.

A kinesthetic (tactile) individual, when positioned for meditation, can feel the energy channel and sense if it is centred or out of alignment with the physical body. If an imbalance is detected, such as an increased awareness in only one side of the body, then it is likely that the channel is partly out of alignment with the physical body.

In a meditation recently I noticed that when I asked to be filled with light I was aware of light entering only the left half of my head. I visually checked my spiritual energy channel and saw that it was partly out of my physical body, held off to the left by two psychic cords. When I cut these cords my channel returned naturally to my physical body once again and I could feel the light entering my whole head and filling my entire body.

If the spiritual energy channel is not aligned with the physical body it may cause poor concentration or restlessness during meditation. A great number of people I speak to about meditation say that they have difficulty meditating and maintaining concentration during meditation. It's possible that realigning the energy channel may resolve most of these instances.

People with a misaligned energy channel are drawing down light and energy into a poorly connected channel. When this happens it is akin to sitting or lying still for 30 minutes with eyes closed, which is not meditation. Drawing down light into an energy channel with a poor connection or access offers limited benefit. It is like being a gardener who digs an irrigation path from a river toward crops but allows the path to go past them at a considerable distance rather than directly to them.

The spirit energy channel is correctly aligned when you ask for the light and can sense or see it entering and flowing throughout your body. It may be seen as a slight brightness above the head, as though there was a candle above. It can be experienced as a gentle tingling sensation as the energy enters the crown of the head. Some people feel a gentle pulsing energy and a warm secure radiance that is both relaxing and reassuring.

When achieving a good clear meditation and connection with spirit, it is like someone holding a torch above your head. At times I've opened my eyes during meditation to ensure a candle hadn't set something alight because the light was suddenly so bright. These instances are infrequent, but do occur when fully aligned with your channel in mediation. Early on in meditation practice it may be difficult to be certain that anything is happening at all. Allow at least 30 days of daily meditation to become familiar with the procedures. Once you're more relaxed with the process it's possible to notice the light entering the body during meditations.

Centering yourself before meditation may involve taking a short walk, completing some physical exercise to release stress or spending time in a garden to connect with nature. A former student Douglas finds that if he spends 10 minutes playing his drum kit he's relaxed enough to meditate. I don't know how his neighbours feel about this but it works for Douglas.

13

Learning to Visualise

Learning to visualise easily with precision is essential. Most small children visualise naturally and easily, yet up to 50% of adults experience difficulties when asked to see pictures with their mind's eye.

If having difficulty visualising, the following simple techniques might help. Seeing things in meditation is akin to remembering. If recalling your favourite food, town or city, it's likely that the images brought to mind are seen with the mind's eye and not with the physical eyes.

Take a moment to imagine or remember a green apple. When you can see it in your mind's eye, make this apple red. Now see this same apple become blue with orange stripes. Although you have not seen such an apple in reality, it is possible to see it in your mind's eye. This is visualization. It is similar to imagining or remembering an object or an event, where the images are perceived not with your physical eyes but in your mind's eye.

This same procedure is used by clairvoyants to predict the future or locate lost objects. Sometimes it is difficult to determine what is imagination and what is a genuine image from a spirit guide or an image from the future. This is a valid concern. With more than twenty years of experience as a clairvoyant and seeing regular visual images in meditation, I still sometimes find it difficult to be sure. Sometimes I see images for a client during a reading that make no sense to me. I explain these to the client and seek help in making sense of the image.

In one instance I saw a client, Lazlo, inspecting a 1970s car with a view to buying it. What puzzled me was that he was particular about carefully examining the body panel inside and above the rear wheels. When I asked aloud why he should do this, he explained that he collected cars and the particular model he was looking to purchase often developed rust in the inside panels above the rear wheels which is costly to repair. Later in the same reading I saw a black box with electronic components which Lazlo was perfecting. I noticed that he was attempting to find a way for the unit to function without overheating, which was a difficult puzzle for him. I knew nothing about the box nor its intended use yet I was able to describe its appearance and to a limited degree, its use. Because I had never seen anything like it before I knew that these images were not my imagination.

This confirmed that what I saw was genuine clairvoyance. In situations where you see images of the future without the confirmation of the client, be patient and allow life to unfold to confirm your images. Don't discard an image because it does not make sense to you. If the image recurs a few moments or even days later, note it down. An example of this happened to me recently.

When working on a book and a project involving the use of hypnosis to move others forward in time, I was testing out the technique for myself. I wanted to purchase a new car and I had spent many hours searching and testing cars from auto showrooms trying to decide what was suitable and within my price range. I used the hypnosis technique to move myself two weeks into the future to glimpse the car in my garage. I saw a new car with long rectangular headlights but none of the cars I liked had these headlights. In fact, the car I really liked had teardrop-shaped headlights. I ignored the hypnosis progression and purchased the car I liked a few days later. A week passed and the dealership had not delivered my new car, as they were having difficulty locating an air-conditioning unit for it. When I rang the salesman to complain, he offered to lend me a car until mine was ready.

I collected the loan car and drove home. The following morning I looked out from my living room and noticed the car in the garage. It had long rectangular headlights and a week later it was still sitting in my garage. This was the day I had progressed forward to in my self-hypnosis. I had seen clearly what was to occur in two weeks but had I progressed forward four weeks I'd have seen my new car with its teardrop-shaped headlights.

Some images are merely glimpses and they make little or no sense at all when first seen. Keeping a journal may assist to record these and if they are later confirmed, this can build confidence with visualisation skills.

When I was 13 years of age I had a vivid, recurring dream which later occurred exactly as I had dreamt it. In this dream I was sitting in a big armchair in an enormous room. I turned to a man on a settee close by and said to him, "It's great, isn't it?"

It was nothing meaningful or particularly memorable, except that I dreamt it four times within a week and that I had no idea who the man was. When I was 17 years of age the scene occurred. I was sitting in a friend's enormous living room, listening to a record on his new sound system. The music was as loud as we could tolerate and I could feel the pounding drums reverberating through my armchair. I turned to my friend and said, 'It's great isn't it?'

I was determined to train and discipline my visualisation abilities and with practice, you can too. Visualisation requires practice and one of the simplest practice techniques is to close your eyes and recall your living room in precise detail.

Working slowly around the room remember each colour, shape, reflection, texture and detail, even the size and shape of the television. Notice if anything is beneath the TV. What colour are the walls? What sort of floor coverings? How many shapes or how many types of timber are visible in your living room?

When you have done this carefully and accurately several times, move on to the living room in a previous home or the home of a close friend. For further practice, read a novel. Story books are designed to create a clear picture in the readers' minds. In a single paragraph the writer creates a scene that is individual to the imagination of each and every reader.

Above me on the wall as I write is a painting of my dream home. It is a graceful country cottage with an orchard garden seen from the living room via the open French doors. The neat rows of fruit trees are covered in a pale pink blossom and a long white wooden garden seat awaits someone with a book and a cup of tea. There is an old pianoforte with a pair of brass candlesticks to one side of the room and a highly polished round table carrying a vase of the garden's blossom and a tea setting for four. A bright red cushion is plumped up on the settee and a series of paintings adorn the deep green walls. The sun streams in through the windows and the open doors, inviting the viewer outside into the glorious garden. In your mind you probably held or developed a vision of what that painting looks like, which is exactly the technique you can use when meditating. Practice makes visualising easy, so when you daydream remember that it is good practice for your visualisation skills.

Steps to improve visualisation skills

1. Close your eyes and take a deep breath, releasing it slowly.
2. Imagine or remember a scene of a beach, with gentle waves lapping at the shore,
3. In your mind, notice a golden orange sun setting and feel the gentle breeze against your face.
4. Feel the sand beneath your feet and smell the sea air, a combination of salt and sand and seaweed.
5. Ahead of you on the beach someone has lit a small fire and you can smell the smoke as the twigs burn
6. Three brightly coloured kites soar in the air. A group of children laugh and call out to each other as they struggle to keep hold of the strings. Notice the colours and patterns on each kite.
7. Now see yourself happy and healthy as you successfully live your life.
8. Open your eyes again.

The above exercise can be varied to improve and maintain visualisation skills. The kites can vary from box kites to oriental dragons or three-tiered kites with coloured tails. For those who simply cannot see anything when they close their eyes I offer this technique:

1. Close your eyes and take a deep breath, releasing it slowly.
2. Count in your mind from 1 to 10 without thinking of a tree.
3. Do not think of a single tree, particularly ensure that you do not imagine or see in your mind's eye a pine tree.
4. Open your eyes again.

Sometimes the act of trying too hard prevents a person from succeeding, as anyone who has tried to fall asleep can attest. To remove the struggle when visualising, simply reverse the exercise and try not to visualise. The results might surprise you. Everyone can visualise and with practice, it is possible to visualise with precision.

The simplest method of developing visualisation abilities is to begin with objects that are easy to imagine, such as memories. Remember your partner, your children or your best friend and go from there. Recall your most treasured memory, an outrageous experience or your favourite meal and from there move on to more difficult scenes. A good comedian or storyteller relies on the imagination of the audience. It's what the audience creates in their minds that makes a storyteller successful.

In essence, learning to visualise involves learning to see, although both abilities involve different types of sight. Visualisation requires peripheral vision, whereas seeing or noticing things in life requires central vision. When developing better ability to truly see what is before you, it becomes easier to recall it when needed.

Central vision is the sight or focus that is used to read or to examine minor details. Peripheral vision refers to objects that are noticed at the edge of awareness but are not central to your point of focus.

An example of well-developed tunnel vision happened to me in France. My partner and I were motorcycling through France in August looking for accommodation in the holiday season. Riding into a large deserted village one Sunday morning we scoured the streets and the village square for signs of life. There was no one about except for an old man sipping a coffee at an outdoor table, with his dog. My partner parked the motorbike and walked towards the old man. She beckoned me to follow and striding straight past him, she pushed an old door open to reveal the whole town, eating and drinking amidst a thick blue haze of cigarette smoke.

"How did you know this was here?" I asked her incredulously. She pointed to the small glass of cloudy liquid alongside the old man's coffee cup.

"What happens when you add water to Ouzo or Pernod?" she asked me.

"It turns a cloudy, milky colour," I replied.

"Exactly," she smiled and continued, "Besides, it's Sunday morning and after Mass what do you think the locals will be doing but eating and drinking."

When we first arrived in the village I was looking for an open boulangerie or patisserie but being a private investigator by profession, she was looking for evidence of life. She employed her vision to focus upon the details that might reveal what she sought; the locals.

14
The Purpose of Meditation

One basic purpose of the meditation outlined in the following chapter is fulfilling one's destiny through spiritual awareness and growth. This can occur in many ways, including knowing when and where there is a need to serve others and discovering how to be useful in the spiritual plan.

Meditation also serves another important purpose. It centres people and enables them to withdraw their focus, spiritual energy and spirit bodies from outer preoccupations. This helps the person to become centred within the physical body and to reclaim outgoing senses or awareness. This is not selfish, for scattered energy depletes a person of spiritual strength and diminishes awareness of individual purpose in life.

This is one of the reasons why clairvoyants or people who venture out of their physical bodies with spirit energy, deplete themselves. By all means take a look at what's out there but be aware that there are enough wonders on earth to hold your interest for several lifetimes.

There is so much that needs to be healed and channelling and transmuting energy is best used for the purpose of self-healing. Some spiritual masters emphasise the importance of withdrawing awareness and energy into the channel and the physical body to fully focus upon spiritual development. Psychic readings and general exploration involve outward direction of energies, whereas meditation involves directing personal energy inwardly to conserve it.

When meditating regularly it is possible to build up reserves of spiritual energy or to habitually conserve your spiritual energy. As a result, you are able to cleanse yourself of some past karma and achieve deep, lasting inner peace.

Meditation allows for a centering of energy and when more spiritual energies are present at one time, you become capable of great realisations and deep understanding. Many regular meditators choose not to see clairvoyantly. This is to conserve their energy and to prevent them spending their lives exploring what is out there in the spirit world.

Mental and spiritual restlessness sometimes occur when energetic parts of a person are missing and the remaining parts of that person are attempting to retrieve what is lost. When more parts of yourself are present, you can be more useful. Being useful does not only necessarily include championing causes. In the spiritual scheme it can involve attending to incidentals such as physical health, diet and earning an honest living.

Respect for nature is necessary for the part it has to play in supporting spiritual development. Caring for animals and people who need encouragement or support is one way of being useful spiritually. Kind words of encouragement when desperately needed can make a huge difference when facing obstacles.

Part of the purpose for spiritual development may involve briefly opening up to areas of life that may be unfamiliar, such as the nature spirit kingdom. This realm includes faeries, elves, gnomes and goblins. Aside from their mythical descriptions, they can take on different shapes according to the environment in which they live e.g. forests, rivers, moss-covered rocks. Spending time in a garden or a park filled with trees and plants is time spent amongst the elemental faeries, elves, gnomes and pixies. Although you may not see them, they see you.

During a meditation years ago I mentally scanned my back garden and was surprised to see a short, potato-shaped figure sloping about at the edge of the garden beneath a tall tree. When I zoomed in for a closer look, he became startled and disappeared underground. Two weeks later, a friend visited and I mentioned the gnome-like creature I had seen. He laughed and said that he had seen a similar creature several times previously when making his way through my back garden to visit me at night. His partner, who doesn't meditate, didn't see anything.

At these times you are in the kingdom ruled by the god Pan. His purpose is to oversee the growth and development of trees, shrubs, plants, flowers, vegetables and the earth. Before some religions superimposed their saints upon the gods, the pagans and other groups worshipped Pan for the work he did. Pagans believed that without this beast with a human upper body and a goat's lower body and his myriad of workers, the earth wouldn't bear fruit or flowers and trees would wither and die. Pan ensures that humans maintain an awareness of nature.

Superstitions arose and a fear of Pan developed—the word 'panic' literally means 'a fear of Pan'. It is better to be thankful than fearful of him. Due to his grotesque, frightening appearance, Pan has been judged as evil. In black magic, witches sometimes use Pan to do their bidding but nothing can harm you unless you fear it. This is also confirmed in the belief systems of the Kahunas, the ancient medicine men and women of Hawaii, who believe that guilt is the doorway to disease. People who wish you harm can be more successful if

Fig 5.
The energy channel aligned
with the physical body. A
cord from the heart chakra.

you harbour guilt or fear.

When familiar with Pan and with your own root chakra, you'll be safer and more balanced. Knowledge and understanding is protection. To perceive Pan it may be necessary to meditate and move downwards in your channel. Before doing this successfully, it is important to be familiar with your root or base chakra. This energy centre is found at the base of the spine in men and between the ovaries in women. The lowest of the seven main chakras, it relates to physical vitality, nature, material survival and survival of the species. It is closely related to the animal part of humans.

If the base chakra is weak an individual usually has poor survival instincts, low physical vitality and often has a poor connection with nature and the physical world. These aren't great sports-people as they tire easily. Individuals with strong base chakras are usually very present in their physical bodies, enjoy nature, the outdoors and sports. They have great reserves of energy and endurance and exude sexual charisma. The stronger the base chakra, the more noticeable the physical presence the person has.

Pan rules the earth and the lower realms (elemental kingdom, etc.) and to explore these realms it is necessary to operate from the root chakra. It is like taking an elevator to the basement. Everything that is around us is also within us energetically, including fine spiritual energy and coarse energies. To discover the depths of the elemental kingdom it is important to descend to the depths within yourself first to access that kingdom.

Most meditations for exploration encourage only upward development, or the strengthening of particular chakras such as the navel and the solar plexus chakras. For well-rounded development it makes more sense to develop and strengthen all chakras.

When a group of people (or group consciousness) believe in a myth, a fable or a fictitious creature, it comes to exist in another dimension. Although not apparent in the physical dimension, it is possible to meditate and visit the place or dimension where it exists. These are thought forms, made strong by the beliefs of many people. They can also be made by one person, through habitually thinking the same thoughts. Aside from the variety of monsters and heroic creatures, I presume that there is a thought form of hell, purgatory or heaven as many people believe these things but I'm unable to confirm these from personal experience.

Developing communication with spirit and expanding personal awareness to include other life forms on this planet can put a person in touch with true abundance. Beings of the nature spirit kingdom tap directly into a spirit or god force for the energy they require for their work. They work with the light and in the light, producing forms that we can see with our naked eye, such as flowers, trees, etc. One can choose to consciously communicate with them or even to work with them to fulfil spirit's plan.

I grew up with poverty firmly imprinted upon my brain. I meditated to overcome this and was told in meditation to 'Open your heart to the true abundance surrounding you, not simply financial abundance but true abundance.' I puzzled about how to open up to abundance when I was poverty-stricken (by my standards). It was simply an excuse on my part. One day I opened my heart to my back garden and its energy poured into my heart. It was a glorious experience, feeling the gentle, radiant sun illuminating the garden and being aware of all of the movement of bees, insects, and earthworms industriously finding food. Everywhere there was movement, from the gentle rustle of leaves in the tall tees, to the demanding calls of tiny birds in a nest, high in a tree top. For a brief moment, I felt as though I was the only living being in the garden that was still.

There were bees working hard in dozens of tiny flowers and thin lines of ants on the ground scouring the soil for remnants. I felt the peace in that garden while hearing the gentle breeze rustling the soft wall of bamboo cane beside me. Like a tall green curtain, it swayed constantly, screening my view of the neighbouring gardens and affording me quiet privacy. It's a beautiful place to be and immensely different from the view of the garden from my window.

Opening your heart to someone close to you, to your home, garden or work is a small step but one which may lead to greater understanding. As I became aware of nature in its many forms, I noticed life supporting itself and supporting me. How can someone feel poor when experiencing so much of life contributing to his or her wellbeing? The trees and plants produce oxygen, shade, shelter and sometimes fruits and nuts. It is strange that despite the support received from nature we sometimes insist upon taming it by tearing it up and covering the earth with cement to prevent re-growth.

Time spent with nature nourishes us and is essential for a balanced base chakra. Some days, after too many hours spent staring at a computer screen, it's a joy to be able to walk in the park and stare off into the distance. When standing beneath a 60 metre tall gum tree, these walks remind me how small I am in the greater scheme of life.

15
Awakening to the Light Meditation

With energy cords extending out to other people and situations, it can be difficult to remain attentive to the meditation process, as a co-tenant Roxanne illustrated some years ago when she ventured into the mountains to complete a ten-day silent meditation retreat. After a few days there was a message on my answering machine from the receptionist at the retreat centre, requesting that I check Roxanne's Australian visa expiry date, as she was on a holiday visa from England.

Realising that Roxanne had probably found something to worry about and that she needed to remain focused, I phoned the centre and left a message for her, as she was not permitted to speak to anyone until the tenth day. The message? 'Keep meditating.'

A friend spent the first seven months of her meditation practice training her family not to interrupt her, to respect her privacy during meditation times. It took patience and strength but eventually they understood and allowed her the space and time to replenish herself through meditation. It is understandable that a family might take some months to adjust to a new routine such as a parent's daily meditation but perseverance brings rewards.

The results of meditation vary from person to person. Success for some takes many months, while for others is arrives sooner. Kevin spoke enthusiastically of the feelings and the clarity of his meditation in the third Sunday of a course I was conducting and by the end of the day he was positively glowing. He talked, too, of quitting a particular psychic development group he was attending, as they were training to complete 'soul rescue' work, which he realised is dangerous if the participants are not extremely developed spiritually.

Not all meditations are clear, simple procedures. On the third Sunday of a course Caroline experienced two negative meditations in a row which frightened her to the point where she wanted to leave early. However her final meditation for the day was positive and she left feeling relieved. Not all meditations are the same, depending on many factors. These factors include the energy in the room where you are meditating, unresolved personal issues at the time and distractions around you.

During one meditation period a CD of pop songs is played when the group are in meditation to add to their distractions. It is intended to prepare them for life at home. As they had been made aware of the impending musical distraction most of them were undisturbed by the CD. Two students even went higher in meditation with the music to guide them.

If you have a religious background, it may be necessary to keep an open mind to fully benefit from this chapter. When you have mastered this meditation take the best parts of what you have learned from this book and what you already hold as spiritual knowledge and combine them for personal benefits. When first hearing this next part I also had difficulty accepting it, so I ask that you have an open mind.

Throughout history there have been a number of enlightened beings who, in walking the earth, have stood out as such evolved souls or bright channels that long after their passing we hear stories of them and their teachings. Some of these include, but are not limited to, Zoroaster, Buddha, Krishna, Moses, Jesus and Mohammed.

These beings, now in spirit (deceased) can be called upon for support, protection and guidance. These beings are masters, for they have mastered the earthly lessons and need not return to the earth plane. I believe we are all ultimately headed in the direction of becoming masters, in our own ways. The various paths we take are not without sacrifices, tests, disappointments and rewards. If we do our utmost to develop ourselves, spirit usually meets us halfway.

However, once you make the spiritual connection and commit yourself to spiritual development, there are limited options for giving up. Deep within you know that you can be more than you are and part of you wants to strive toward fulfilling that potential. I attended a talk by an Indian master who was touring the world and was surprised to hear him repeatedly voice beliefs and concerns about following a master. He mentioned that we can each find our own way up the mountain in search of our spiritual fulfilment and none of us needs a master. He pointed out that a master is simply someone who has been to the mountain top and can act as a guide for others.

He then explained that the only way to know if what a master or others say is true is to go within, where all the answers are. Although the journey is individual, being part of a group of like-minded people may help when encountering obstacles. Hearing how others overcome such difficulties gives hope as well as valuable techniques for the journey.

There will be times when you may feel inclined to quit, to sulk when you don't get your own way, to lose faith or patience in the process or feel overwhelmed. You might long to return to the innocence before the journey but those in spirit know your limitations and a week of sulking is not going to deter them. When it dawned on me the things I'd have to relinquish if I truly wanted to travel this path, I was depressed.

These included alcohol, which disturbs the balance between spirit bodies and the physical body, parties, which are populated with people who are drinking to escape their desires, and any crowded places where large amounts of alcohol or drugs are consumed. Also certain foods such as onions and garlic which, being root vegetables, are suitable for grounding but they limit the ability to achieve high meditations - hence the folklore about vampires avoiding garlic. I realised that I'd need to cleanse more thoroughly or reduce clairvoyant readings as they deplete spiritual reserves of energy.

I reduced or gave these things up reluctantly. I enjoy carrots and other root vegetables, so I have them in moderation. In fact my friend described this process as "Kicking and screaming your way to enlightenment." After you've given up these, easier foods and habits, spirit asks you to give up more entrenched habits.

I was asked to give up my pride, a very difficult task for me. Soon afterwards they asked me to open my heart to the whole world. I almost choked in my meditation. One by one my blockages, fears and grudges were being rooted out and I had to forsake them before proceeding. It can take a long time.

You may be required to purge yourself before each new step. I can assure you that on the days when you are alone, stuck and completely frustrated, the good old days of getting roaring drunk around an old piano, squeezed into a local pub with 125 other non-sober types seems very appealing.

I occasionally enjoy a glass of champagne and awaken the next morning with a thumping head. Life can't be all work and sometimes it is necessary to remind yourself what your life used to be like by re-experiencing it. It can be a lonely, long path, difficult to negotiate but if it is your unique path, silently or not, it calls you.

Naturally such a steep and lengthy path must offer rich rewards for your efforts. Few of us would forsake immediate gratification to pursue a steep, difficult path to the mountain's summit without the expectation of a deep sense of stillness or happiness.

The process encourages a deeper understanding of yourself and the worlds around you, both physical and spiritual. An awareness of the rules of these visible and unseen worlds can help you to master these realms. In the process, you'll discover your strengths, talents and your true purpose for being here. Although a deep sense of peace and happiness may initially be a goal, these end up being a byproduct of the journey.

Recognising your deeper purpose for being here can make the stresses of daily life subside. Traffic delays won't suddenly disappear but your frustration levels may diminish. A deep relaxing meditation every day is like a short holiday, whenever you need one. It's your afternoon in a hammock under a tropical palm tree, being carried off to sleep by the gentle whisper of a series of placid waves lapping at a nearby shore.

If life is a marathon, then it's important to have rest stops. As marathon runners pause briefly for refreshments, meditation is life's pit stop. It offers a chance to pause momentarily to make sense of the day, the week or your life's direction.

16
Meditation Procedure

In the following meditation procedure, the term 'God' refers to what you feel God is. For some people the term 'God' is a religious term, for others it is a source of energy or Goddess from which all of life derives. Whatever you know God to be is what matters personally.

Firstly, you'll need a map. Then some direct experience, discipline to avoid becoming distracted and courage to face the energies you have to contend with along the journey.

1. Find a comfortable place where you will remain undisturbed. Sit or lie down and settle your mind and body.
2. If necessary, write a list of your concerns and put it aside until after the meditation. You can do this mentally if you prefer.
3. Take three deep breaths, releasing each breath slowly.

You can record the next section onto a CD to play, so that you can guide yourself through the process without having to refer to the book.

4. Now ask: "Source, (or Heavenly Father) please send me protection on all three levels (physical, mental and spiritual). Thank you, thank you, thank you." This is a thank you for each of these levels.
5. As you release the third breath, mentally say to yourself:

"In the name of the Source (alternatively - In the name of the Father, the Son and the Holy Spirit...) please send the light down through my crown, through every cell of my body and out through my feet and into the earth. Thank you, thank you, thank you."

Now in your mind visualise the light entering your body through your crown chakra, and feel it gradually penetrating each cell in your head, down your neck and then through every cell of your body. Feel the light enter your legs, flow down to your ankles and then pass through your feet and out of your body and down into the earth. The energy passes through you, sweeping away all negativity and leaving you feeling peaceful and calm.

It doesn't matter if you're five floors up in an apartment block. The energy passing through you is fine enough to pass through all material objects on its way down to the earth below.

Now build up a ball of energy in your brow chakra from the incoming energy and mentally say to yourself: 'May every cell, every molecule of my head, face and ears absorb love, the strength, wisdom, power, humility, peace, joy and harmony.'

6. Now ask: "May all of the cosmos support me."

7. Feel your head absorb this light, power and love.

Moving down to your throat chakra, build up a ball of energy from the incoming energy in your throat and neck and say mentally to yourself:

"May my neck and throat overflow with the light and may every cell and every molecule of my throat centre absorb the love, strength, wisdom, power, humility, peace, joy and harmony."

Feel your neck and throat absorbing this light, power and love for a few minutes.

Now move down to the heart chakra and repeat the process.

Next move down to the solar plexus chakra and repeat the procedure.

Now move down to the navel chakra and repeat the procedure.

Finally move down to the root or base chakra and repeat the procedure. Hold the light in your base chakra area for longer than the other areas to ground yourself. As you do this, see or feel the light overflowing at your base chakra and filling your legs and feet.

Having this light and love within each cell of your body is very strong protection against darkness or negativity.

Now silently ask: "Can my spirit guides please appear before me and support me."

When you can see, hear, feel or sense the presence of a spirit guide, ask if he or she comes to you through the Source (alternatively – through the Father, the Son and the Holy Spirit.) The Father or Source represents God, the spiritual source or what- ever you choose to call it. The Son represents the earthly manifestation of the Father's energy, such as Jesus, Buddha, Krishna, etc. The Holy Spirit is the higher self or essence and spiritual self.

The Hawaiian Kahunas (traditional medicine men and women of Hawaii) refer to this as 'Aumakua' or the conscious mind spirit. In modern times it is sometimes referred to as the 'higher self.'

Ask your guides to state clearly that they come to you through Buddha, Jesus Christ, Mohammed or your preferred master. This process is to eliminate imposters and time wasters. In the spirit realms the aforementioned ascended masters are so well respected that spirit entities rarely pose as these beings to fool people with inaccurate information.

Have the guide tell you directly and clearly that he or she is present before you in the name of Jesus/Buddha/ Krishna, if you have any doubts about what you are hearing or seeing. In situations where I have imposed this test, occasionally mid-sentence, the guide disappears, to be replaced by the real guide. There was no difference in the image but a vast change in the quality of the information I was receiving.

When satisfied that your guide is genuine, ask the guide to show you where your channel is, relative to where you are physically sitting or lying (see Fig 6). If you cannot see clearly you may feel it, e.g. it may be off to one side of your physical body.

It is important to request assistance to align your channel, to benefit from its source of energy. You may see a shaft of white light appear. This could be in front, beside or behind you. The light might not be very bright at first but as you channel more frequently it strengthens.

8. Now ask your guide to assist you to line your physical body up with your spiritual channel. You will notice a gradual movement of your channel toward your physical body, until it is in alignment. The reason why so many people cannot find peace and stillness when they meditate is because they are often away from this energy channel and cannot benefit from its calming, restorative influence.

9. Once inside your channel, familiarise yourself with it and with the feeling of being inside this light. With practice, it is possible to achieve this link with the cosmos in the waking state, wherever you are.

This process may seem long and drawn out, yet it is necessary to know the basics before taking shortcuts. When you're more experienced, if you have difficulties with a quicker method you can always revert to this full procedure, knowing that it works.

Repeat this meditation procedure once daily for two weeks before proceeding to the next part of the meditation. In two weeks you'll probably feel familiar enough with the procedure to incorporate more into the process. The ten steps are listed below in point form:

1.	Make yourself comfortable.
2.	Remove any concerns you have before proceeding.
3.	Take three deep breaths.
4.	Ask for protection
5.	Ask for the light.
6.	Allow the light to flow through your body from your crown chakra down to your feet.
7.	Ask the cosmos to support you in what you are about to do.
8.	Ask for your guides and ask them to state who they come to you through, (which ascended master).
9.	Ask your guides to realign your channel to your physical body.
10.	Familiarise yourself with your channel.

Once this procedure has been repeated a few times you can familiarise yourself with your energy channel. This channel of light is like a long tube. While inside the channel, look up and notice that it extends far off into the distance. It is the same sight if you look down. This is your private passage off into the universe and beyond and back to God, the Creator or whatever you choose to call It. Although this channel extends this far it doesn't mean you can automatically travel off to meet your maker today. You require familiarity with personal limitations, a close connection with and a deep trust of your guides.

If you experience difficulties with any part of this meditation it is important to practice it before proceeding to the next stage. It is essential to be completely comfortable with this technique before effectively cutting psychic cords.

Remember light attracts darkness, so procedures for self-protection need to be very carefully followed. If not fully protected you may collect negative energy. There are written examples of this throughout the life of Jesus Christ. Darkness gathered during the agony in the garden (St Mark 14:32-43). Doubt filled him as the time of his physical death drew near. Buddha faced his own darkness, both within and outside of himself on his road to enlightenment.

If your physical energy is low or if you feel negative after a period of meditation, ask for protection on all levels again and offer thanks three times. This is not a reference to evil entities or ghostly shadowy figures, although they do exist, for darkness can assume the form of inertia. Negativity can manifest as sluggish laziness that prevents a person from being bothered to meditate in the first place.

There are many excuses to justify inward resistance to developing spiritually. It may manifest as preferring to keep yourself in the dark about your spiritual worth and true identity. This part may reason that you're on a path of deprivation, whereas there is immediate gratification awaiting you somewhere else.

Naturally effort is required and at times it's not easy. If it was an easy path, everyone would take it. The reason why the view from the summit extends so far is partly because it's rarely crowded at the summit. When finding your place at the mountain's peak you'll feel at peace, partly because of being among likeminded people who share your dedication, determination and spiritual philosophy. It's a process of awakening your deeper spiritual self and coming home to your tribe, who can nourish and support your endeavours.

It's easy to be distracted by the physical demands of life such as a successful career, creating a comfortable home or raising a family. This need not be at the expense of your deeper, spiritual purpose for being here. It's possible to choose a physical path, a spiritual path or both. Living life in the physical world while attending to deeper spiritual needs requires concentration, until you have a range of effective methods to nourish yourself physically, emotionally, mentally and spiritually. Then each set of demands balances the other. If you forget about daily life in the pursuit of spiritual bliss, then health issues, work demands or an annual holiday arrive to bring you back to the present.

If financial or family demands keep you from attending to spiritual needs, the inner hunger eventually serves as a reminder about life's bigger picture. Each level of existence is essential and how you blend them together is what makes you unique.

17

Simple Meditations

A simple, straightforward meditation involving bringing down the light and flushing it through your body is worthwhile. Leave the more complex techniques aside for now and become familiar with the basics. Meditation is a basis for contact with guides and masters, seeing the energy channel and tracing psychic cords. These practices are added gradually to strengthen meditation abilities.

Often the most suitable and effective time for meditation is after sleep when refreshed. It's possible to use meditation to refresh yourself but calm, clear meditations usually occur when you are refreshed and easily able to focus.

Meditation is not effective for people who drink or take drugs frequently. In these circumstances, meditation can lead to a lack of focus or becoming un-grounded. Alcohol or drugs consumed three days prior to a meditation may affect the quality of the meditation. Meditation is simply an opportunity to look inside and find what is there. For some people this is inner peace. For others it is creativity or answers to questions they have. Meditation is primarily a technique to draw personal focus within and to centre yourself.

One result of regular meditation is increased congruence, as many different parts of yourself are gathered together in harmony. When different parts of yourself are harnessed towards a single purpose, much more can be achieved with less effort. A team that works towards a common purpose is usually more effective than a scattered, chaotic group or even an individual working alone.

At a recent public talk I decided not to refer to my notes continuously but instead to speak my from heart and my experience about the subject. Looking out at a room of a hundred curious faces it was an opportunity to take them on a journey, an exploration of unseen worlds. In the hour that followed we laughed, cried and marveled at how easily volunteers confirmed descriptions of people connected to them by cords I traced out in demonstrations. Because I felt congruent at that moment, I was able to explore cords along with audience and not have to watch the clock or tick off relevant points.

Life with its demands can scatter us, drawing our thoughts and attentions in many directions. Meditation offers an opportunity to return to centred, peaceful balance. In this balanced state it's possible to make sound decisions, reflect on past issues and remember that in 100 years, none of this life will matter to us anyway. The best part is that meditation is free, portable, simple and effective.

The simplest meditation is to sit or lie down and focus within. When thoughts wander away to outside demands, simply guide them back to being focused within. If momentarily distracted by a sound, accept the sound and release it. This process includes repeatedly focusing upon what you are aware of within yourself and within your immediate surroundings. One effective way to do this is to state aloud or to yourself in your mind, those things within and without that you are aware of at that time. An awareness meditation might go like this:

"I am aware of my breathing. I am aware of tightness in my throat. I am aware of the sound of a plane flying overhead. I am aware of my socks pressing against my feet."

"I am aware of my throat relaxing now. I am aware of the warmth of the sun on my face. I am aware of some tension in my calf muscles. I am aware of the sounds of traffic off in the distance."

This is a simple, effective meditation technique that brings personal awareness to the present. It can be done almost anywhere while standing in a train, waiting for a bus, or on a line in a sandwich shop. When all or most of the parts of you are in the here and now you have what others might term 'presence'. When present in the moment there is great power, because all power lies in the present.

At first your mind might wander off in many directions. When this occurs, relax. Each time you become aware that your mind has wandered off to unresolved conflicts, unpaid bills or something that happened yesterday, simply state what you are aware of within your physical body or your immediate physical surroundings.

When I first taught this technique to Clare, she found it almost impossible to do. I asked her to say aloud to me what she was aware of within herself and within the room (my office). During her first attempts she had difficulty keeping her awareness in the present or in the room for more than 20 seconds. However Clare was determined to succeed with the technique, so during her drive home she practised the technique with statements such as:

"I am aware of my hands upon the steering wheel. I am aware of the red traffic light ahead. I am aware of my back pressed against the seat and the music on the radio."

After Clare practised this technique aloud and silently several times a day for five weeks, I noticed that she was more present in her physical body. She was more attentive, her cheeks lost their pallid appearance and she seemed more positive about life. I asked her what benefits she had found from the technique.

She told me, "I've become more efficient at work, so that I have an hour or so spare each day for other tasks. I've been present enough to see what my children are actually like. They've grown so much and I don't know where I've been these past few years. But do you know the most bizarre thing? I've realised that for almost a year now I've bought a tinned salmon and salad sandwich at lunch each working day and only last week I was present enough to realise that I don't like tinned salmon. As a sandwich it was a soggy, lumpy mess and I'd never noticed before, as I was busy working while I ate or thinking about something else. Some days I didn't even know if I'd had lunch at all, as I couldn't remember it. I had to check my wastepaper basket for the sandwich wrapping to discover if I had eaten that day."

There are many reasons the mind wanders away from the present, habit being the most probable cause. Learning a new habit takes practice, vigilance and effort but the rewards are often worthwhile. Small children usually live fully in the present, which can be seen in their immediate reactions to circumstances. They cry when they are frustrated or disappointed and they stop crying when they feel better. They laugh when something amuses them and stop when the moment has passed. Although children may be less effective at achieving long-term plans because they live in the present, it is also possible that they are better at the art of living as a result of actually noticing the present and its opportunities.

Another simple meditation involves focusing thoughts and attention on the third eye area, which is between the eyes in the centre of the forehead. This brings the focus back to yourself and after repeated practice, brings your senses back into your physical body and up to your third eye. This meditation is popular with masters and is often done at ashrams or meditation centres.

The process involves breathing in while focussed on the brow or third eye chakra. On the outward breath gently focus on sending some of the energy of your breath out the front and back of this chakra. As you breathe in, draw energy into this area with your breath and release it through the brow or brow chakra with the outward breath.

The simple techniques outlined here can be used in a regular meditation. The purpose of this meditation is to restore balance between the physical, emotional, mental and spiritual aspects by quietly stating what you are aware of within your physical body..

In the rush of modern life, meditation provides a chance to pause, breathe and re-set yourself. It also offers a glimpse of the underlying issues in life, unresolved issues from the past and opportunities that lie ahead. With practice, meditation can bring a person back to the present moment or take an individual out of the physical body to help him or her to glimpse the bigger picture of life. It can also enable connection with those spiritually evolved parts of yourself that offer clear advice about the consequences of your actions and decisions.

Although it begins with stillness, the inner calm found in a deep meditation is the basis for self exploration. Learning to slow the mind and experience deep stillness is a wonderful way to replenish spiritual reserves of energy. Drawing down the light is a more thorough way to cleanse yourself and to top up energy reserves.

This light can then be used to purify yourself and the immediate environment or to cut psychic cords. When cleansing and cord-cutting is complete, it is possible to explore your channel, travelling out into the universe. For some people, stillness in meditation is sufficient for their needs. For others however, it's just the beginning of exploring the universe and other unseen worlds. To be able to travel out of the physical body and be conscious of the journey can be an amazing experience. Although many people travel astrally out of the physical body during sleep at night, few recall their travels when they wake up. Learning to travel consciously when meditating can open doors to hidden, fascinating worlds.

18
Your (Astral) Traveller Body

Once familiar with the meditation process, it's time to begin dealing with psychic cords that link you to others and to parts of yourself (or your awareness) that you may have left in the past. The technique outlined below is not required every time you meditate but can be useful. It is worthwhile at the end of each day if working in situations where you collect dross such as healing, hospitals, counselling, psychic readings or emotionally charged situations. Someone who works in a calm office environment might only require to use this process one a month.

It is necessary to begin with the main travelling body. This astral body is the one that travels off through time and space continuously. Its purpose is to travel the cosmos and to learn, returning with knowledge via the connecting cord to one of your chakras.

The main traveller or astral body, relays information back to you continuously, although people are generally unaware of this. It is beneficial to consciously connect with your main traveller body to know what trials it encounters. If the traveller body is weighed down by a difficult travel experience you may unconsciously feel weighed down in your life despite having a supportive environment and a comfortable lifestyle.

Colin's former wife, Lynne, lived interstate and he was often too wrapped up in his manufacturing business to keep in touch with her and his two daughters. He forgot to send her a card one Mother's Day and during his dreams that night Lynne appeared. She told him that she was returning overseas as she felt completely unappreciated. The following day Colin telephoned Lynne to apologise for not recognising her efforts in raising the children and found that Lynne was as angry and hurt as he had seen her in his dream. Colin would not have known about this for weeks had it not been for his close connection with his traveller body. The traveller body also provides information that assists in day to day living. An example of this is when meeting someone new and feeling an instant rush of recognition.

This can sometimes be the result of the traveller body travelling forward in time to survey the future. It then returns with memories of names, faces and situations. It's an adventurous part of you, visiting places you may not dream of going but it accumulates knowledge that can assist in your life when needed. When developing a close communication with the main traveller, it is possible to notice when its explorations are contributing to your circumstances on the physical plane.

The main traveller is constantly learning. Staying in touch with it keeps you up to date with what it is learning. Some of this knowledge may not seem to benefit you but it can be a great help in keeping a perspective on life's big picture. When encountering obstacles in life, the traveller body can depart in search of viable solutions that are sometimes relayed back to you through dreams.

The main traveller may be linked through any of the chakras. As the traveller explores the universe it encounters the energy of the different planets and needs to pass through their energy fields to proceed further. In passing through a planet's energy field the traveller blends with this energy, absorbing some of it in the process. Whatever your traveller encounters 'out there,' you experience to some degree here on earth. For example, if your traveller is passing through the planet Jupiter, you are likely to feel the effects of this planet. Jupiter increases vision of opportunities and enthusiasm to pursue them, resulting in improvements in career, relationships and life generally. This is unlikely to be an overnight experience, as such journeys can take months or years.

Bringing the main traveller back to your channel to recharge it, allows you to build a stronger conscious link with it. This then enables understanding of what is going on 'out there' and assists the traveller to resume its travels recharged.

When contacting and retrieving the traveller (or astral) body for the first time it may seem lost or disoriented, having been out in the cosmos for some time. Be patient; allow it to come and go as it pleases, for it is a traveller at heart. This is a friendship worth cultivating because this body can teach what is out there in and beyond the universe.

An example of the traveller body operating close to your physical body in the short term occurs when you visit a friend. As you drive to your friend's home your traveller body travels on ahead of you to survey the destination and returns to report. This accounts for the feelings you may experience when approaching your destination, e.g. a sinking feeling in the pit of your stomach when approaching the home of two friends who have been arguing bitterly.

To avoid any difficulties the traveller may experience, you might decide to try to keep your traveller body in your channel but this is not easy. It's not called the traveller body for nothing. It loves to roam and being stuck in your channel stifles its curiosity. It's akin to keeping a boisterous teenager indoors on a stretch of rainy days. It's not possible to keep an eye on the traveller body indefinitely, as you have to sleep sometimes. Before uttering your second snore, it is gone, without even a short note as to where it is or when it plans to return.

Physical repetitive routines of daily life don't interest the traveller. It travels to work with you for a few days and soon becomes bored. If you're a pilot or travel regularly to exotic places it may accompany you more regularly but this is only one country, on one planet, in one galaxy of many, which is why it seeks greener pastures.

This traveller remains connected to each person by a cord of energy and before proceeding with cutting cords, it is important to retrieve this body. Repeatedly cutting the cord connecting your physical body to the traveller is like slamming the door after your child has run out of the house to play with friends. If you accidentally cut this cord it is likely to be reformed rapidly but repeatedly cutting this cord is not the aim. This cord is broken when we die and isn't likely to be permanently broken by the cord cutting procedures outlined in this book.

Cords to others vary in size, shape and form according to the person perceiving them. Some appear as a silver thread, others resemble a thick type of hose. Sometimes they'll even look like chains or rope and the colours may vary. Strong, deep, long-standing cords can appear like the roots of a tree as they cling deep into the chakras. These cords often require assistance from guides and concentrated effort if you want to dislodge them.

When requested, guides may cut cords using a variety of implements. Native American Indian guides might use a tomahawk. A friend has a Chinese guide who uses a sharp dagger while other guides may choose to use machete knives. The implements are not as important as the task of cutting unwanted cords to others.

19
Procedure for Cutting Cords

Energy cords can appear at any point in the physical body and are not limited to the chakra areas. If there is a weak spot in the physical body it makes an easier entry for a psychic cord. When clearing cords it is wise to check the whole body not simply the chakras.

1. When you have protected yourself and asked for the light (as explained in chapter 16) silently ask:

"Please connect me with my main travelling body."

If you cannot find this body, ask for a guide to appear and explain that you are seeking your main travelling body.

The first time you seek your travelling body is often more complicated than subsequent times, as the process is foreign to you.

2. When locating the traveller help him/her to return to your channel, cleansing it first with a flush of energy. This energy is formed by taking a deep breath, then as you breathe out mentally sending a stream of energy stemming from your brow chakra into a miniature tornado. This vortex of energy is released and mentally directed to sweep across your traveller, collecting any negativity attached to or surrounding the traveller body.

Have this energy, in the form of white light, spiral around and through your traveller until it is clear and clean. When it is clean, visualise the tornado spinning off out of sight and into space.

3. Ask your guides which chakra the traveller body wishes to return to and then request that protection for that chakra as you open it wider, by visualising it opening to accept the traveller back home.

4. Close the chakra behind the traveller, leaving no holes. If any other

holes are apparent in that chakra, close them off at this time. If experiencing difficulty in clearly seeing chakra energy, ask your guides to ensure that the chakra is well sealed or ask them to assist you with sight.

5. Now scan your body, starting with the brow chakra, for any cords which may be present.

6. If you identify any cords from a chakra, enlist the assistance of your guide to cut each cord, one at a time. To cut a cord, take an inward breath and visualise a small whirlwind of white light extending outward from your brow chakra. See this whirlwind break free from your body and cut the cord or cords. It's possible to use this whirlwind of energy to slowly encircle the physical body cutting all cords at once.

7. Once a cord is cut, it will fall away and dissolve. Don't allow the size of the cord to put you off. Simply ensure that the cord has been cut before proceeding. Recently I felt uncentred during the day and in meditation that night I saw a cord almost 20 cm across leading into my heart chakra. I asked to see the originator of the cord and a client came to mind. I cut the cord and she phoned me two hours later. She needed energy and after I had cut the cord, she phoned to re-establish it. I used the phone conversation to help her to better use her own resources then cut it again after the conversation.

It is possible to burn a cord back to its source or simply close it off by diminishing it in a clockwise direction. This is effectively spiraling it back upon itself. As long as it is pushed back out of your energy field you are doing what is necessary. It is unnecessary to follow the cord back to the person it originates from, as this may cause your traveller difficulties and take time locating and freeing it.

In rare instances the person sending the cord has some unresolved issue with you and wants to maintain a connection to you. If this occurs, your guides may assist by reasoning with the spirit of the other person, helping it to understand why you want the cord dissolved. As a minimum measure push cords back to the outside of your aura. If you cannot see it for yourself, your guides may indicate to you how far that is. This sight develops with practice and some people feel or sense these cords before they learn to see them.

8. When tracing the cord back to the person who sent it, stop just outside her aura and explain to her spirit that you don't want the cord. Make sure that you see the person turn away from you when you have told her this, as it is a symbol that she has taken the cord back again and is not interested in re-cording you at that time. If you have no vision of this, ask your guides to indicate when she has turned away or you may sense when that person's attention has been directed elsewhere.

9. It is sometimes worthwhile asking the person at the end of the cord or your guide, exactly why she has corded you. This allows you to adjust your actions if a reason is given for cords consistently reconnecting. When the person at the end of the cord has turned away, your traveller body and guides may return to your channel. When intact, the channel resembles a fine white shield surrounding your body. It is evenly formed, without thin patches or holes.

10. When removing cords, repeat the above procedure with every cord in the crown chakra area, both front and rear, including the sides of the head. When you have completed the crown chakra and there are no cords remaining, move down to the brow (or third eye) chakra, removing the cords here. When this chakra is clear of cords, proceed through each remaining chakra until you have cleared the base chakra. Then enjoy a few minutes of bliss.

In these moments I have experienced peace, balance and harmony that runs so deeply and powerfully throughout my body that I feel myself radiating joy. This is one of the rewards for efforts and commitment. It may take the form of deep stillness, fulfilment and contentment. This can last for hours after a deep mediation and with practice, each daily meditation replenishes your spiritual body and provides emotional nourishment. As a result, life seems less stressful and sources of joy and happiness are more readily available.

When completing this exercise there may be a block in one or more chakras, making it difficult to move below that chakra to clear lower chakras. This is natural and with repeated attempts, these blockages disperse, allowing you to work your way down to the base chakra.

Some people spend years meditating regularly, trying to raise their consciousness while ignoring their lower chakras. As a result they find it difficult to reach and clear cords to the base chakra. It's not as simple as thinking you are getting down there to clear cords, it is important to feel it too. For people who have difficulty seeing cords, you may feel where they are by a tightness where the cord enters your body. Try not to be too hasty in deciding that tightness in the throat is always the result of a psychic cord to the throat. Eliminate any physical causes first, such as an allergy to certain foods, unexpressed anger or the start of a cold. If you have excluded likely physical causes and the tightness persists, check for cords. If you cut any cords to the area and the pain remains, consult a medical practitioner.

Over a dinner of hot chilli one night, I took my first mouthful and promptly lost my voice from the burning chillies. I was gasping for air when my friend burst into laughter and said, "Don't tell me. A cord to your throat chakra, eh? Looks like a bad one, too."

Always check physical causes before looking for energy disturbance. In another instance I awoke one morning with my spine locked up and pinching a nerve. I was in severe pain which four treatments with my osteopath did not alleviate. Every day for three weeks I awoke at around 5 am in pain. After trying the physical approach, I meditated and sought a possible energy disturbance. In this situation it was the result of energy depletion, weakening my energy field and allowing many cords to areas I didn't usually find them. After increasing the regularity of my meditations and conserving my spiritual energy, the pain subsided.

11. When you have cut a cord and closed off your aura by sealing off the hole left when the cord is removed, close your aura down by visualising it shrinking a little. Next pull it back until it is level with your physical body. Sometimes auric energy fields extend outwards from the physical body and if you have pulled your chakra energy

back to your physical body it finds its own natural level.

A chakra does not close fully when there is a cord still attached. When forcing a chakra to close you may experience pain in that chakra region or find it springs open again when you move on to another chakra. Ensure that you cut cords from the front and from the back of your body and close the front and rear openings of each chakra.

Most people do not have the energy or the ability required to fully close their chakras in the early stages of using this technique but complete success comes with practice. There is a tendency to favour one or two chakras but it is necessary to cleanse and close every chakra when meditating. The more familiar you become with your chakras the more balanced personal development is likely to be, as you're less likely to favour one chakra while ignoring another.

To travel throughout the universe astrally and return with knowledge and function effectively in the day-to-day world requires mastering chakra energies and removing any psychic cords that may impede development.

It is common for materialistic people to be unable to function well in spiritual circumstances and it can be difficult for spiritually inclined people to be effective in physical or material situations. As we are spiritual beings who have chosen a physical dimension to master new concepts and to strengthen ourselves, it is important to tend to both physical and spiritual needs. Without losing spiritual identity, we are challenged to master the material world. Tracing cords out to the person at the other end of each cord is not necessary once you have done this once or twice. The technique is merely to provide proof that cords lead somewhere.

When cutting cords simply create in the mind a small whirlwind of white light and direct this light across each cord to cut that cord. This whirlwind, which may be only 40 cm tall and 10 cm across can also be employed to cleanse the energy field.

Larger versions of these whirlwinds can be employed to sweep a room to cleanse it of negative energy. When the whirlwind has swept the room, mentally direct it out the window and off into the sky so that the dross isn't left in the room.

During a course, Jacinta complained about being unable to see any cords when in meditation despite stating that after cutting unseen cords in the first week, she had felt much better about herself. To confirm to her that she did in fact have some cords I asked all the other students to send their awareness out to her during meditation to examine her for cords.

With her consent we examined her during a meditation and most students confirmed major cords from her third eye chakra and from her solar plexus chakra. Six of us described a short, bespectacled Asian man in a business suit linked to her solar plexus chakra. This technique is not generally recommended (as it is possible to form cords or leave your awareness outside yourself) but it was necessary to show Jacinta that she did have cords while confirming to those who saw these cords that they were perceiving them accurately.

Group consensus is a powerful tool in developing trust in personal abilities. This is also true for the quality of meditation. Ashrams and group meditation centres are popular because group meditations can help a person go higher when meditating and can build a sense of community for consultation if experiencing difficulties with the procedures.

After having practised the full cord-cutting technique above, you can use the simplified version as shown below.

Simple cord-cutting technique

1.	Centre yourself through meditation.
2.	Ask for protection on all levels.
3.	Scan your body to sense where you feel less present, perhaps due to a cord pulling you out of your physical body.
4.	If you see or sense a cord, create (in your mind) a small whirlwind out of the white light pouring down into your crown from above.
5.	Direct this whirlwind to slice the cord and break the connection. The cord will fall away naturally.

6.	When you feel that you have cut all necessary cords, direct the whirlwind slowly around your body and your auric field. This helps to collect any residual dross, leaving you feeling lighter and centred.
7.	Then direct the whirlwind out of your aura, out of the building you are in and off into space.
8.	Return personal awareness to your physical body and complete the meditation.

Students usually report feeling better and lighter after one week of meditation and cord cutting. Although many had meditated previously, they acknowledged the difference cutting cords made to their meditations and to their lives.

Initially I was surprised at the results being achieved so quickly, as I did not expect anybody to see a difference for a month or two. One student noticed that, after cutting cords to particular people, several people remarked how they felt that she was emotionally detached. After cords have been cut, people who have corded you may notice the difference if they are sensitive to surrounding energies.

Jacinta described a symptom of cord cutting when she mentioned that her ex-husband had telephoned her twice in the past three days, when he usually calls only once a month. Both times he was mistakenly told that she was not at home when she was indeed in the house. She had cut the cords linking her to him and if there is no outstanding karma between them he is likely to fade out of her life quite quickly. If there is unresolved karma between them, he will probably continue to telephone Jacinta until he re-establishes a cord with her.

People who want to remain corded to you usually attempt to re-establish a cord soon after you have cut one but in time with regular meditation, it is possible to strengthen your auric field with the added protection requested every time you meditate. Initial attempts at re-cording may be avoided through using voicemail instead of answering the phone personally. Only the most determined person continually tries to re-cord you when any cords they send are repeatedly cut.

When people tell me that they are lost in their lives or that they have forgotten what they came into this life to do, I usually search for psychic cords because longstanding cords can take us away from our intended purpose in life.

In a recent psychic development course a student in his late thirties volunteered for a cord demonstration. I was specifically looking for cords to past partners or people he had yearned to be with (unrequited love) but not pursued. Starting at 15 years of age I described a school friend, then two other slightly older men when he was 17 a long term partner at 22 and another partner at 28. He confirmed each of these people and explained that he had a crush on a school friend at 15 years of age but nothing eventuated between them. Sometimes when a person is unable to release the hopes they have built up around a potential but unrealised relationship, they find it difficult to move on and embrace new opportunities.

When demonstrating how cords can be seen, it helps to ask for volunteers who can stand in front of the audience and confirm people I describe at the ends of cords protruding from their bodies. I shuddered when describing a former partner of a woman in her thirties. She agreed that he had dark, curly hair and a small upturned nose. When I described his fierce temper and his need to control her every move, her eyes widened and she nodded her head.

Sometimes volunteers don't even remember the person I describe to them. After describing a short, stocky man with a receding hair line and deep dimple in each cheek that appeared when he smiled, the woman before me shook her head. I explained that he had deeply tanned skin and was of a muscular physique due to his physically demanding job but she still didn't recognise him. At this point a voice was heard from the third row as a young girl called out. "Mum, that sounds like dad." My volunteer laughed and nodded, explaining that she was trying to forget her former husband.

20
Spiritual Protection

Achieving high meditations regularly leaves a person clear-minded but to get there it is essential to be free of cords and negativity. Psychic cords to others can be un-centering and oppressive when attempting to still yourself in meditation. This is why it is important to cut cords before bringing down the light. To ensure all cords are cut I usually cut cords before drawing down light and again afterwards after I have filled my body with light. The second cord cutting is usually more effective as the light is stronger and the whirlwind is spinning more rapidly when cutting cords.

Everyone is protected spiritually and the inner sense of peace that stems from knowing that we are safe is an integral part of well-being. When dealing with spiritual matters and completing meditative exercises, protection is as important as it is in daily life. Protection helps a person to feel safe while increasing concentration on meditation.

The subject of psychic protection often arises in classes and there are usually several students who declare that their form of protection is impenetrable. To demonstrate the unlikelihood of such claims I conduct a test in the form of a simple exercise.

I ask the student to stand up and step forward so that the whole class can clearly see us both. I then ask the her to seal herself off with her choice of psychic protection. When she indicates that she is protected I proceed to penetrate her psychic protection and can usually do so within four seconds.

Some people protect themselves by surrounding their bodies with white light but fail to ensure that the light covers the soles of their feet, allowing an easy entry point. For others who have psychic cords leading into or out of their energy field, these are easy entry points. In one demonstration I noticed that the student was effectively closed off psychically, so I gently clapped my hands together to arouse her curiosity, as her eyes were closed. She became curious and sent a cord out to me which then became an easy entry point.

In another instance a woman sealed herself up tightly while I inwardly asked a guide for the way into her auric field.

"Look at the fine crack in her auric field," he said to me. It was an accessible entry point.

"I'm in," I said.

"How do I know?" she asked me.

"Well, I can see a silver-haired woman with a small black dog. It looks like a Scottish terrier. The woman is lonely but patiently sits by the window hoping that someone might be along soon. She misses Geoff, despite their differences."

"That's my mother and Geoff is my father who died three years ago."

"So am I in then?"

I feel like a safe cracker when completing this exercise but it is necessary to illustrate that many of us believe that we are completely protected when in fact we're not. Many students have a measure of protection that might be suitable for most situations. However they are not entirely protected.

The strongest form of protection against attack or general negativity is to bring light and the love down through every cell and molecule of the body. Some people opt for elaborate rituals, including the strategic placement of candles and crystals, talismans and even sacrifices. I believe that by regularly bringing the light down into the body properly and travelling in the company of your guides, you are safe.

If you can carry a symbol of your particular calling master you have that master's protection, e.g. for Jesus, a cross. For Buddha, the Tibetans use the bell, a spiral cross (shaped like a swastika) and other branches of Buddhism use Buddha statues, blessed string and ribbons which are worn around the wrist or the neck for protection and also the string of 108 beads used when chanting and sometimes during meditation. Individual masters have unique symbols.

Any protection that requires a time, a place or an object can limit its usefulness and its application. A simple straightforward technique that provides inner and outer protection is all that is usually required. Naturally there are tests. There are times when you may experience fear or confusion and at these times the meditation technique can offer renewed strength, allowing you to emerge stronger and better able to cope in the future.

If you perceive people who attack you spiritually as your teachers and thank them for doing an admirable job, while learning the lesson they have come to teach you, these test and trials may benefit you. It's not always easy to recognise the lesson contained within a situation, which is where your guides can help.

Several years ago I awoke one night from a deep sleep, feeling hyper-alert and aware that I had been defending myself. I lit a candle and meditated for 20 minutes before returning to sleep. In the morning I awoke and realised that whoever was attacking me was simply allowing me to reassure myself that I was safe and capable of protecting myself.

One of my guides is a Chinese man of indeterminate age who smiles constantly and only answers a question with a question or a story.

"Why am I going through this situation?" I asked him in frustration one day. He smiled before replying:

"There was once a blade of grass and this blade of grass thought it was so special and so independent that it needed not the other blades of grass but from a distance it was apparent that this blade of grass shared its stem with many others and its roots with even more."

By this time I was fidgeting, aware that the story would finish—with a question. In answering his question I'll be answering my own. If I am lazy, as I was when he told me that story, I'll meditate the next day and ask the same question again. When I do so he is not put off for a moment but begins patiently again.

"There was once a blade of grass." He politely tells me that there are no short cuts and no easy ways; either I walk the full distance or stay behind.

His way of protecting me is to help me to strengthen my weaknesses. It is not a sanctuary he offers but a process of thought whereby I can overcome the obstacles before me.

Attacks and negativity are only energy. It is possible to either take the negative energy directed towards you and transmute it, transforming it into a positive more usable force or direct the energy around you back to its source.

My friend Christine became aware of a stream of negativity being directed towards her from a jealous friend, Julianne. The friend didn't mean any harm and was unconsciously attempting to suppress her feelings but Christine felt the energy. At first she tried to talk it over but Julianne avoided the topic. Christine then contacted her in meditation to explain that she had no reason to be envious. Julianne was not interested in hearing, so Christine simply visualised the negative energy emanating from Julianne and returned it to its source.

One of the simplest method of returning negativity is to say "Return, return, return. All negativity return." This can be said in the waking state and is very effective. The repetition of the word 'return' covers the physical, mental and spiritual levels.

Some people believe that by accepting that you are safe, you are safe, which often works for those people. There are others who believe that it is important to go through a ritual or a procedure to become safe.

It's possible that the procedure actually makes them safe or that they become convinced of their safety by the ritual of the procedure. It is likely that both aspects combine to increase their safety. By believing that you are generally safe and then enlisting a range of simple procedures to ensure continued safety, you're covering both bases. If a small child, believing himself to be completely safe, walked out on to a busy road, he may not realise the potential threats to his safety. By accepting that he is presently safe and then acting to ensure his continued safety by avoiding traffic he takes charge of his circumstance to improve his safety.

Some people fear the devil, perceiving evil to be temptation lurking around the next corner or in dark shadows. Perhaps evil includes inertia, which slows us in our pursuit of all that we can be. Evil may also include doubts about our ability to succeed, which prevent us from even trying, as well as fears about rejection that cripple our attempts to reach out to spirit, to one another and to life itself. Evil may be the thousand tiny impulses, crushed in their infancy by the negativity which exists around and within us all.

Meditation increases the chances of a thousand tiny impulses reaching the light that nourishes them. Recently a person told me about her partner, who was a 'decent, God fearing Christian'. For 10 to 12 weeks in a row he's a narrow-minded, biblical zealot who stands condescendingly in the church each Sunday. After this period however, he disappears interstate to indulge his desires for sex, gambling and alcohol. Upon return he woefully admits that 'The devil made me do it'. When I first heard this I laughed and asked if I could use the line myself or better still, copyright it. This justification is merely a licence to indulge base desires and yet maintain an appearance of righteousness among surrounding sinners. It begs the question - Does heaven have a blackjack table?

In some periods of meditation it is possible to experience an exceptional connection with spirit and be able to travel up your channel (as detailed in Chapter 4) past your guides to meet your master or even higher. When doing so, your vibration is raised and great amounts of light and energy pour through your being. A sense of inner peace or a deep spiritual stillness descends, surpassing anything previously experienced. As a result you may desire to remain peacefully in meditation.

Being human and unable to maintain such a connection for long periods, you fall to earth eventually. The more you meditate the better you are able to maintain this connection. The first experience may last a minute or two which may not even occur until you have been meditating using this method for several months.

Then with each opportunity it is possible to extend the experience into minutes or even hours. The after-effects of deep meditations usually last for up to three days, as it usually takes that time for a spiritual connection to fade away.

As light attracts darkness, be aware of the possibility of drawing negativity towards yourself in the days that follow a high connection. This negativity can take the form of friends or acquaintances telephoning you to unconsciously link in for some of your brightness. Negativity may be collected while riding a bus, walking through a shopping centre or standing in a queue.

High meditations can be cyclical. At particular times of the year that vary from person to person and through certain periods of your life, meditation is relatively easy and high, clear connections are made almost effortlessly.

Make the most of these opportunities, for they are the times it is possible to make rapid spiritual progress. To mirror these highs, there are times when your traveller body (the spirit body that travels off to explore the universe) is going through a difficult period and high meditations become rare. At these times, cutting cords and spiritually cleansing yourself may be the best you can manage.

Even this is worthwhile, because personal negativity is generally kept to a minimum. It enables more effective functioning than if you've done nothing at all for yourself. I recall a friend who managed a very high connection once and when she spoke with me the following day she was still spiritually high, despite being wide awake. This is an example of living meditation. She was positively radiant for a short period.

Within eight hours she had received telephone calls from five energy hungry people. These people, who unconsciously wanted a link with her, phoned for a conversation. As a result of these links her energy soon plummeted. It takes about three days to dissolve cords completely after they have been cut and removed.

The Kahunas or 'keepers of the secret' of the Hawaiian Islands practice ancient healing and medicine believed to originate from Africa. The African connection, is due to the similarity of the Hawaiian words and references to the African words in magic, despite the differences between the two groups in culture and native languages. Traditionally the Kahunas request that once balance has been restored, don't think about the person or the situation that has caused the imbalance. This is because thoughts form links and these links may uncentre you again. That's why it's important to maintain positive thinking.

Others, especially people who are attempting to develop themselves spiritually, know on some level when you have managed a high connection with spirit and they consciously or unconsciously try to link in to this energy. It is probable that their traveller body has been out to see you and realises that you are clear and balanced.

I have an acquaintance who telephones me only when he is off-balance and it is usually when I feel good. Recently he phoned at a time when I was frustrated with my computer. He closed the conversation early and said he'd call back in the evening. I did not hear from him for several weeks. It seems that since I had little spare energy for him, he had no interest in a conversation.

Spend the next few weeks noticing who leaves you feeling good and who leaves you feeling drained. Then you'll have a clear idea who will be calling when you achieve a clear connection with spirit in meditation. By practising cord cutting and self cleansing you'll be prepared if someone drains you or un-centers you when you need to be balanced. This is not to suggest that you don't help a friend who is in need but that you notice the people around you who always seem to be needy. Choosing to help someone by sharing your energy is different from someone helping him or herself to your energy uninvited. Awareness is important.

21
Spiritual Cleansing

While psychic protection is one part of the equation, psychic cleansing is the other part. There isn't much point in protecting your energy field from dross if your energy field is already choked up with negativity. Periodically it is important to cleanse yourself and your home and work environment.

Psychic cleansing techniques range from simple, three-minute procedures for light cleansing to intricate meditations for deeper cleansing. Basic psychic cleansing techniques include:

• Swimming in the ocean.

• Taking a bath containing natural sea salt (to replicate the ocean).

• Dusting yourself down in the garden.

• Prayer.

• Meditation.

Swimming in the ocean helps to dissolve dross or negativity as salt water is an excellent cleansing tool. When stepping out of the water after even a short swim a person usually feels relaxed, despite being covered in salt.

Adding a cup or two of natural sea salt to the bath water can replicate the ocean and help to cleanse dross. If you work as a healer, a clairvoyant, a bartender, a nurse or in other emotionally demanding professions, you might have a salt bath every day after work but if you work in an office, once or twice a month is usually sufficient for maintenance cleansing.

The process of dusting yourself down in the garden takes on a minute or two and is something many healers do between clients. It offers a mild cleanse, equivalent to washing your hands compared with taking a shower. This process involves using both hands to dust yourself down, beginning with your head, your neck and shoulders, each arm, your torso and your legs and feet. Each time you dust an area of your body, flick the residual dross away like flicking water from your hands. When completing this process take a deep breath and stretch to ensure becoming grounded again.

Prayer offers a chance to still your mind and focus on deeper needs. Lighting a candle before prayer or meditation improves the energy in the room slightly, therefore improving concentration.

Meditation for cleansing varies from a simple white light meditation in bringing down white light and having it surround and flow through every cell of the body to more complicated meditations such as the Awakening to the Light Meditation detailed in chapter 15 or a Cord Cutting Meditation in chapter 19.

Simply believing that you are protected is usually not enough. Thinking positively only takes you so far and if you believe you can swim before you've learned to swim, good luck when the currents are strong.

There are some simple methods for cleansing a home environment including opening the windows to allow fresh air to circulate through the home. As clean air passes through the home it takes light dross with it. For more residual energy clean all the surfaces such as window panes, window sills, floorboards, kitchen bench tops, tables and other surfaces using products that are safe for those materials.

A 5% solution of cloudy ammonia in a bucket of soapy water is usually effective for cleaning floors, windows and window sills but more gentle products may be required for polished table tops and kitchen bench tops.

Meditation using a whirlwind of white light can be effective for cleansing a home too. When in meditation, draw down the light, sending it out through the brow (third eye) chakra as a whirlwind. Visualise snapping the whirlwind of light off from the brow and making it vertical. Widen the whirlwind to around a half a metre in diameter and stretch it out so that it reaches from the floor to the ceiling in your home.

Send it in a sweeping motion around the room you are currently in and then room by room around the home. As the whirlwind spins, it collects stagnant energy, cleansing any space into which you direct it. When you have swept your home or a particular room that you want to cleanse, send the whirlwind of energy out a window and off into space, taking the dross with it. Momentarily think about your physical body to ensure your mind doesn't remain connected to the whirlwind of energy you've sent away from yourself. End the meditation and then take a moment to notice how different your environment feels after this cleansing process.

If you've been experiencing bad dreams at night and you're not sure if they are a result of dross in your bedroom or internal issues being processed during sleep, salt water may help. Fill a mixing bowl from the kitchen with tap water and add a cup of natural sea salt. Mix the salt into the water and place this bowl in the bedroom. It's usually best placed on a bedside table or off the floor so that you don't end up with a clean bedroom and a limp from stubbing your toe in the middle of the night.

Change the water (and salt) every two days for a week. If your dreams settle down in a week then you've cleansed dross from your room. If not, it's likely that your dreams are not the result of dross but internal issues. Most people return to peaceful sleep within three days. This is an effective technique if stressed or worried about work, a relationship or financial issues and bringing these worries to bed at night. The salt water helps to clear away the energy of this worrying and allows a fresh start each day.

If there has been an argument or someone has been ill for several weeks, bowls of salt water placed around the house are an effective way to cleanse away residual emotions or negativity. Combined with opening all the windows (weather permitting) and a physical cleanse using a cloudy ammonia solution it can be a wonderfully uplifting spiritual spring clean. When a home or workplace is thoroughly cleansed the people in that environment usually feel more focussed, clear-minded and calm.

22
Maintaining Energy Balance

It is a challenge to feel radiant and avoid cords. Unless you live in a cave or on a deserted beach, you probably communicate with people every day. After a wonderful meditation you may feel so good that you'll seek out the company of others to share it with. What better gift to offer friends and loved one than the best you can be.

When striving to savour the residual energy from a clear connection with spirit and not wanting others to pull you down immediately, here are some tips:

1.	Don't open your email for a few days.
2.	Leave voicemail to answer the phone.
3.	Don't answer the door unless you feel inclined.
4.	Spend a few days away from home; in the country or by the sea.

It seems to be drastic action to maintain a feeling of wellbeing but it's your choice. In most situations you'll realise that you'll lose some energy now but will be able to reach the spiritual connection again. When you have felt low or drained for a long time, you may wish to savour these feelings of clarity and inner peace. If you've worked hard to feel centred and positive and know that others can make their own spiritual connections, then you may choose to experience this joy and peace alone.

You may use this private time to outline some relationship, career or spiritual goals. If you do lose this energy through a psychic cord to someone else, they'll probably only lose it through one of their own cords.

It is similar to pouring one cup of hot water into a cold bath; it has no noticeable effect.

Several years ago I was instructed by spirit guides to write this book. At the time I didn't want to because I felt I didn't know enough. I also didn't fancy the idea of looking down the barrel of a long book with 'only 100 pages to go'. I was content to write short stories.

One guide was brutally clear with me. "You've not been getting much work lately and you won't be getting a lot in the future, so you might as well write." I was stunned.

"This is blackmail."

"No, it is your path."

"I'm sick of this spiritual stuff," I replied, scowling. "I want things to be easy and I just want to be happy." His final words on the matter are printed indelibly in my mind.

"The price of peace of mind is effort." So, reluctantly I began. Occasionally I returned to moping with the rationale "I can write it and I can type it out but that doesn't mean that I have to publish it. In fact it doesn't mean that anyone has to read it at all."

I sometimes wonder where I'd be now if I'd opted for the gentle, scenic spiritual path. The one that allows you two turns at being a prince or a princess, a turn at being a king or queen, five chances at being a man or woman of the cloth, a short stint as a peasant followed by several chances as a popular artist, musician or craftsperson. I'd probably trade my turn in politics for a shot in the circus and reflect upon all of these during my stint as a Buddhist monk in a Tibetan monastery on my way to a try or two in a native African village.

Life as a nomad might be appealing but after all that moving about I'd need a life where I could sit down a lot, such as a clerk in a government office. During morning tea I might be struck by lightning through the lunchroom window, where a string of masters appear to me to give me the option of leaving there and then for good. I'd say "Yes" naturally and be off to that big lunch room in the sky for the long morning tea.

Instead, I feel impatient. The spiritual part of me wants to go home, return to spirit and the human part of me believes that I have a life to live and it is a pity to waste it on meditation when adventure calls. Perhaps being conscious of my traveller body as it explores time and space is enough adventure.

Exercising discipline over physical, emotional, mental and spiritual bodies can offer rewards of good health, inner peace and a harmonious life. Balance is a delicate issue, for too much emphasis in one area can leave another area unbalanced. If there are any doubts about your current state of balance, ask in meditation.

Long-term rewards and fulfilment are usually the result of disciplined spiritual practices. Discipline is the key. If you discipline yourself to meditate every day you'll feel the long-term benefits. When I complete a long day of client-based work I am usually exhausted. My initial urge is to flop into a chair and do absolutely nothing until my energy levels pick up again.

Experience has taught me that if I take a hot bath

Fig 6.
Channeling energy through meditation. When centered and without psychic cords, energy passes through your body easily.

and cleanse myself quickly, energy levels return to normal within 30 minutes. Some days it is four hours before I take that bath and in that four hours I have done nothing except flop in a chair without any energy. When I lack the necessary discipline to run a bath I pay for it by having no energy after work. Specific meditations and cord-cutting procedures are designed to achieve particular results. They are not half-hearted techniques and need repeated practice, which requires discipline.

If poor spiritual hygiene is maintained, sooner or later it will not be possible to reach high meditations again because collected dross and cords will hold you down. The resulting inertia may even cause you to cease meditating.

Negative energy can manifest as inertia, laziness or procrastination regarding positive beneficial habits. Since most people have decided not to renounce their present lives, they have to find ways of coping with everyday surrounding negativity. It might emerge as feeling too tired to meditate at the end of the day and then spending 90 minutes trying to fall asleep at night. A ten minute meditation and cord-cutting exercise can help a person to fall asleep immediately and enjoy a deeply relaxed, restful night. A few nights of restful sleep can sometimes help an individual feel years younger. Instead of struggling to tackle everyday demands, it's possible to sail through the day with enthusiasm and energy.

23
Symbols for Protection

When meditating, a lighted candle assists, along with burning incense prior to commencing, as this cleanses the meditation room. The mind is a very powerful tool and when a great number of people believe that a particular object has a certain effect upon people or circumstances, their beliefs can become reality. The communal belief grants these objects the power ascribed to them. Christian people throughout history have believed that the cross is a powerful protective symbol and it has become what they believe it to be. For Buddhists a statue of Buddha or a photograph of a lama may be used as a protective symbol. Ancient Egyptians used the Ankh which is a cross with a loop at the top that depicts the human body.

In serious psychic attack or periods of heavy energy, a cross hung in the room or worn can offer powerful protection. The cross is not merely a Christian symbol, for the Rosicrucians have used a similar cross to the Christian cross for over 3000 years.

Symbols can be powerful. The swastika used by Hitler's armies during World War II is also seen in some of the ancient Thai temples, as it is a spiral and a variety of spirals have been used by ancient cultures the world over. Spirals draw energy to their centres, that can then be channelled into a suitable or unsuitable purpose.

A healthy life-balance is the purpose. What is the point of reaching great heights in meditation if daily work brings you into contact with negativity on a grand scale? Unless you don't mind being a hermit, you have to come down sooner or later and can be corded by friends, lovers and strangers. It's all a part of the business of living. Blaming others for cording you is futile if they are unconscious of their actions on an energetic or spiritual level.

When tempted to help someone by introducing them to meditation, be aware that when they have difficulties meditating, they may unconsciously send a link to you for help. In time, they may end up strongly linked to you, becoming the energetic baggage that holds you down. Consequently it is important to be rigorous with cleansing and protection techniques.

Actively pursuing a spiritual purpose can be a lonely path, so if people around you are reasonably content, leave them alone. Once a commitment is made to this path and spirit guides commit themselves to your process, there is limited chance of going back. If you change your mind or rescind your commitment halfway, they are unlikely to be lenient with you. That is, if you choose to return to your life as it was prior to meditation, they don't assist by making it easier in any way.

Spirit guides are usually patient with you and your journey. They are also gentle but occasionally forceful. They never set a task or give you a challenge that you are not fit to complete. This is a universal law. You may feel that life has given you a challenge too great to endure but it is unlikely. Sometimes when I've been taking myself and my life too seriously, they've laughed heartily and shown me the absurdity of my concerns. In this way they have helped me to focus on the big picture.

Opening up to spirit in unfamiliar surroundings requires caution. It is not always possible to know what energies surround you or to know who has opened up in that same spot before you arrived. During a holiday in the Greek Islands with Christine, I visited an ancient temple devoted to Poseidon, the Greek god of the sea. It was in rubble, a victim of time, nature and careless locals, except for a circle of stones sunk slightly into the ground.

The moment I saw the circled stones I sat inside them and opened up my channel.

"What are you doing?" came the incredulous cry from Christine. I closed up and opened my eyes to explain.

"I'm tuning into the energy here." Her next question stopped me dead in my tracks.

"Would you like to guess how many people before you have done exactly that and how many of them might still have links to this spot?" Perhaps she was being overcautious but I decided not to take the risk.

Psychics, clairvoyants, witches and mediums generally cannot resist certain places and usually open up to fish for information. They may dump their own negativity there and often leave cords. This means that when I opened up, I risked being linked to dozens of people I've never seen before. It may have been okay but why risk it?

There are some pitfalls to becoming more sensitive when raising personal energy through regular meditation. Think for a moment about how many people spend considerable effort deadening their senses through alcohol, long working hours or simply ignoring their feelings. When opening up and remaining open psychically and emotionally, you are likely to become more aware of the heavy, negative energy fields surrounding others that they probably take for granted. The energy of their unresolved issues, unfulfilled desires, fears and regrets linger around their physical bodies like a thin fog, restricting their vision of life's opportunities. This resembles background noise that they may fail to notice or simply take for granted. It eventually can become a lead weight for an individual that is sensitive, especially when regularly psychically cleansing. It's similar to the experience of attempting to have an intelligent conversation while being the only sober person in a room full of drunk people.

Finding the symbols that work best for you is part of the journey and spending time with people who use these symbols may also be rewarding. Group meditations can offer powerful experiences, both during the meditation process and afterwards when discussing the shared practice. After a busy week at work or with family concerns, the act of spending an hour or two in meditation with like-minded strangers may offer a safety net and a reminder of how we are all part of a larger, spiritual family. It can act as an energetic re-charge when daily life is demanding.

The contemplation process is not the only reason why people drop in to an ashram during meditation periods. When Melanie accompanied Sandra to an ashram, she spent considerable time out the back scanning the shoes each person had discarded before entering the hall. She needed a new pair of sandals and sought inspiration at an ashram. After trying on a dozen different sandals she found a suitable pair and it was clear what she had to do. At the end of the evening Melanie asked the owner where she had purchased her shoes and two days later she bought herself a pair.

24
Energy Dumping

When meditating, be aware of friends and acquaintances who 'drop off' energy. Those who do so are often involved in psychic or spiritual development and yet are unaware that when they open up and bring down the light without any protection, they may end up with more than they bargained for.

Gross energy (heavy, negative energy or sometimes stagnant energy) or disembodied spirits who are attracted to light can be attracted to your light. This energy stays around if cleansing isn't completed regularly. Friends spending time with you or near your channel can unconsciously drop off this energy or disembodied spirits, in your home, leaving you to deal with it. The important thing is that it can be cleared away and the more you cleanse the less likely any residual energy will be hanging around.

This dropping off can occur over the telephone and it is usually an unconscious process. However, many years ago, in a psychic centre where I was working, someone deliberately visited to drop off energy. Two or three psychics worked seven days a week in this centre, giving readings and we had many visitors through the course of a week. One of the regulars was a man who wanted to be a clairvoyant who visited at least twice a week. Each time, he managed to off-load all the gross energy he'd picked up. He was unaware of dumping negativity; he only knew that he felt better when he visited the centre.

It became such a routine with him that if I wasn't busy with a client, I left the building when he arrived. He was attempting clairvoyance and astral projection techniques without proper grounding or protection. It wasn't too much of a problem for him because he could always clear himself with a visit to the centre.

Whenever a person finds a brighter light than his or her own, which is someone who has a stronger spiritual connection or one who cleanses more regularly it is possible to unconsciously drop off any negativity. When in the presence of a spiritual master it is possible to experience negativity lifting or dissolving. This can be the result of your passing this energy to the master whose job it is to pass it back to its source.

I first saw my master in meditation and he was in his mid-thirties with a head of thick black hair. When I saw him at a talk two years later he was almost entirely grey, as a result of all the karma he had taken on from his disciples.

This is why an energy channel is and must remain a private place. It is not the location that is important in itself, for a person can channel anywhere but it is essential to protect your regular place of channelling from outside negativity. This protects you from people who dump negativity in and around your channel.

It is also important to shield yourself from people who deliberately link into your energy. They are sometimes referred to as "psychic vampires" and they are rare. However, a former employee of the psychic centre, Lisa, deliberately sought the energy of others when she visited a psychic centre where I worked.

As she appeared in the doorway my instant feeling was one of impending trouble. As it was ten minutes before closing, I packed my cards away and prepared to depart. I packed my cards quickly, as a person's tools make an easy link to that person.

Lisa only had to handle my tarot cards and she'd have a link with me, something I was keen to avoid. Lisa was making a fuss of the other readers as she touched everything she could lay her hands on. I saw her making her way around to me, so I completed packing, donned my coat and departed with a short goodbye over my shoulder. She spun around as I left, saying "Oh, you must be the new reader. We haven't met," as she reached for me. I didn't falter as I explained that I had a tube to catch and perhaps we'd meet again.

It was rude perhaps but no more so than arriving on the pretext of a friendly visit while covertly linking in to all those in the centre for as much energy as she could steal. Later I discovered that Lisa visited every three or four months and that all the psychics knew she was visiting to steal energy but nobody bothered to stop her or to point out what she was doing. Because Lisa pretended not to see what was actually going on each visit, the other readers also chose to ignore reality. Their reasoning was simple. Why stop her when a stranger can walk in off the street and do the same thing during a reading?

People walking in off the streets rarely deliberately send out psychic cords to siphon off energy from clairvoyants, whereas Lisa visited expressly for the energy she could collect, having squandered her own reserves of energy. There is a particularly recognisable energy surrounding people who practice negative magic, called a vortex. It is a hunger within that continuously draws the energy from others, yet it never seems to satiate the hunger within the person. When near such an individual it's possible to feel drained as your energy is drawn into the vortex created by that person's spiritual hunger.

Some weeks in the psychic centre we received five calls a day where the caller hung up the receiver when we answered. Ordinarily you'd think that it was a wrong number, a prank, or a mistake. However 30 calls a week for three or four weeks made some of the readers paranoid that someone was phoning simply to form a link with a reader.

These are extreme examples and it is possible to experience similar situations when you have been meditating with a clear channel for a year or more, when you possess a bright, radiant aura. It's not life-threatening but merely inconvenient or destabilising. It's important not to write off the human race simply because they might cord you.

Newborn babies are filled with spiritual light and love, which makes them appealing to most people. To hold a newborn you can feel the powerful channel of light and an unpolluted auric field. Caroline explained her bewilderment at being in a hospital bed beside the wife of a Hells Angels motorcyclist when a group of bikers arrived to see the new baby. Even the roughest looking man melted when holding the infant. Arms littered with tattoos held the baby so tenderly that she wanted them to hold her own child so that she might have a rest.

Often the most frustrating person to be around with regard to cording is a healer, clairvoyant or alternative therapist who is involved with deep energy work and yet has little or no understanding of cords, protection or cleansing. Often five minutes in such a person's company is all it takes to become completely drained by powerful cords.

If an individual chooses to deal with these energies in his or her career, it is important to understand energy flow. When spending any period of time in the company of such a person, it is possible to walk out with more than you came in with. This occurred when I visited my osteopath one morning. It was his busiest day of the week and he had a young girl giving a preparation massage, which allowed him to get straight down to the business of back adjustment.

As she directed me to a room I sensed that I'd need protection, because her energy felt chaotic and scattered. She seemed distracted and mentally vague, as though only a small percentage of her had made it to work that day. I guessed that this was due to her current emotional difficulties. It is difficult to protect yourself from cords or from another's energy when that person has their hands on you for ten minutes. After she completed the massage she left and my osteopath entered and made the required adjustments.

As I attempted to stand I found that I couldn't. My energy was completely depleted. When I was finally able to dress and leave, it was ten minutes before I could see properly. I had to sit on the footpath outside the treatment rooms and work hard to re-balance my energies. After that incident I decided that before undergoing a massage from a stranger, I'd scrutinise his or her energy beforehand and refuse the treatment if I felt that I might become unbalanced me through touch.

Receiving positive touch from someone who is balanced and centered can help you to become centred too. A deep relaxing massage from someone who is centred and focussed can help bring personal awareness back into the physical body, leaving you feeling peaceful, calm and relaxed.

For several months I received a weekly shiatsu massage and after each session I felt positively radiant. The therapist explained that shiatsu – a fully clothed Japanese massage which includes plenty of stretching, is a bit like yoga but with someone else putting you though all of the stretches. Using a low, un-sprung mattress on the floor, she stretches the limbs, digs into the organs with her elbows and gently stretches most of the tension out of the body.

"So it's yoga for lazy people?" I asked. "Exactly," she replied, laughing. She is very conscious of keeping her own energy clean and balanced for her clients and disciplined in regularly cleansing herself and her workplace. As a result she is able to re-balance her clients weekly. The rewards of these efforts include having enough energy after work to live her own life and being able to build a thriving business because her workspace is a sanctuary from the chaos of modern life.

25
Spirit Guides

Spirit guides are beings in spirit without physical form or body, who are prepared to guide people on a quest for spiritual development. Spirit guides can be accessed through meditation or in dreams at night. Clairvoyants can sometimes contact guides through shifting their focus or awareness to see them (in the mind's eye).

Everyone has guides in spirit but many people have not seen or contacted them. Although spirit guides cannot live life for you, they can assist by showing you the path to personal fulfillment in life. They can also help you gain insight into individual circumstances and lessons in life.

Although spirit guides can greatly assist, there comes a time when a person needs to grow and develop independence. To achieve this, guides may encourage you to read the energy of a situation and decide for yourself what is the most appropriate course of action. This is the way to develop confidence in personal abilities. Eventually a person doesn't need guides to continually advise when choices are offered.

If lacking in confidence or not wishing to become independent of guides, they may take to answering your questions with questions or simply not answering you at all. If you become too reliant upon them for advice, this can be very frustrating. It is akin to being punctuality obsessive but not having a watch.

Spirit guides are not personal servants and they are unlikely to force or coerce you into a course of action. If there is an attempt to force you into a course of action it is vital to test to ensure that they are your guides and not imposters or simply your imagination (see Chapter 20, Psychic

Protection). Any guides who appear and proceed to lay down the law or expect absolute obedience need questioning and further investigation until they can demonstrate why such strict approaches are required.

This is often a symptom of personal energies not being properly aligned or not following the meditation procedure correctly. In rare situations, there may be a being who resembles your spirit guide but is a different entity altogether.

There are occasional exceptions (see Chapter 4, The Journey Homeward) where a guide requests specific tasks. This may include a change of diet (either temporarily or permanently), a series of exercises, the addition of a particular vitamin or mineral to your diet or the development of a particular quality such as compassion, humility or confidence. If in doubt, ask the guides why they advise such changes and make certain that you receive a clear explanation.

If they are evasive or non-committal awaken from meditation, stretch your legs, light a candle or some incense (if you don't already have them burning) and begin again. Sometimes a period of exercise before meditation releases tension and allows a person to relax more easily into the meditative state.

If when returning to meditation, you experience the same guide who issues the same instructions, ask the guide if he or she is there in the name of the Father, Son and Holy Spirit, or Buddha, Mohammed or whoever your ascended spiritual master may be. Don't accept a 'Yes' answer. Insist that they say it in full. Imposters do not usually say that they are present in the name of the Father, Son and Holy Spirit when they are not, for in spiritual realms, the Son, as in Christ, Buddha, Mohammed and Krishna are well respected.

This is why it is important to learn to read energy. If imposters turn up, it is possible to move them along quickly. Reading energy comes with practice. It is similar to the way many of us read the energy of others when we first meet them. You often get a 'sense' of whether you like or trust someone on first meeting. If you have tested your guide and he or she is still there making the same requests, you have a choice as to whether or not you comply. Free will is an important part of life and these procedures are not designed to replace personal decision-making ability. The first, or lower guides contacted are often more talkative but with progress the higher guides tend to say less.

If still unsure as to whether to trust your guides after completing the previous procedures, ask someone who is in clear contact with their guides to check for you. If there is no one who can effectively do this for you, wait a day or two before contacting your guides again. This doesn't mean that you need to skip meditation; it's possible to meditate without guide contact and still receive positive benefits.

Those in spirit are there to help when you are trying but unable to find your way in life. Several years ago, during a period when I was experiencing a prolonged bout of exhaustion and loneliness, I awoke to find that I had no appetite for food or for life. I wondered if the day would ever arrive when I would actually want to eat and to be alive again. That night as I cried myself to sleep, I asked spirit to give me some joy. Even if it had to be when I was sleeping, I didn't care. It would be worth it to wake up rested. The following morning I awoke laughing heartily. I was enjoying a dream so much that my laughter awoke me. Although I soon forgot the dream, I was grateful that my request had been heard. For the rest of the day I felt buoyant, cheerful and confident of being supported.

It is important that the information given by guides is accurate. Accuracy decreases when a person is stressed and experiencing a poor meditation. It can also result when a person is restless, unable to focus clearly on guides or when there is an intense desire to hear particular information. If meditating expressly to have personal plans confirmed as worthwhile then expect occasional disappointments. If advised by guides that a particular course of action is unwise, ask why. You can ignore their advice and act as you wish. Desire for a particular outcome can lead to imagined contact with guides, resulting in illusory advice.

If you ask an important question and need to be sure about the advice or information you have received, ask your guide for information about the next 48 hours. If the details you are given about the next 48 hours eventuate as advised then it's likely that the other information given to you during that meditation is correct. If not, then you won't spend a year or two waiting for something to occur that won't happen. Instead another deeper meditation later may provide more accurate information.

Spirit guides are found within your channel. An energy channel is similar to a tube and it is important to keep this tube of energy intact. Time spent in meditation checking the channel for holes is worthwhile, for any energy that is prevented from leaking can be used for living and personal spiritual development. Shining a torch into the night sky creates a tunnel of light. An energy channel looks very much like the shaft of light emanating from the torch.

The procedure for channel checking is as follows. When in a clear meditation, direct the flow of light coming down through the crown chakra, out through the third eye. This opens the third eye chakra, enabling you to see (clairvoyantly) your channel and anything you need to see for this exercise.

Then request a guide appear before you or if you have a name for him or her you can ask for that guide by name. After greeting each other, ask the guide to accompany you on a check of your immediate channel.

When beginning, examine the channel for holes or weak spots in your field of energy. If you find holes or thin places throughout the channel, these can be remedied simply. Direct the flow of light that is entering your head through your crown chakra out through your third eye chakra into the hole or thin spot, filling it in. Ensure that the energy you are directing is blending with your channel wall, strengthening it and becoming one with it. Rotate your awareness 360 degrees to see your channel from every angle.

You may not be able to cover the entire length of the channel, as it is very long and requires experience and practice to travel its length. If there are any holes or weak spots in the energy field they are likely be grouped around the seven chakras or energy centres of your physical body. As the channel is your source of light and energy, any holes allow this energy to leak out, depleting your supply and attracting negativity with its brightness. At this stage focus only on the part of the channel around the physical body and first metre above your head and below your feet.

It is possible to access spirit guides through your channel. These guides are unlikely to appear together but they appear at each chakra or energy centre and in groups with a common background, e.g. American Indians grouped at one chakra, Chinese at another, etc. (see Fig. 7). Guides are found up and down the energy channel. There are seven guides or groups of guides, corresponding with the seven chakras. It is rare that a person will perceive all seven groups until very experienced with the process and able to achieve very high meditations.

The nationalities of each guide group vary and no particular group is better than another. It is likely that your guides are representative of the different groups of people you have spent time with in previous lives.

If you find a group of American Indian guides, you have probably spent a life amongst these people and these guides have spent time with you. "When you are ready, you can ask your guides where you know them from. They can take you on a journey, which may be exciting or painful, into the past that you have shared with them. My experiences of such journeys have taught me about myself, my guides and the way of life of other people.

My native American Indian guide has recently been pointing to two horses every time I visit him in meditation. He wants to take me on another journey but these journeys take time (sometimes two hours in meditation) and I've been busy with other projects. We will go together soon, for I have reason to believe that what he wants to show me relates to my life at the present time. In previous sojourns with him he has carefully shown me the benefits of group interaction and team spirit in the everyday activities of the tribe. He has asked me how I can apply the same principles in my own life. His approach is to show me instead of telling me something. It allows me to make up my own mind and reach independent conclusions. Each meditative journey offers a chance to explore another aspect of life or an issue currently presenting itself. Almost every journey results in a deeper understanding of my choices.

Each guide and his or her group relate to one chakra. "When identifying the chakra each guide is related to, it is possible to know exactly where you are (high or low) in your channel. So while travelling up and down the channel that surrounds your physical body, it is possible to see guides or groups of guides for each chakra. The physical equivalent is moving personal awareness up and down your spine from chakra to chakra.

As there are seven main chakras in the physical body, there are seven guides or groups of guides (see Fig. 3). Don't expect to meet them all in one meditation. If there is a blockage in one chakra or there is difficulty in moving up and down the channel, you may not meet all of your guides for years.

Some clairvoyants, healers and people who meditate regularly who have met one guide, think that they have found all that there is to find in spirit. Even professional clairvoyants who communicate only with one guide sometimes feel that they have sufficient contact with spirit. Persist until meeting all seven groups, because then you have successfully moved up and down your channel through all seven chakras. You'll also have access to seven different perceptions of life and guidance with spiritual nourishment and development.

The exploration doesn't stop there either, for when you have met guides on each level there is an opportunity to reclaim knowledge from the life or lives you have shared together. There is plenty to learn from each guide and from journeying into the past, for you are the sum of your past actions and decisions. The guides for the lower chakras are useful in giving information about everyday situations, whereas the guides for the higher chakras, the heart chakra or higher, usually deal in more abstract or spiritual terms, relating more to your soul's journey than to current physical circumstances.

After several weeks of meditation and no sight of guides, Emma discovered dozens of people during one meditation. They were a blur until one woman spoke to her and stood out from the rest. The moment she spoke, Emma felt a tug on her solar plexus chakra, that she interpreted as a confirmation of the connection with this guide.

It is not necessary to meet guides in any particular order when contacting them in meditation. It's possible to meet the guide for the base chakra and then a guide from the heart chakra group. With practice it is possible to meet them all and enlist the aid of the ones you have met to help you reach others.

My Thai guides are always in a group. It is impossible to single out a main guide. The warmth radiating from their collective energy is an inspiration of a harmonious community. Conversely, each time I have seen or spoken with my Chinese guide he has been alone. I have never seen another member of his group. I haven't asked if there are others and I expect that if there are, he will introduce them at an appropriate time. These journeys into the past have been both short sojourns and epic journeys taking weeks of regular meditation to complete. When interrupted during a deep meditation it's possible to return to the conversation with a particular guide a day or two later in another meditation. When a guide takes you on a journey in mediation to show you something, the process may require several mediations to complete the process. Sometimes I can't wait to finish the day and return to meditation to discover where the next part of the journey will lead. It's like watching a powerful film. The difference is that you often feel a part of the whole experience and can ask questions about what you're seeing.

There have been occasions when I was overwhelmed with emotion and unable to continue and other meditations where I simply ran out of time. In each instance, when I returned to meditation and sought out the guide, we immediately became immersed in the past and continued the journey. These explorations are not simply for the purpose of proving the existence of past lives, despite the possibility of gathering enough information from them to authenticate a particular incarnation.

They are an opportunity to grasp personal history here on this planet and clearly perceive individual purpose here this lifetime. There may also be some unresolved incidents or situations from previous lives that require resolution before proceeding with this life's lessons. Although there is no obligation to seek out unresolved issues or learn from them, there are usually significant rewards for doing so. These might include the chance to recognise what particular people in your current life have to teach you and what experiences you've shared together previously.

When first introduced to this range of guides from many different nationalities I became defensive.

"Why can't I have my usual guides? Why all these foreign guides?" I asked Christine. I was familiar with two guides who were Caucasians whose first language was English. Christine explained that these guides had shared lives with me in previous incarnations. Gradually I recognised their importance. They were reminding me of lessons shared together and different perceptions of life. In a way, it helped diminish my ignorance regarding other cultures.

Marco is a friend, whose 15-year friendship with Joanne was in turmoil. He explained how they had taken a holiday together and it had turned out to be a disaster. Instead of snorkelling in the sun on a tropical island, they spent almost two weeks huddled inside avoiding a series of tropical storms. 12 months of saving and planning for this break left them frustrated and disappointed. They bickered continuously and returned home exhausted. Two weeks later Joanne had not returned Marco's calls and he felt that their friendship was in jeopardy.

Marco was advised by his spirit guides not to jump in to sort out the problems but instead to allow Joanne to bring them to him in her own time. The guides explained that Joanne needed time to rest after the trip and to make sense of the difficult experience. The wait was challenging for Marco, who urgently wanted to resolve the conflict and restore their friendship. Marco repeatedly asked his guides, who were happy to allow him to pursue the forthright approach but cautioned him that it was not a wise choice. They reminded Marco that he had asked them to highlight the wise approach, so in effect he was carefully advised but free to act as he pleased. He immersed himself in his work as a distraction and waited. Eventually Joanne brought the unresolved conflicts to him, resulting in resolution without emotional cuts and bruises. They discussed the disappointment over dinner and ended up laughing about it. At the end of the meal they had decided to open two travel agencies named "Holidays From Hell" and "Give Me a Break."

During a recent psychic development course, Margaret spoke of rarely glimpsing guides and when she did, the guides would not confirm that they were coming to her through the Father, the Son and the Holy Spirit or the source, the manifestation of the source and the energy behind the source. It occurred to me that she had possibly turned her back on those in spirit. I asked her if some painful incident in her past had driven her to feel abandoned by God or spirit. She confirmed that there had been two devastating periods in her life where but for her children, she might have given up the will to live.

As she described the events her eyes brimmed with tears and the memory seemed to age her in a matter of moments. I asked Margaret what she needed to restore her faith in spirit but she didn't know. She agreed to think about it. I reasoned that it was possible that her decision to cut off from the source (or spirit) during her times of great pain may have caused her present inability to see guides in meditation.

Katie mentioned that she, too, had experienced pain so great that she had lost her faith in God and all those in spirit. She also experienced difficulties with seeing guides in meditation. I asked her what she required of spirit to restore her faith in them.

She didn't seem to want to restore her faith in them. Fellow class members were supportive and the fact that she was present in the course meant that she was stronger than the trial she had faced. In her own time and way, she might work on rebuilding trust with those in spirit. An alternative is to thank the guide for appearing and simply ask for another guide to come to you through the source, the manifestation of the source and the energy behind the source.

A Guide-contacting Technique

1.	Make yourself comfortable and enter meditation.
2.	Cleanse your aura, using white light in a miniature whirlwind to sweep your energy field clean of debris. Visualise the whirlwind of energy disappearing off into space.
3.	Request protection on all levels.
4.	Request that your guide/s appear before you in the name you feel most comfortable with such as the source, the manifestation of the source and the energy behind the source (or the Father, Son, and the Holy Spirit (Buddha, Krishna etc.).
5.	If they do not appear after a few minutes, it may be necessary to move your awareness up the energy channel. To do this, take a deep breath and at the same time draw down extra light through your crown. As you release your breath, push this energy down through your body to thrust your awareness upwards. The sharp release of breath through the nostrils as you force your awareness upwards is a simple process. You may have to repeat this procedure to raise your awareness enough to contact your guides.
6.	Ask your guide if there is anything that you need to know at this time. Listen inwardly for the reply. It sounds like remembering a voice.
7.	Ask your guide questions about one subject. Asking about too many subjects may lead to confusion.
8.	Thank your guide for the assistance.
9.	End your meditation.
10.	Write down your question and what you were told by your guides while it is still fresh in your mind. Details that are not written down may soon be forgotten. Date the page for later verification.

You might ask a simple list of questions, including:

What is my next step?
What can I learn from this person or situation?
Why is this situation repeating itself?
Would it be wise for me to ... ?
Why am I not receiving the results I had hoped to receive with... ?
What can I do to resolve / release / achieve / understand / help?

If unable to see your guides in meditation, be patient and persistent. There are many reasons why some people experience difficulties with this technique. It is an intricate technique and requires regular practice to familiarise yourself with the process enough to settle into it naturally.

Personal visualisation skills may need strengthening through practising the visualisation exercises described in Chapter 15. These may be limitations resulting from recreational drug use that passes when ceasing taking drugs or alcohol and allowing the physical body to detoxify.

There may be subconscious fears surrounding the technique that require resolution before proceeding successfully. You may have turned your back on spirit as a result of some traumatic earlier incident. If so, it may be necessary to resolve the feelings and attitudes surrounding the incident to allow spirit back into your life again. It is not possible to exclude spirit entirely, as spiritual energy exists everywhere but it is possible to exclude direct communication with spiritual beings when feeling that you have been abandoned or ignored when pleading for help.

Don't assume that you are unable to master the exercise when experiencing setbacks. There are many reasons for delays in being able to achieve the results these techniques offer. You are establishing lines of communication with parts of yourself and with those in spirit that have not previously existed in this way and building trust takes time. It is like establishing a friendship. Expect the first steps to be tentative. I know of people who have meditated for years before being able to see their spirit guides. After we returned to Australia, Amanda meditated every day for more than three months. One afternoon she walked in from a garden meditation looking dejected. I sensed that she was ready to give up her attempts to contact her guides because she wasn't have any success in seeing them.

Remembering the Chinese guide Christine had described, I sat down to meditate and contact him. In meditation I found him and explained that Amanda might give up if she didn't experience any real progress soon. He nodded silently and thought for a moment. He then told me to instruct her to return to the garden, sit cross legged on the lawn facing the back fence and meditate. After 15 minutes she might see him beneath the lemon tree. I finished the meditation and explained what she needed to do.

She disappeared outside into the late afternoon sun. I returned to reading my book as an insect buzzed in the window. 30 minutes later she returned with an expression of disappointment. I asked what happened and she explained that she had meditated as requested.

"Did you see him under the lemon tree?" I asked tentatively.

"Yes but he didn't say anything to me," she sighed.

"What? For three months you've been meditating without a glimpse and now in 30 minutes you're complaining that he hasn't said a word? You've seen him! You've seen him. There will be other meditation for conversations."

Time spent practising the Awakening to the Light meditation is not wasted. It can help to raise awareness in meditation and prepare for guide contact. Try to avoid the practice of comparing yourself with others. It is not a race. If it is, each of us has a completely different starting point.

26
Clairvoyants

We all have the ability to be intuitive because we all commenced life as sensitive people. Small children sometimes blurt out sentences that are surprisingly insightful, while learning to think before they speak. In teaching them to think first, we give the message that their minds are more reliable than their feelings or instincts. The less they rely upon their feelings and intuitions, the less their intuition develops.

The term 'clairvoyant' literally means one who is clear seeing. Clairvoyance is sometimes called 'second sight', referring to the ability to see situations and events that are not readily visible to the naked eye. These can include situations in other parts of the world or past and future events. There are three basic methods for receiving information psychically.

Clairvoyance is developed ability to see images of events at a great distance, in the past or the future. These images can be symbolic, requiring the clairvoyant to interpret them or in realistic terms, as occurs when you recall a past situation in your mind or mind's eye.

Sometimes a clairvoyant perceives situations that make no sense to them and the client is enlisted to help unravel the significance of the images. This happened to me one day in a demonstration to a class. I described some stainless steel farming machinery that the student was examining before delivering to a customer. In my mind I saw him looking around this rectangular metallic box-like structure, which made no sense to me. He later explained that the particular machinery I had described was something he was thinking of retailing for use in dairy farms.

Clairaudience means clear hearing. This is the developed ability to clearly hear the voice of your guides in meditation or in the waking state. During a reading for a client a clairaudient usually states "I am being told that" or "I can hear this music that sounds like..." Those with less developed clairaudient abilities may experience a voice in dreams at night, telling them what to do or something they need to know.

Soon after the death of a close friend I was alerted to her astral visit during a dream one night when I heard her calling my name. She visited to reassure me that she was fine which helped with my grieving. Despite knowing that she was in a better place I was sad because she wouldn't be a part of my daily life. We conversed in dreams a few times after that until she felt that it was time to move on and allow me to live my life.

Clairsentience describes clear feeling. It is the developed ability to handle an object and read the energy left in it by people who have owned or handled it previously. More obvious examples of clairsentience occur when a person has a positive or negative feeling about a house when walking into it. The feeling in the house is usually left there by present or previous occupants.

Clairsentients read the energy of rings, watches or other personal objects belonging to someone. They often combine this with clairvoyance and receive images after touching an object. During a recent psychic development course students paired off to practice psychometry – the sensing energy from objects such as a ring or a watch. Nathan complained the following week that during this exercise he had felt a twinge of back pain, that his practice partner Jade confirmed. This pain reoccurred throughout the week, interrupting Nathan's sleep and affecting his concentration at work. Jade bounced into the room that morning explaining how she felt fabulous now that her chronic back pain had disappeared. During this process Nathan had inadvertently collected Jade's back pain. He asked how to return it. I explained that all he had to do was to state "Return, return, return; all negative things return" and then mentally release it.

During the morning tea break I asked Nathan how his back was feeling and he explained that he felt much better. "I did hear Jade complaining about her back again," he said and grinned as he sauntered off in search of another chocolate biscuit.

It's important that clairvoyants take responsibility for what they see and what they tell their clients and also for maintaining their clarity of vision. Often clients consult a clairvoyant when the outlook is bleak, seeking reassurance that life will improve. Some clients seek advice about an appropriate course of action to ensure a positive outcome from their present situation. When a reader is able to tell a client that circumstances are likely to improve, it helps the client persevere.

An important task of the clairvoyant is to remind the client that the current situation will pass. It is a fact. Good circumstances come and go. Trials also come and go. Predicting the future is a delicate process as there exist many possible futures. The clairvoyant's task is to illuminate the most beneficial path to take from the opportunities available and to describe the most likely path the client will take. We know which path we have taken when we look back but the clairvoyant's task is to know that path before it is taken and the results of taking it. The client has free will. Sometimes the clairvoyant's task is to remind the client how to exercise this free will constructively.

One basic stereotype of a clairvoyant is of a silver-haired woman in her fifties with a foreign accent and an odd assortment of curios in her workplace. These might include a collection of thimbles, teapots, tarot packs or religious artifacts. I have a friend who, as a clairvoyant, fits this stereotype perfectly. When clients arrive at her home where she reads, Audrey puts the kettle on for 'a nice cup of tea'. They chat for a few minutes as she finds her glasses "because I can't see a bloomin' thing without them luv." Audrey produces a tiny pack of cards and starts talking.

One day when I was visiting her I noticed that some of her cards were missing, and that she did not have a complete pack.

"Your pack is a bit short," I remarked and she laughed.

"I don't know a thing about those cards anyway, darling. The problem was that I used to simply look at people and read them but they became so paranoid about what I could see that they'd close up tight, making it hard for me to get any information at all. So now I splash a few cards on the table and remember to point to them occasionally as I read the way I've always read. It's easier that way."

Her clients don't expect her to simply look at them and read their energy. They come with the expectation of a technique, a system or a performance, which is what she delivers.

27
Clairvoyants and Meditation

One metaphor for life might be that we are all in a forest and one person asks another "How do things looks from where you stand?" The answer is usually the same. "Trees. It's all trees from here." If clairvoyants influence the life directions of others by telling them what might be, they risk limiting their clients' openness to other possible directions. They can also limit the clients' ability to determine their own direction.

Although many clairvoyants work diligently at their profession, it is possible for anybody to do what they do, see what they see, by making time and finding the discipline to practice the techniques. Many people consult clairvoyants without wanting to know about life patterns. They come with more immediate problems requiring urgent solutions or directions to where solutions can be found.

The spiritual supply of energy available to everyone is to enable an individual to return home to the spiritual source after death. It can be depleted through giving clairvoyant readings. Helping others is sometimes an important part of growth but it is possible to help others constructively without depleting personal spiritual energy.

Considerable amounts of spiritual energy are expended during a clairvoyant reading, energy that can be used for the clairvoyant's own spiritual development. Some people believe that it is selfish to refuse to read for or help others with personal spiritual energy reserves. However, when life here on the earth is over and it's time to cross the line into spirit, who is responsible if spiritual energy is squandered giving clairvoyant readings for others instead of preparing for a personal spiritual voyage?

Why give others spiritual reserves of energy when it is easy to show them how to access their own source of energy? Encouraging people to be responsible for their own spiritual development enables freedom and independence. Everybody wins. While clairvoyants continue to read for clients, depleting personal reserves of energy, the clients can either retain their own energy or worse, fritter it away in a non-productive manner. This is not suggesting that clairvoyants should avoid giving readings but that this spiritual energy better serves them in travelling out of their physical bodies and all the way back home, to their eventual spiritual abode (see Chapter 4, The Journey Homeward).

If they have travelled this distance through meditation, they can access a greater source of energy, which can then be used for giving readings if it seems important to do so. This means that the clairvoyant needs to be a bit of a juggler throughout the reading process. The reader has to seek and retrieve information and then find the most appropriate way to tell the client what she sees. She then has to find a way to relay her findings to the client in a language that the client understands.

Sometimes clairvoyant's receive information that doesn't make sense to them, such as mathematical equations or scientific formulae and it's important that they pass this on to the client without altering its meaning. The clairvoyant needs to be aware of the client's questions and their own spirit guides simultaneously. This can be difficult, especially with guides who are less than tactful in their appraisal of the client's circumstances.

I often work with two guides when giving readings and for practical questions about my own life and a different set of guides for personal development. The guides present when I read for others have unusual and sometimes blunt ways of looking at life. I am sometimes forced to edit what they say to me, to avoid offending my clients.

An example occurred recently with a young woman who was desperate to be married to a particular man. In her mind she had decided that being married to this man meant the end of her loneliness and a guarantee of happiness and fulfilment. The man in question had run away from her to Africa. He told her that if he returned, then he'd marry her. I asked my guides to explain the situation more clearly to me.

"She's driven him away with her obsession to be married. She's only 22 years old. What's the hurry?" he said to me. I pressed him for more detail.

"Will he return to her?"

"He'd be a fool to come back."

"Yes, but will he come back?"

"Of course. He's addicted to her as she is to be married to him. Take a look at this other man. He's the one with whom she'll be happy."

At this point I was shown a scene of the woman before me laughing and talking with a curly-haired man and who was not the man she wished to marry. Later I saw another scene of two children, one of whom looked like a small version of the curly- haired man.

"Can I tell her about this?" I asked.

"Yes, she'll need this information in a year from now."

Having spent about five minutes staring away from my client at the wall, I turned to give her the edited version of events.

"The man you have asked about is coming back to you. There is, however, another opportunity for fulfilment. Another man is going to enter your life and he has brown curly hair, a big build, well-defined muscles and hazel eyes."

"But I don't want another man," she replied.

"Yes I realise that but when the time comes, he is an opportunity that you may consider. It's always a nice feeling to have more choices than you need, after all. You can say 'no' when he arrives, especially if you are happy in your current relationship."

At this point my guide burst into laughter with, "Happy! Happy to cling together in the shadow of their own hunger. Dwarfed by their own desires." I declined to repeat what he said.

"Where will I meet this other man?" she asked. As a rule, I don't answer this question as it usually doesn't help the client. If I told her that she'd meet him at a bus stop, she'd probably spend the next five years loitering at bus stops and still not meet him one day earlier than life intended. I explained to her that he would arrive at the appropriate time and that she'd benefit more from focusing on current issues.

When clients are laid low by life and their outlook is bleak, a clairvoyant who gives them something positive to look forward to, actually motivates them to shake off their negative attitudes. When a clairvoyant gives the client some positive events to anticipate but none of the steps required to reach these circumstances, problems may occur. Instead of being motivated to take action to achieve individual desires, the client slips away from that present hardship into fantasy, picturing the eventuality described by the clairvoyant.

Recently Astrid asked about her love relationship with a man who had recently left her. After refusing to remain on his medication for a psychological disorder, he was sinking into mental chaos. I explained that this relationship wasn't giving her what she wanted and was distracting her from pursuing her new career but she was desperate to be told good news.

"I had two other readings from another clairvoyant who told me that we are soul mates. She said that there is a baby waiting to come into the world for us to raise, but this child is waiting for him to resolve his issues and commit to me." I sighed and searched through her past and into the future to glimpse some of the patterns of her life before I spoke.

"Is it fair to say that your father was self-absorbed when you were growing up?" I asked tentatively.

"Yes. He was an alcoholic."

"Is it fair to say that sometimes you were invisible to him as a child?"

"More like always than sometimes." She said as she began to cry.

"Let's look back at the past three men in your life. It seems to me that although different from each other, these men were all self-absorbed and unable to acknowledge how hard you worked to make them happy. Is this a fair assessment of the situation do you think?"

"Yes."

"Looking ahead five years I can see you sitting on a balcony with a partner, raising a glass to the fantastic year you have had together. You seem astounded that so many positive opportunities arrived in a relatively short time and you're glowing with happiness."

"Is this partner my recent partner?"

"No. It's someone new."

"But what about the baby?" she asked.

"What age are you now?"

"Forty eight."

"And at what age did the clairvoyant tell you that this baby was to arrive?"

"When I'm fifty."

"How many women do you know who have given birth at fifty years of age?" I asked. There was a long silence before Astrid spoke.

"Are you saying that she was wrong?"

"I can't comment on another reader's findings as I wasn't present for the reading and I don't know how she gleaned her information. I can only tell you what I see. From what I can see today. Your most likely future includes this other man, however you have free will with all of this."

If a clairvoyant does not encourage the client to remain in the present and deal with the current obstacles, the person may not resolve or learn from the circumstances. The result can be that the conditions drag on unresolved. Sometimes people sacrifice spontaneity to seek certainty in their lives and there can be underlying comfort in being told what to do. It absolves some of the responsibility for personal choices in life.

The original seers were the high priests and the religious teachers in the community. Who better to instruct people on spiritual values than someone who is in direct communication with spirit? This is an important step toward personal spiritual growth and connection or communication with divine energy.

Why be continually dependent upon others for information, when those in spirit gladly give directly? It may serve a person to consult others for convenience or if there is a lack of time or discipline to maintain meditation practices. Some people pay others to communicate with spirit on their behalf when, with effort, everyone can learn to do this themselves.

In giving readings to clients, clairvoyants are sometimes accused of removing opportunities for their clients to learn by telling them the most likely outcomes. Sceptics believe that when clairvoyants predicts the future, they plant the seed of that outcome in the mind of the client. The client, who then, consciously or unconsciously, moves towards the predicted outcome, due partly to their individual beliefs in the clairvoyant's powers. While this is possible, it does not account for psychic's ability to correctly confirm what has occurred in the client's past when he or she was not present to plant suggestions or to witness what occurred.

An effective clairvoyant can also search back into a client's past to glimpse important decisions and turning points that have shaped that individual's life. In a recent reading I took a few minutes to scan back through the client's past for incidents that affected her self-confidence and shaped her attitudes to love relationships. Karen sat quietly while I sifted through the details, noticing which specific events had influenced her attitudes to relationships. I described these to her and she thought for a moment, before nodding in agreement. They included her watching how her parents resolved conflict when she was a small child and the longstanding influences resulting from her first love relationships. In maturity, it can help an individual to reassess attitudes when knowing the incidents or situations that helped to originally shape those beliefs. If attitudes are not questioned periodically, they can exert an influence on personal decisions below your conscious awareness.

28
The Senses

There is a tendency for people to lose their senses or awareness through the seven main chakras (see Fig. 3). The chakras serve as connections between spirit and the physical body.

Mental awareness may travel from the physical body when curiosity or desires are triggered. The main traveller or astral body has a will to travel and although it can be influenced by the mind, it has a great strength to resist personal mental abilities. This means that it is not possible to simply ask it to return to your physical body and expect it to do so. The astral traveller connects the physical body with the higher, causal self. The causal body is the highest or finest of the energy bodies, that is less restricted by time or gravity etc.

The Traveller body investigates, seeks wisdom and relates all that it finds back to the physical body through a thin invisible cord or thread. This is attached to the physical body through one of the chakras. The chakra through which the main traveller is centred differs from person to person. It's possible to discover where spirit energy is leaving the body by asking your guides or by simply focusing upon each chakra individually. This method is outlined in the next chapter.

The senses are directed by your mind, emotions and incidents in life and may wander about while your physical body is sleeping at night. This is especially true of the traveller body. Part of the purpose of meditation, aside from contacting guides and travelling up and down the energy channel, is to purify and rebalance yourself, to make your body a comfortable place for the astral traveller and the senses, so that they can reside peacefully within you.

If a person allows the physical body energies to fluctuate wildly or to become very unbalanced, some of the particles may vacate the physical body. This individual is unlikely to notice the senses straying from the physical body when experiencing great physical or emotional upheaval.

Prolonged trauma upsets the balance between the physical body and the spirit. If you retrieve your senses or scattered thoughts and desires and are still experiencing great physical or emotional turmoil, your senses are unlikely to remain with you for long.

The actions or circumstances that can upset the balance of energy and open up the way for senses to scatter include:
• taking drugs, both recreational and some prescription drugs or consuming alcohol.
• an accident or a severe illness.
• a sudden shock.
• a surgical operation where a general anaesthetic is used.
• alcohol abuse.
• prolonged severe physical or emotional pain.

Generally, people live with a degree of scattered awareness and a reduced level of spiritual energy in their physical bodies. This causes no harm other than to make them less present or centred. To be centred, balanced and completely whole, it is necessary to be 'all there'. All senses are needed to be present. To achieve this, a still mind is required.

It's possible that some people fall in love to make themselves whole again. When something is missing (their own spiritual heritage of infinite love and peace) they seek fulfilment elsewhere, even if it's temporarily. There is a natural inclination to fill the void due to unconscious awareness that something is missing.

If a person is losing energy through the base chakra, there may be a natural inclination to fill the void due to an unconscious awareness that something is missing. This triggers a desire to fill the gap to restore balance.

If the desire to fill this gap in the base chakra is not pursued through meditation, an individual may choose to fill the void by finding someone (a partner) to compensate for this deficiency. Another method involves seeking people or circumstances to satisfy personal hunger, based upon the particular chakra that is unbalanced. Continuous hunger results in attention dropping to the base chakra, increasing desire for sex, food or whatever makes one feel complete again. Sexual desire or excessive eating can gradually become a constant pastime as a temporary replacement for long-term spiritual fulfilment.

A person may eat more food than is necessary due to spiritual hunger. This is exemplified by spiritual masters requiring much less food due to their spiritual needs being met. Sometimes it is important to hear the spoken word due to inner spiritual needs. Through spiritual discussions, a positive conversation or listening to someone reading a spiritually uplifting text, it is possible to be spiritually and emotionally nourished. When the senses are drawn in through meditation, physical pleasures are less important as an individual becomes fulfilled on deeper levels.

In a psychic reading recently, Narelle was be weary with living, as she had not experienced an easy life. She suffered with severe, sudden mood swings and was oscillating between exhilaration and despondency. Throughout the reading she seemed to completely lack enthusiasm. As the reading concluded, I thought that perhaps Narelle had not received what she sought.

Narelle had been undergoing therapy for nearly two years and as she departed she explained that she felt that she had not progressed very far. That evening when I was cutting cords in meditation and rebalancing myself, I noticed a manifestation or spiritual entity with me that was not my own. I asked this manifestation, the product of a cord from someone else, to accompany my travelling body and together we traced the cord attached to this spirit body back to its owner. It was Narelle.

As it was attached to my second or navel chakra, that connects with passion for life and enthusiasm, I interpreted it as meaning that she wanted some of my enthusiasm, that she lacked within herself. This manifestation was created by Narelle's desires and mental despair.

It was not an easy task ensuring that the spirit body remain with her physical self while she was feeling so desperate, for there was no nourishment there for her. In meditation, I explained to her manifestation that these emotions belonged with her and that there was no room or place to remain with me, the spirit became upset and began to cry. A manifestation can take on every emotion.

When I explained that without her spiritual energy returning to her physical body Narelle's spiritual progress might be impaired, it became almost hysterical. It was adamant that it didn't want to go back as there was no nourishment there for it. I was momentarily at a loss as to what to do, when my own traveller pointed out that all Narelle's efforts with therapy were about to pay off. Eventually her needs would be nourished.

The manifestation accepted this and reluctantly returned to Narelle. I cut the cord and pushed it back, sealing the chakra behind me. In the physical state Narelle was probably unaware of what went on. I didn't think it was necessary to tell her.

My responsibility to myself is to remain balanced and whole. Had I allowed that manifestation to remain within my aura it might have added that desire to me and restricted my own spiritual progress. Narelle would not benefit from her senses leaving her and remaining with me. Instead, she may have experienced a deep hunger on that chakra level.

When it is difficult to forget a lover, an ex-husband or wife there may be several reasons for this in spiritual terms. I refer here to thinking obsessively about another person, perhaps even years after the relationship has ceased.

The first most obvious reason might be that the karma (or unresolved learning) between the couple is not yet complete. That isn't suggesting that a full relationship needs to be resumed to complete any outstanding karma, as there may be other ways to resolve the karma. The simplest way is to ask your guide what lessons are involved and the most suitable approach to mastering them.

A second possibility is that the individual and his or her former partner are still corded psychically to each other. This can be as a result of unresolved issues in the relationship or through thinking continuously about each another. Angry thoughts about a former partner result in a psychic cord being sent to that person or strengthened if one exists already.

Considering the number of people who leave relationships experiencing unresolved anger and resentment, it is common for former partners to have cords between themselves. As long as a person blames another for his circumstances he remains corded to that person.

The Kahunas of Hawaii believe that amends must be made with people you have offended, not with God. In this way, making an effort to restore harmony between yourself and others helps to reduce the need for cords by offering resolution.

A third possibility is that some spiritual energy has been left with a former partner and the desire to see that person again may be an unconscious desire to reconnect with this spiritual energy. Naturally, if a person has not rebalanced or not made a more suitable home within for spiritual energy, spending time with a former partner will not bring inner peace.

To retrieve spirit bodies (energetic parts of the self that may have been left behind), it is not necessary to spend time with a former partner who, consciously or unconsciously, has possession of them. The retrieval of spirit bodies can be done through meditation while accompanied by a spirit guide. These steps are outlined in Chapter 29 Retrieval of Your Senses.

Retrieving parts of yourself left with parents, former partners or friends can be liberating. Depending on the reason why those parts have remained with someone else, retrieving them and reuniting them with the rest of your spiritual reserves can lighten the mental or emotional load carried every day.

Results of spiritual retrieval may also include clearer thinking and less fuzzy-headedness, enabling successful pursuit of dreams and life goals. If the part missing is from the throat chakra the results of retrieval may include a reduction in chronic sore throats or a stiff neck.

When Phillip retrieved a part of himself he had left with a previous partner, his bad back eased up and he gradually discovered an increasing sense of personal power. As a result he finally took the necessary steps towards a better career which he had been talking about for years. By retrieving this part of himself he was more available for relationship and after being single for 18 months, eligible women began to notice him again.

Improved passion and enthusiasm for life were the noticeable differences when Miranda retrieved parts of herself that had been absent since she was a teenager. It was a drawn out process for her, lasting more than six months but the rewards included a new passion for life. To the surprise of friends, at 49 she took up Latin dancing and water skiing before spending three weeks camping in the Pyrenees mountains in south west France. The change in her attitude was so

Fig 7.
Spirit Guides

profound that one friend accused her of being on drugs while another asked if she had won a lottery.

Her partner Christos noticed the changes and asked Miranda to show him how to change his own life by retrieving lost parts of himself. His progress was slower, taking over a year but eventually his physical vitality and enthusiasm for life increased. He also began to feel more whole and present for life's opportunities, which was fortunate, as he had to keep up with the new revitalised Miranda.

29
Retrieval of the Senses

Retrieving lost awareness, in the form of spiritual bodies, is similar to marshalling a force of people who are committed to working towards your goals. Personal awareness escapes the physical body through desire or mental restlessness. When all senses are fully focused, a person is much more powerful than when those senses are scattered. It is possible to achieve more with much less effort because more parts of yourself are working towards your goals. The difference might resemble three people working on a project suddenly swelling to 30 people working on the common goal. Progress is generally accelerated when additional people work together.

It is surprisingly easy to scatter mental energy and lose a sense of spiritual purpose. An example of this occurred in a small way recently. I awoke with a clear idea for a chapter in a book I was writing. As my first client wasn't due until 11:00 am, I decided to write the chapter while it was fresh in my mind. I turned on the computer and put on the jug for a cup of tea. The phone rang a few times and soon I was engrossed in writing.

After an hour I took a short break and put on a load of washing, answered the phone and remembered that I had to write and fax a column before lunch. My focus was steadily ebbing away in many directions, until I looked up to see my first client walking down the path. I was still in my bathrobe and I didn't want to answer the door with tussled hair and a bristly face. If this scenario is extended over sixty or seventy years, it's easy to see how people lose awareness of true purpose, when the mind seeks new horizons to fulfil its restless nature.

One of the benefits of retrieval of the senses was shown by Deborah. Having struggled with long periods of listlessness and a general lack of motivation, Deborah decided to do something about it. After learning meditation techniques she discovered that her solar plexus chakra and her navel chakras both contained psychic cords leading out to people and situations from her past.

Over a period of several weeks she repeatedly retrieved these parts of herself and cut the cords. As a result, her passion for life and her energy levels soared. Her best friend jokingly asked if she was having an affair as she seemed so joyful. Deborah effectively restored her energy levels by collecting lost parts of herself. Because some of these cords extended from her solar plexus chakra (a chakra that represents personal power) Deborah also became more assertive and capable of achieving her goals. Her partner, Rodney, wanted whatever she was taking, thinking that it must have been due to a vitamin supplement. It was difficult for Deborah to explain to him that his energy levels might also improve if he meditated regularly.

Regular meditation, as outlined in Chapter 16, Meditation Procedure, enables a gradual reclamation of many parts of yourself that may have split off for a variety of reasons. Alternatively, you can use this specific method.

> Start by meditating, using the method outlined in simple point form in Chapter 16. Complete the cord-cutting procedure, and then ask your guide to identify why your awareness was lost to the person or object at the other end of the cord.

The next exercise requires the traveller body. Ask your guide whether your traveller is currently within your channel. If it is not there, request assistance in locating and retrieving it. To assist with this exercise, ask that whatever your traveller perceives you will also see, hear and feel.

Spend a few minutes observing what your traveller is viewing and sensing what that part of you is sensing. Ask your guide if you can recall your astral traveller body. If the answer is yes, proceed to cleanse it before bringing it into your channel. To bring it home, simply ask it to return to you. Concentrate upon your physical body and it usually returns rapidly.

If your guide indicates that you cannot retrieve your traveller, it may be stuck somewhere or in the middle of an important process. This is not necessarily cause for concern, for the traveller may have to proceed through its present circumstances for some days or even weeks before it can return to your physical body.

Channel some love and light out through the connecting cord to your traveller, to refresh it and replenish its energy. It is useful to repeat this daily in meditation until guides tells you that you can retrieve your traveller.

At any time you can ask guides what is the most appropriate course of action. When your traveller is back inside the channel, seal the hole in your channel walls as you do when cutting cords. This is done by drawing down the light through your crown and mentally pushing this light into the hole on the your auric energy field to seal it off. Ask your traveller to spend some time with you and request that he/she communicates with you when out and about. Ask also if your traveller requires anything to function more easily.

Once the traveller body has been retrieved it is time to complete a check by asking your guide if there is any part of your awareness that is currently out of your channel and needs to be retrieved. If your guide confirms this, then identify through your own sight or through your guide which particular chakra the cords flow through.

You may wish to experiment with your traveller body for a few weeks before proceeding with the following exercise or choose to read this book and complete the exercises when you feel ready.

Retrieval exercise
(A simple version follows this complete process)

Beginning with the crown chakra using the following procedure:
1. Make yourself comfortable.
2. Take three deep breaths, releasing each slowly.
3. Mentally ask "Please send me protection on all levels. Thank you,

thank you, thank you."

4. Mentally ask "Source of all life please send the light down through my crown, through each and every cell of my body and out through my feet and into the earth. Thank you, thank you, thank you."

5. Sense the light entering your crown and flowing gently throughout your body, cleansing, restoring and re-balancing you. As this energy passes through your body it is sweeping away tension and negativity, restoring a sense of inner peace and calm. The energy passes through the floor and directly down into the earth.

6. Take a few moments to familiarise yourself with your auric energy field. Mentally scan your physical body and begin to notice the first of your energy bodies. This extends a few inches beyond the physical body in the same shape. (There are several energy bodies including the emotional body and several mental bodies).

7. While scanning your body, notice any psychic cords of energy extending from the body. These can enter or leave the body at any point but are most likely to extend from the front or back of the body via the chakras. Sometimes it's easier to feel cords than to see them. You might feel a tightness in one chakra or be less aware of yourself at one point in the body due to a cord pulling your awareness from your body.

8. Select one psychic cord to deal with during each meditation. It is important to be able to clearly see or feel this energy cord to be effective with this process. If you can't clearly see or feel a psychic cord simply enjoy this meditation and repeat it daily or weekly until you can clearly sense psychic cords.

9. Focus your attention on this cord extending from your body and mentally trace it out to its destination. Try not to have any expectation of what's at the end of this cord as expectations can be confusing.

10. When reaching the end of the cord there might be someone you know or a part of yourself that you have left with another person or left in a particular location. If you find someone you recognise, you

may be corded to this person by your desire or he or she may have corded you. If you see a part of yourself it is important to reclaim this part, bring it back to your physical body and cleanse it before accepting it into your auric energy field. Sometimes when a part of you has been away from your physical body for many years, it no longer resembles you. It can appear as a child, an adolescent or at your current age. The age it appears to be can give a clue as to when it left or what it's needs were when it left.

11. Explain to this part of you that you plan to bring it home and that you'll take responsibility for meeting its needs in future.

12. Ask this part of yourself what it needs and why if felt that this other person might better meet its need?

13. Try not to judge or to make excuses. Both parts of yourself will be rewarded if reunited. This part can have its needs met and you can reclaim the lost energy of this facet of yourself. You may need to negotiate a workable solution before this part is happy to return. It is likely to leave you again if you don't keep to your commitments so don't promise what you are unlikely to deliver. If it departs again it is usually easier to retrieve it a second or third time.

14. Ask this part of yourself to accompany you back to your body and stop just outside your physical body, to cleanse it first.

15. Drawing down some white light through your crown, force it out of your third eye chakra into a small whirlwind of energy. Break this whirlwind off from your third eye and send it around the part of yourself you have collected.

16. Send this whirlwind of light through your past self or spirit-self in a sweeping motion, ensuring that the whirlwind collects all of the dross or negativity your spirit-self may have amassed while away from you.

17. When you've done this, mentally direct the whirlwind off into space and return your awareness to your past-self. You are now ready to accept this part of yourself back into your body.

18. Notice where the cord originates from your body as this is where

your past-self will re-enter your body. Gently tug on this cord and pull your past-self back into your auric energy field. You may see your past-self turn around and fit into your body.

19. Draw down some white light through your crown and mentally direct this light to close off the hole where the cord exited your aura.

20. Mentally state "Thank you source of all life for sending me the light. Please stop for now and please continue to protect me on all levels. Thank you, thank you, thank you."

21. Mentally shrink the chakras in the soles of your feet where the light left your body on its way into the earth.

22. Now mentally shrink each chakra, beginning with the base chakra, ensuring that the you close the front and back. Shrink each chakra to around 2 centimetres in diameter.

23. Finally, shrink the crown chakra and take three deep breaths as you bring your awareness back to the present.

24. Open your eyes and reflect for a few moments. You may want to record this experience in a diary for later reference.

Simple Version of the Retrieval of the Senses
1. Take three deep breaths and ask for protection.
2. Ask for the light. Feel the light sweeping down throughout your physical body.
3. Scan the physical body for psychic cords. Cords to parts of yourself may be a different colour to cords from others.
4. Select one cord and trace it out to its destination.
5. If it ends at another person then retreat and cut this cord.
6. If it ends with an energetic part of yourself explain to this part that it's time to come home to your physical body.
7. Ask what it needs to feel happy to return. Negotiate a workable solution.

8.	Return to your physical body, stopping just outside it to cleanse this part first.
9.	Forming a small whirlwind of white light from the Brow (third eye) chakra) send this around the energy body to cleanse it completely. Then direct the whirlwind off into space.
10.	Pull the past self back into your body and allow it to settle.
11.	Close off the hole left by the original cord leading out of your body.
12.	Ask the source to stop sending you the light. Thank you (three times).
13.	Close down your chakras, starting with your feet, base, then navel, solar plexus, heart, throat, brow and finally the crown chakra.
14.	Take three deep breaths and open your eyes.

What to expect when retrieving your senses

Your manifested self may not look like you do at present, for a variety of reasons. It often appears to be the age it departed your physical body last, so it could be an adolescent, a child or even a baby.

In rare situations it may appear as an animal. When a friend reconnected with one of his manifestations for the first time, it appeared slightly wolf-like. He could see a part of himself in its eyes but its appearance was wild. It may take the appearance of a child or appear out of shape or out of focus.

The longer this awareness has been away from your channel, the less it is likely to look as you currently do. Desire, jealousy or anger may appear as an ugly manifestation but this is nothing to fear. Your channel is a connection with spirit. It is the path through which spiritual energy reaches and replenishes you. It is your connection with the rest of you or the source from which you spring.

If your senses have left for any reason, they are not regularly replenished spiritually along with the rest of you. They have probably left because you were distracted by fears or desires. The longer your senses are away from your physical body and your channel, the more spiritually depleted they become. If energetic parts of yourself left your physical body suddenly, as a result of a shock or an accident, these parts of you are unprotected while away from your channel. Their brightness can attract dark or negative energy from their surroundings. This negative energy can cause changes in appearance.

It is possible to heal these manifestations and restore their depleted energies and also change their appearance. This is done by recalling them back to your physical body, cleansing them, absorbing them back into yourself and then taking care of spiritual needs through replenishing this energy. Meditation, prayer, yoga, bush walking, fishing, surfing, art, dancing music or poetry are some sources of replenishment. How you nourish yourself spiritually is unique to you.

When telling the lost parts that you are about to bring them home you may need to first reassure them that the love and spiritual fuel they need can be supplied if they return. You cannot order your awareness to return, as it may have left in search of what was missing in your channel. You can, however, encourage, support and reason with it.

It is prudent to resist promising too much to those parts that have departed, as disappointment can damage the rebuilding of trust between the past and present selves. This is the conscious beginning of an important friendship, which if started with honesty can reduce complications afterwards. It is the process of becoming integrated. In assimilating scattered parts of yourself it's possible to end up with astounding integrity, focus and peace. As a result, it is possible to achieve more life goals with less effort, as you have organised more parts of yourself to help. When you're present in the physical body you notice opportunities and threats more readily, enabling better choices and the chance to avoid some of life's pitfalls.

Often people who achieve great goals in life have a certain energetic presence. Presence can be a sign that most of the parts of that person are present and are working together towards goals. Sometimes this manifests as charisma which successful actors and singers exude but it's possible to be present and focused and yet still be unnoticed by others. When Ted arrived at a course he seemed somehow different from his fellow students. At 45 he had the appearance of a man who had already climbed a mountain and achieved a major personal life goal. His relaxed confidence seemed to stem from having nothing to prove to others. During a conversation in a tea break he mentioned that he had travelled the world for two years after selling a business he had founded to a large corporation. He took two years off to decide if he was to work again and if so in what capacity.

If your past self appears to be much younger than your present age, its departure may be due to some trauma or incident that has occurred in the past. It is unlikely to continue developing outside your channel.

If it appears to be an adolescent or an adult, cleanse it using a small whirlwind of white light from your third eye chakra and encourage it to return to you. It sometimes helps to know what triggers these departures of awareness from the physical body, as those situations require resolution on spiritual, psychological and emotional levels.

Some types of counselling have a similar purpose, to reclaim parts which are split off from your centre. If your past self resembles a child or a baby, it requires great love and light. Bring it back to your channel, cleanse it and become reunited.

In reclaiming lost awareness it is possible to heal the past. This is likely to have a most profound effect. Imagine having no past to weigh you down or to call you back for resolution. A resolved past is equivalent to feather-light emotional baggage. Instead of being hampered in every pursuit by emotional baggage distracting or slowing your progress, you can proceed steadily towards personal goals with clarity.

Leo seemed overwhelmed at having to return to past incidents to retrieve energetic parts of himself. He suggested that this task might take years, which was a valid complaint. I reminded him that each time he retrieves parts of himself, he is more available to live in the present.

The more he lives in the present the more joy, peace and fulfilment he can expect. If many parts of you are not present in your body, then you miss experiencing the full spectrum of life events, perhaps missing out on some of the emotional and spiritual dimensions of life. Another aspect to retrieving your lost parts is to overcome patterns of behaviour that limit you or are simply outdated.

Alice had a compulsive, destructive relationship with Richard when she was 16 years old. Richard was a tall, red-haired man and this imprint stayed with Alice. In the ensuing 15 years she had a succession of relationships with tall, red-haired men who resembled Richard, because she had left many parts of herself back with Richard throughout that relationship. Instead of returning to Richard in meditation to collect those part of herself she had left with him, Alice began new relationships with men of similar appearance while searching for her own missing parts. It wasn't a conscious decision but subconsciously she was searching for the rest of herself. If parts of ourselves are left behind with a partner we are less available for opportunities in present day life.

During the months that she mastered the meditation techniques, Alice returned in meditation to her past relationship and retrieved many parts of herself. At first it was a difficult process. She could be sure that she wasn't imagining the whole process, but gradually she noticed that she thought about Richard less. Instead of thinking about him five time each day, Alice averaged three thoughts of him each day.

As Alice became more familiar with the process it seemed less daunting. Then it became a goal, to retrieve any parts of herself she had left behind and to re-collect those parts of herself that returned to Richard despite being collected recently. She gradually lost her desire to revive her relationship with Richard as she retrieved what she was seeking - those parts of herself. She now has a relationship with a man who doesn't resemble Richard. She is much more present in her life as a result of dealing with her past.

At first it seemed a daunting task but it is now a daily habit. Where Alice once left parts of herself in situations for years, she now meditates daily and collects those parts of herself that have strayed throughout the day.

Leo eventually realised that the next ten years would pass whether he resolves his past or not. If he doesn't, he may feel as he does now in ten years. Problems don't usually resolve themselves. As a counsellor, I see many older people with habits I previously had. I resolved to change some of those negative habits and worked hard to eradicate them earlier and now they are merely memories.

Clive reaped the rewards of healing himself of his past. When I first met him, Clive looked physically worn out and his eyes betrayed someone who was haunted by his past both day and night. At 35 he looked 60 and unhealthy.

He began a course of therapy and took up the daily practice of meditation for inner healing. We lost contact for almost five years but when I saw him again I couldn't believe my eyes. He was positively radiant with enthusiasm and his eyes sparkled with humour and a love of life.

"What became of the other Clive?" I asked him laughingly.

"He was very sick but he's better now."

"What was wrong?"

"He didn't realise that the past was over. Now there is room for some joy."

"Are you sure you're not Clive's younger brother?" I teased.

With power comes responsibility. Using power without responsibility increases the risk of stumbling in the pursuit of knowledge and spiritual development. The law of karma is also the law of understanding and to truly understand something it may be necessary to experience it from many different angles. When you have done to another person what someone is doing to you, it is often easier to forgive others when they trespass.

In his youth, Simon occasionally purchased goods that he knew to have been stolen. Several times Simon was also a victim of household robberies. At first, he didn't link the two. His reasoning was that if others were to be dishonest, then he'd be a fool to be completely honest himself.

In time, he began to question his reasoning and gradually became more honest in his dealings with others. This newfound honesty was reflected back to him and he ceased to be a victim of robberies himself. This is not to suggest that honesty alone protects a person from the ill intent of others but it is usually a good place to start.

'You reap what you sow' is an old saying that illustrates that we are all planting seeds continuously. It is wise to become more aware of the seeds that you are planting even today.

Although it is possible to trespass into the psychic energy fields of others without immediate consequence, the karma of your positive and negative deeds is layered into your own aura. This gradually makes its way deeper into your energy field needing to be resolved at some later time, perhaps in another lifetime. Parents sometimes intuitively sense the needs of their children without permission, believing that by meeting those needs they are being better parents. Instead this is often an example of not respecting the child's personal boundaries.

When Clara explained how she and her husband had purchased an apartment for their 30 year old daughter Sethi so that she might live without the burden of a long term mortgage it sounded like generous parents looking after their child. Later in the session when I mentioned that Sethi was likely to move to New York and then settle in the US with a partner, Clara was horrified.

"We bought her the apartment so that she wouldn't move away from us and so that I could drop over for coffee on Saturday afternoons. If she moves to America I can't see her every weekend. I'll have to move there too, when she settles down." The gift was a way of controlling her daughter. Clara agreed that she was a 'helicopter parent' hovering in the background. Perhaps eventually she will become a long range helicopter parent.

30
Rewards of Being Centred

When resolving the past through reclaiming lost senses, it's possible to take knowledge and understanding and leave behind painful situations. Healing each past manifestation enables an individual to complete the more challenging spiritual exercises that follow.

The rewards are inner peace and a deep sense of happiness resulting from being centred in your body. Being centred requires that all the parts of you are present, resulting in an integration of those parts into one whole. This integrity means it is possible to achieve and experience much more in life with significantly less effort. When completely centred while playing sport, it is possible to play with grace, precision and accuracy.

When an actor is centred, he or she is completely convincing in the role. If an individual is centred while running a business, she is an effective, astute manager, organiser and leader. People make better decisions when centred, often avoiding expensive mistakes and dead ends. This is because they are more directly connected to intuition, which is a positive guidance tool.

Even when becoming temporarily centred again through meditation, life becomes effortless and there is a sense of joy that comes from feeling secure within. Opportunities are more apparent and there is a choice of playing with them instead of struggling. When tracing each cord and retrieving scattered senses, it is important to ensure that this newfound awareness is maintained. If becoming scattered again, retrieval is a simple procedure and reintegration is less involved, as your awareness has not been away from your physical being for too long.

The more a person meditates the stronger the connection with spirit and the more likely it is that personal awareness remains with the physical body. If you have a desire that takes a part of yourself out of your body and steadfastly refuses to remain with the physical body for long periods, find out why. Ask your guides or seek a way that you can quench that desire through meditation. If in doubt, ask a guide.

The traveller body does not usually stay with the physical body for very long, as its purpose is to travel, so it is vital to allow it free reign. If setting off on holiday, the traveller (if not involved with other issues) travels ahead to visit the destination, before reporting back to your physical body to give you unconscious information about the holiday destination ahead.

When retrieving cords from another person, find out why they are there. During my studies with Christine I experienced problems with my second chakra. Several times I lost awareness through my second (navel) chakra and when tracing the cords, I found a manifested image of myself with Christine. She explained that my self was not being fully supported or replenished the way it needed to be. Being in her company I realised that Christine had already resolved the problem I was working through and that her second chakra was much more balanced.

Her balance was unconsciously appealing to some part of me, so that when I physically returned home for the evening, a part of me stayed with Christine. Each time I retrieved it, replenished its energy and channelled the light through my whole being it remained for a short while. A few days later it was gone again. This is what occurs when the cause of the senses seeking fulfilment is not dealt with properly.

When a sense leaves and manifests with someone else, it forms a psychic cord from your body to the part of yourself that is with that person. If a part of you leaves your body and enters the throat chakra of a friend, you may experience tightness in your own throat if your friend experiences throat issues. If your friend has a number of cords to his or her throat chakra, you are corded to each person via your friend's throat chakra and the cord back to your physical body. This means that it's possible to drained by people you've never met as you are linked to them through their cords to your friend.

Next time you develop a sore throat, a headache or lower back pain, before assuming that someone has corded you, check to see if any energetic parts of yourself have left to be with someone else. Obviously if you suspect a cord you can cut it but if there is no noticeable change immediately or within a few minutes, look for another cause. Resist the urge to cut cords every hour or two, as it is unnecessary.

For people who consistently meditate, the same process occurs naturally. Regular cord cutting is necessary for those involved in spiritual work, such as healing, counselling, clairvoyance, etc. but for the average person the act of meditating regularly is usually sufficient to draw the senses back.

Spiritual masters rarely speak of cords because their disciples are regularly meditating and this process eliminates much of the need for cord cutting.

After learning about cords, b e g i n n e r s sometimes step into a garden to open up, channel the light and cut cords. They might step outside, cut a

Fig 8.
How clairvoyants use psychic cords

few cords and return within ten minutes. This is overdoing it. Anywhere a person opens up, a channel is established. Although these channels are weak, a stranger may sit or stand in them afterwards. Places like bus stops, bus seats, trains, waiting rooms or the sofa at a friend's place are not suitable places to open up to spirit. Any temporary channel dissolves in a few days or weeks but it is better to exercise caution.

This explains why commuters who stand at a bus stop continuously asking themselves when the bus will arrive are setting up a thought energy field. If you have ever arrived at a bus stop feeling patient and relaxed but soon found yourself asking 'Where is that bus?' it is because you are standing in the energy fields of fifty other impatient people who were thinking that same thought.

Thought forms exist anywhere repetitive thinking has taken place. The more powerful the thought, the more entrenched the thought form energy. Fearful thoughts, such as those experienced in an ambulance on its way to an emergency ward, remain with that vehicle long after it is decommissioned as an ambulance. The same goes for a home, office or a car.

Christine often experienced energy-hungry visitors, particularly in the psychic centre where we worked. One particular visitor had an uncanny knack of entering the waiting room and sitting in the chair that Christine had just vacated. No matter in which of the seven chairs Christine had been sitting before this man arrived, he would automatically stride straight for her chair if it was vacant. He knew unconsciously where to seek any possible residual energy Christine may have left in that seat.

A channel is a corridor of energy surrounding the physical body and running through an individual from head to toes and beyond. This energy channel connects a person to the earth and to the universe and because of this, it must be private. Obviously it is necessary to sit down sometimes in public places and there is no harm, as long as you don't open up to spirit randomly. Opening up to spirit involves drawing down light into your channel or meditating to open your awareness to your surroundings. Doing this in public can be like turning on a torch in a dark night. Moths and insects are drawn to the light. People who are spiritually hungry are unconsciously drawn towards the light filled energy channel to replenish themselves, which may cause you energy depletion.

The ability to control the chakras (to open them or close them down) is usually diminished when under the influence of drugs or alcohol. When temporarily losing control of the chakras in this way it is likely that they open (not necessarily fully), allowing the senses or awareness to wander away, simply leaving an individual wide open to psychic disturbance through surrounding negativity.

Considering the type of environments in which people consume alcohol or drugs, the risks are amplified. The average drinking place, be it a bar, hotel or restaurant, is not usually a spiritually balanced environment, especially when there is loud music, cigarette smoke and huge desires present or fear being released through the ingestion of illicit substances. Yet due to the consumption of alcohol, when people congregate they automatically open up.

There are specific drugs, such as MDMA or ecstasy, which are designed to force open particular chakras. Ecstasy can open the heart chakra, increasing positive feelings toward others for hours at a time. Imagine the potential effects of a collection of surrounding energies because the heart chakra was forced open for around five hours while dancing away at a club or a party with hundreds of other people. It is understandable why some people have limited spiritual awareness. In these (extreme) examples it is easy to sympathise with those parts of the person's energy that prefer to leave to seek alternative fulfilment.

When more centred within your channel, life becomes balanced inwardly and outwardly. It is possible to remain calm, focussed and effective in daily life, putting more inner resources towards personal goals and life's purpose. Sometimes karma prevents a person from being completely present and remaining on the earth plane but when fully present, less effort is required to achieve individual aspirations. It is as though there is more commitment and energy focussed towards the same objective.

For some people the process of becoming centred and remaining centred on a daily basis can take months or years. For others, it is a slower process, lasting a lifetime. It depends upon what occurred in the past to separate you from yourself and how long the senses have been away from your channel. It isn't a race. It is important to take all the time needed to collect yourself.

All that a person needs to know about him or herself is located within the personal aura that surrounds the physical body. Before charging off to examine the auras of loved ones or work colleagues, remember that retrieving this information without permission is trespassing upon the aura of the other person.

Although trespassing without permission sounds as though it is only a minor intrusion, it may be necessary to accept it when others trespass upon your aura in return. With clairvoyants, the fact that the client has sought their services is confirmation of permission to enter their aura but only for the duration of the reading.

We arrive in the world centred and over the years, life events can scatter parts of us. Through meditation we can reassemble these parts to become whole again. When we are whole, separating our true purpose from life's distractions is easier. By remaining focused on personal purpose in life, we are usually happier and more successful in physical and spiritual quests.

31
Finding Your Master

We are all masters in the making. The master is a reminder of what we once were and what we will be again. As senses and desires distract us, it is vital to be continually reminded of perfection that awaits us.

There are two types of masters, living masters and ascended or calling masters. Living masters are physical people who have mastered themselves spiritually. These range from gurus who live in ashrams in India and meditate every day to business men and women or retirees who tend to the needs of the underprivileged. Sometimes living masters teach others, through formal courses or by example.

Ascended masters are people who have lived in the past and are recognised as having mastered their spiritual lessons on earth. These might include Buddha, Jesus, Moses, Mohamed, Krishna and many more. Ascended masters are available for guidance through meditation or prayer, to teach us or serve as an example of positive role models.

Each person has a calling master and many share the same master. A calling master may be Buddha, Jesus, Zoroaster, Krishna, Mohammed or one of many saints who have visited the earthly plane. Their energy is familiar on meeting them. You have probably shared history together and they have energy that is easily recognisable to you. It's like recognising your child's energy in a dream, even if the child is much older or younger.

It is likely that each person has an ascended master who is responsible for guidance towards a long term spiritual destination and a living master who is responsible for guidance on the path in this lifetime. The living master is the history teacher, helping an individual pass each assessment and successfully complete the year. The ascended master is like a professor and head of the history department, guiding one towards a greater purpose beyond studies.

It is possible to pursue a spiritual path without guidance from a living master but there are times when the support of someone more experienced is welcome. This guidance may be gleaned through meditation, not necessarily with a face to face meeting.

Before meeting a master, relying on guides is essential because it is their purpose to prepare each person for his or her master. It's not possible to meet your guides every time you meditate for they are not always available. To meet and converse with a master it is essential to aim for very high meditations.

A spiritual master is one who has usually given up worldly possessions and desires, retrieved all personal awareness and centred him or herself at the brow or third eye chakra. When doing this, all chakras below the brow chakra automatically close and he or she works solely from the brow chakra.

When spiritual masters radiate energy, they do so from the third eye or brow chakra. Their disciples cannot usually reach the brow chakra, due to a combination of their own desires keeping them limited to the lower chakras (see Chapter 11) and a lack of awareness as to how to raise their energy to reach the brow chakra. This is so that they cannot deplete the master's energy through psychic cords. He or she is too high for them to reach. This doesn't prevent them from trying however, as disciples sometimes try to make a master their surrogate parent. As a result they desire his or her love and attention.

During a talk given by a visiting master some years ago the cold draughty room was packed with devotees, disciples and the nervously curious. After a 45 minute discourse the master opened the floor to questions and a middle aged woman stood up and sang him a song she had composed. On an on she went, singing of how she loved him and how much deeper she loved him than yesterday, while the master looked more and more uncomfortable. When it occurred to me that she was probably straight out of central casting, it took all of my discipline to control my fits of laughter. While he had spent decades detaching himself from his desires, she was seizing her one chance to gain his attention to satisfy her desire to be noticed.

It is traditional that the master appears when the pupil is ready. Hence the saying, 'When the student is ready, the teacher will come'. Many people search for a master, some shop around for the best deal to suit their needs and their lifestyles. Choosing a master intellectually might result in selecting a master who is not right for you this lifetime who may not necessarily advance your spiritual growth.

Your living master is likely to be alive somewhere in the world. If he or she has recently died another master takes over his or her responsibilities and becomes your new living master. It's possible to be introduced to them via their books or photos or to meet him or her in meditation or at night in a dream. When you are ready he or she arrives.

This may seem like a lot of work, to meet a person spiritually whom you have never met in the flesh or who may not have existed in the flesh in your lifetime. It's natural to wonder if the imagination is being brilliantly exercised while seated in the lotus position with a candle burning. However, when a master appears and says something simple, if anything at all, you feel the enormous power of love radiating throughout your entire body. All current concerns and desires momentarily slip away and are replaced with a deep, peaceful calm. You are unconcerned with the past or the future, embracing the stillness and joy of the present.

Bathing in a master's energy or surrendering to peace, joy and harmony, can result in wondering why such simple, deep stillness makes you feel so happy and contented. When you are ready, your living master may introduce previous saints or masters with whom you have been in contact. The living master is responsible to see you safely home after a lifetime on this earth.

When meeting living masters or calling masters who are not your own, although it's natural to sense their purity, power and love, you are unlikely to be affected emotionally in the same way as when meeting your own master. When I first met my calling master in meditation I did not know who he was but I fell to my knees and could not look at him, such was the power and love that he radiated for me.

Kneeling before him I cried tears of joy into his open hands. His love and compassion overwhelmed me. He continually reassured me but I felt like a lost child who has been reunited with his family. Although my ego told me that I was a grown man acting like a groupie, it did not matter. I wept and as I did so I felt my burdens lift from me and doubts being replaced by love. It was a though a heavy winter cloak had been removed and I felt light, peaceful and calm.

His energy was so pure, so radiant and freely given that it made me feel extremely humble. I found myself thinking 'I want to always remember this moment.' When I recall it, several years later, it still brings tears to my eyes.

When I saw him the second time tears welled up immediately and it took what seemed to be forever to summon the courage to look into his eyes. Meeting his gaze only served to make me cry harder and babble incoherently.

I wouldn't recommend that anyone push to meet their master in a short time. The fastest journey is often the least comfortable, so it is important to decide between the rope and tackle or the scenic route when scaling the mountain.

We are all going home eventually but there is no race to get there. Remember that it is possible to glimpse your destination within this lifetime. I was writing this one afternoon when an acquaintance, Sally, came to say hello. Sally has no obvious problems, she is financially secure and enjoys a good family life. She does not ask much of life and is usually relatively contented.

As meditation doesn't interest her, our common interests are everyday matters. Five minutes into the conversation I found myself struggling to speak, as my throat had started to seize up. I was being pulled out of my channel very quickly, presumably by her desires. As I had been writing when she arrived I was open to spirit while the pen was in my hand. I did not close myself down spiritually before answering the front door and failed to do so as we sat down to talk.

I deliberately did not sit in my writing channel because drawing down extra spiritual energy can trigger others to unconsciously dump emotional and spiritual negativity. Consequently by not closing down or protecting myself it took me 24 hours to recapture the peace and harmony I was experiencing before Sally arrived at my door. During that time I was ambitious for money, power, possessions and became extremely materially competitive.

During our conversation Sally had corded me unconsciously and pulled me away from my centre. She was unaware of what was occurring. This often happens with people who are engaged in developing themselves psychically or spiritually.

People involved in spiritual development continuously seek information and their travellers are everywhere but in their physical bodies. Their awareness sometimes remains with others if they find them more peaceful than their own physical body.

A day or two is not long to be out of your channel compared with a lifetime. However, when adding up all the hours and days and weeks spent out of your channel it soon mounts up. In the 24 hours after Sally's visit the decisions I made were not my best. They were not composed, centred decisions because I was uncentred.

There are times in our lives when important choices need to be made that affect our future. These might be a career choice, a relationship decision or a decision about where to live. If we are uncentred when attempting to make important decisions, it is unlikely that these decisions will be balanced and informed.

It is impractical to shun people while pursuing a spiritual journey. This is especially so when family needs escalate. Sometimes a person no longer derives the same level of fulfilment from the social events previously loved. If we knew ahead of time those foods, habits and circumstances we'd be required to give up, the rewards for spiritual development would need to be powerful and appealing. A spiritual journey needs to be something truly outstanding to make parts of a present lifestyle seem unnecessary, uninviting or lacklustre. More than this, it has to be something truly remarkable that an individual might find no real desire to return to a former lifestyle once the process has commenced.

It needs to be something so beautiful, powerful and inspiring that the old way of life simply fades to grey. When people have an opportunity to meet their living masters, calling masters or even simply find their channels and fill their being with its light, it's likely that these processes can strengthen their confidence for the journey ahead.

Cutting cords, cleansing and bringing light down through your channel is enough to 're-set' you after enduring a difficult day or even a stressful month. Having the chance to re-set yourself ensures that you feel grounded, balanced and centred. It also reduces the chance of poor decisions or negative reaction to circumstances while uncentred.

When Fiona arrived for a clairvoyant session she was angry. Her boss was being unreasonable with his constant demands and as a result, she had left her list of questions at home that morning.

"I arrive home at 8:30 most nights and he'll often text me questions until 10:00 pm. This job is eating up my whole life and I haven't been to yoga or meditated for months now." Fiona was uncentred and although she disliked her work environment, she was too frazzled to examine alternative solutions. I requested that she turn off her phone and explained that she didn't need any questions as her issues were self-evident. It was time to meditate, cut cords and then examine her choices once she was sufficiently balanced.

We meditated for half an hour and I took her through the cord cutting process. At the end she was visibly relieved. Fiona had been meditating and cutting cords for almost a year but it was necessary to have someone else guide her through the process that day because she was too wound up and exhausted to focus on each step effectively. After the meditation her choices were clear to her. It was time to find another job and it was essential that she turned her phone off as she left work each day, so that her boss couldn't control her evenings. It was also important for Fiona to remind herself that her life's purpose is more important than her work. Regular meditation offers this reminder in a gentle way.

One evening I asked Christine how important it is to be initiated by a living master and she replied that 'All things come in due course.' She explained that if a master is responsible for you that master seeks you out when you are ready. This prompted an image in my mind of a knock at the door one day and my receptionist relaying a message to me.

"There's a Mr. Master at the door for you."

Screaming "Aaaarrrgggh!" I climb out the back window and slink off into a clump of tall grass. The feature film of this will be entitled "The Master Cometh!" I admit to being master resistant, figuring that I have a master resistance of 84.5% which is not bad considering that I'm a child of the '60s.

Christine assured me that initiation is worthwhile, despite the fact that each disciple of her particular master agrees to meditate for 2 ½ hours every day, avoid eating meat or drinking alcohol and live a righteous life.

In a particularly good meditation one Sunday I went beyond all of my guides to my living master. This is something I had rarely done before without the assistance of Christine in London. The master asked me when I was going to come home; to the path of my destiny with spirit. I looked at him and noticed how solemn he was before suggesting that he play awhile with me.

"If I am to play with you you'll lead me on for a long time."

"You're right," I sighed, realising that there was spiritual work to be done. "Does that mean I have to be initiated by you?" I asked him.

"Yes it does. I'll be in Australia next year and I'll do it then, so prepare yourself."

I sighed again while realising that preparation means regular meditation and spiritual discipline. I had been joking earlier about being the holder of the record for a person knowing their master and resisting following their master's teachings. I think I'm about to surrender to the path. It was a high, clear meditation and I was glowing afterwards. I felt a deep sense of clarity and purpose. It's almost too easy to be distracted by life's shiny toys and temporary goals, forgetting that novelty soon wears off and the deeper, spiritual hunger eventually resurfaces. Finding a harmonious balance between nourishing yourself spiritually and living in the physical world is what makes each individual unique.

32
Organised Religions and Philosophies

Organised religions and philosophies are important because they guide their members towards proper conduct. Religions offer a system and often an example to follow. This can be of great benefit to those who otherwise may not bother with personal spiritual development or give up after encountering the first obstacle.

When embracing a religion, a guru or a particular philosophy we sometimes experience a feeling of community or belonging. A fraternity exists amongst people who share spiritual beliefs and this community can offer support and understanding when members experience hard times. When a religion or philosophy offers an example to follow or a goal to which its members or devotees aspire, faith is still required. This is because a direct experience of God is often lacking.

Individuals can experience God in many ways, through prayer, meditation or noticing God in surroundings. The butterflies of summer or the smile of a small child, can be seen as God's presence. However, religions or philosophies that rely heavily upon doctrine, risk having members who follow the doctrine but who do not necessarily experience God directly. When the members only follow the doctrine, the mysteries remain hidden to them.

While following in the footsteps of others, you may not achieve what those you follow have achieved. What worked for Buddha, Mohammed or the apostles may not work for you. Some of us can sit alone on the side of a hill in contemplation for years while others prefer a different approach.

It seems reasonable that no system, no matter how complete it purports to be, is perfectly suitable for everyone. For some people, the idea of a system is abhorrent. What I have previously described is not a religion, nor is it a philosophy, although it encompasses concepts found in religions and philosophies such as karma. This procedure does not require faith, although perseverance might assist if results are not immediately forthcoming.

When practicing meditation there are different results, that are likely to be as valid to you as my results were to me. You may decide to travel off out into space or to other dimensions and experiences that currently defy explanation. Hopefully you'll arrive at your own understanding of what is out there, where you fit in the greater scheme and where you will go after discarding your physical body.

Obviously a level of belief in the procedure is required for motivation to go through the meditations before getting results. Effort is necessary at times but experience suggests that helpers in spirit are patient and often prepared to go at a pace that suits each individual. It is everyone's right to experience personal origins and the final destination. It doesn't take great vision to see that many people are without life purpose. Some have forgotten or made obscure their real purpose for being here. As individuals expend precious spiritual life force in 'getting and spending', life attempts to prod us to remember. By continually ignoring these reminders, there is a risk of squandering precious spiritual energy on possessions that become redundant when we die.

I suspect that I've already spent too many lives sitting around and I'm increasingly keen to go home. In the past I've spent a fortune on courses, workshops and personal development, all of which gave me what I needed. Those processes helped, enabling me to go within myself to a place with the answers. As I developed, I needed less of these outside objects and novelties to make me whole. Basically, somebody stopped feeding me fish and taught me how to fish for myself. Now when I have a problem, I remember my skills and use them to center myself and replenish my spiritual reserves of energy.

It's possible to take what suits you from a variety of religions or philosophies and combine these beliefs and methods in a manner that works well personally. It's important to thoroughly understand each concept so that it is still effective when taken out of its original context. If there is a lack of understanding why a method works, then simplifying it may render it ineffective. There is a risk of leaving out vital steps in a procedure.

Organised religions or spiritual groups can offer support when needed. Sometimes the conversations over tea and coffee after a group meditation at an ashram are as important as the meditation itself. These provide a chance to bond with fellow travellers on the path and to hear how others blend their spiritual lives with their everyday lives, deadlines and commitments. Although elders can offer inspiration and be powerful role models, sometimes it's reassuring to see fellow travellers have the same doubts and the same issues that you're facing. Sometimes beginners feel overwhelmed when comparing themselves with a teacher but can be inspired by someone who is just a few steps ahead of them on the path. Added to this is the benefit of group prayer or meditation which makes it easier for beginners to reach greater heights in meditation due to the energy of the surrounding group. It can be like singing is a chorus. When you stray from the note there are dozens of surrounding voices to remind you of the notes you're aiming for.

33
Psychic Attack

On very rare occasions people have been subjected to psychic disturbance or even psychic attack. This is an attack by another person that takes place on the astral level. (The astral level is composed of a fine energy substance that contains a second body belonging to each individual.) An attack can happen when the person is asleep.

This occurred to me recently. I awoke from a dream at around 4.00 am with my heart pounding. I turned on a light and looked around the room with disbelief that it was really my room. I felt a strange sensation. I almost believed that I had awoken in a parallel universe and this simply appeared to be my room.

Something was missing. Sound. I live between two main roads and there is light traffic all night. There was not a car to be heard. I lay awake feeling uneasy, until a sound reached me. It was like the sound of rain on a roof but it was not raining. The sound increases until I couldn't bear it any longer. I sprang to my feet and went searching for it. In the kitchen I found the electric water jug boiling. It was a strange coincidence and I reasoned that I probably had not thoroughly disconnected the power lead when I turned it off the previous evening.

I returned to bed and reviewed the dream that had disturbed me. In this dream I was a security guard in a community and had killed a man who was terrorising others. A friend of the man I had killed had vowed revenge and planned to kill me. I explained my position but he wouldn't be dissuaded. He told me that he'd kill me and I replied, "If you can find me," before I skipped out from under his gaze into another dimension. I skipped two more dimensions and lost my name and all energetic identifications that enabled others to locate me. Anyone experienced with the astral world knows that when calling a person's name it is possible to find him or her on the astral plane. It is equivalent to knowing the person's address.

To avoid being followed and located in the dream I became a reflective ball of energy, invisible and nameless. I discared all handles (points where others can attach themselves to my energetic body) or identification marks. It was then that I heard a voice saying, "You can disappear but you'll always be running. Do you want that?"

I pondered this for a minute in my dream and decided to return to the person who was hunting me, to allow him to kill me if he really wanted. I awoke as I was explaining to him that if he killed me he would in turn become the hunted one, as others sought to bring him to justice. Upon awakening I wondered about the methods I had used to escape this person and why I had felt it necessary to be so thorough. It was an unanswered puzzle until the following day when a regular client came and put the pieces together in my mind.

She told me her boyfriend had introduced her to a man who was 'a bit of a guru'. He had a strict philosophy for people who wanted to fast-track their spiritual development. Those around him paid him large sums of money to be taught from his pool of knowledge and very few who joined his sect had successfully left it when they changed their minds.

While talking to this woman I realised that this guru was in fact psychologically unstable and that she wanted to leave the sect. He knew this, despite her secrecy, through visiting her regularly via the psychic cord he had to her. He was aware that she was planning to consult me. I realised that it was he who chased me in my dream. What he probably didn't count on was that I know the rules and am not so easily intimidated.

During my reading for the client I became more and more curious about this man and why he was teaching others at all, when he really disliked people and didn't trust anyone. I also wondered why members found it difficult to leave once they decided to do so. When new devotees join his sect, this 'guru' encourages them to link into him. Their desire to benefit from his spiritual understanding usually results in them sending their awareness out to him.

He gathers this awareness and holds onto it. This is easily done, as he has convinced them that they will benefit greatly from his knowledge. As they are spiritually hungry, these energetic parts of them search outside their physical body for spiritual nourishment.

The devotees' awareness (spirit bodies) don't want to return to them, as these parts realise that there is no fulfilment to be found there. People who follow this guru may feel more whole when they are in his presence, simply because they are in touch with the parts of themselves that he holds. It is difficult for them to leave, because leaving the guru might seem as though they are abandoning a part of themselves. The devotees interpret this wholeness as a sign that they should follow this man.

His threatening appearance in my dream was his way of warning me off and ensuring that I didn't help my client when she consulted me for assistance in leaving him. What attracted my attention when she first sat before me for a reading was this man's ego and his love of money. His energy surrounded my client, which made it difficult for me to push through it to reach her.

Ego and money do not bode well for someone who claims to be a spiritually advanced teacher. I saw clairvoyantly that he had quietly put aside a seven-figure sum of money in a bank account in another country and was planning to disappear one day and retire to a comfortable life. Meanwhile the unsuspecting devotees give him their trust, their money and themselves in the hope that they might gain a speedy enlightenment. It merely confirms that there are no short cuts to spiritual understanding.

This 'guru' also relied on the egos of people who followed him. According to him, those who have left the sect have 'failed and can't find the strength necessary to achieve spiritual completion this lifetime'. It is almost impossible to know with any certainty how others are progressing spiritually. It's difficult enough to monitor personal progress.

I advised my client to lie low and fade to grey. This involves staying out of her 'guru's' line of sight. As this guru is self-absorbed, she only has to become less interesting to him and she will soon be forgotten. If she actively resists him, he might wreak havoc in her life. She said that she could have him investigated but I suggested that it's possible that those who arrived to scrutinise him might also become clouded in their thinking at his instigation. He is not an idle magician and would probably stop at nothing to achieve his ends.

I also advised my client not to meditate for a month or two, then to meditate in a different room in the house than usual, as he had a strong psychic link into her channel at home. I advised that, when she had faded from the notice of this man, she take a trip overseas, as links are harder to maintain over an ocean and over long distances.

This is a very unusual situation and most people are unlikely to ever be in this position but it is important to be vigilant. These circumstances arose as a result of my client's impatience for spiritual enlightenment.

It is possible to reach enlightenment in a short time but such a journey usually requires an experienced teacher and plenty of trust. The steepest journeys requires the least baggage so a short trip to enlightenment may require releasing friends, a job, a home environment or attitudes that restrict growth and development.

Few people are capable of doing this rapidly without going crazy, so we take the scenic route up the mountain. As someone who prefers proof instead of trust, my journey so far has been at a much more moderate pace.

Reaching enlightenment is not a race as everyone has a different starting point. On this personal journey it is difficult to be certain when a path is leading to spiritual growth or to a dead end. Sometimes great personal sacrifice is required for growth and at other times understanding arrives gracefully.

34
A Journey through Love

The shortest spiritual journey is one filled with love. A journey's destination can be obscured by immediate needs and yet some of these urgent desires can be postponed. Love is a requirement that cannot be postponed. Love is essential when pursuing a spiritual path. If a person denies the need to give and receive love, the spiritual journey becomes a physical or intellectual exercise.

If, in attempting be loved we rely solely upon other people for our source of love, disappointment is likely. People can be unpredictable. They are also learning about love and life and it is unrealistic to rely on others to fulfil personal love requirements entirely.

Some people don't rely upon others at all. Perhaps they have been hurt earlier in their lives and have emotionally shut down. They may attempt to meet their needs through denial of love, through fantasy or through relationships over which they have total control. A relationship with a domestic pet is one where you have greater control as your pet relies upon you for food, water, shelter and love and it can derive much of its understanding of life through you.

On a spiritual level, dogs, cats or any domesticated animal are also attempting great spiritual advancement. They advance themselves through close contact with humans, who are more evolved beings. This is because dogs or cats share a group soul, whereas humans each have an individual soul. When owning domestic pets, you take responsibility for their physical wellbeing and for their spiritual progress. It is possible to enable pets to advance spiritually, through loving them and allowing them to love you in return.

People sometimes abuse such relationships by ignoring their animals' needs, by mistreating them or even abandoning them. An animal treated poorly has a limited chance for advancement, as its owner is unlikely to be taking care of his or her own spiritual advancement. When an animal has formed a strong bond of friendship with a human, the two may grow spiritually and help each other. To love and support people who are less evolved than us is often spiritually and emotionally rewarding.

Upon the death of a pet the relationship may conclude but sometimes the animal may reincarnate and share another life with the human. Five years after their dog had died, David and Rosie decided to get another one. They looked through the local newspaper each week to see what was available. One day a litter of Doberman pups was advertised and they decided to look at them.

They were shown a dog and six puppies. They were seven weeks old, crawling all over each other and playing. When David entered the room some of the puppies looked up at him. One particular puppy cocked its head to one side, then to the other, observing David and Rosie closely. After a few moments it stood up and walked over to the door and sat by the door while the couple examined all the other puppies.

It sat watching David, waiting to be taken home. As no puppies had been taken from the litter at this stage, it had no memory of people visiting and leaving with one of the puppies. Still it waited, quietly.

David did not notice it at first, as he was busy patting the mother and examining the other puppies. David and Rosie were not particularly taken with any of them and stood up to leave. When they turned towards the door they noticed the small male puppy looking intently at them. David and Rosie had been chosen by the dog and it had made a wise choice. They love him as one of the family and it is heartwarming to see such a confident and healthy dog.

In mediumistic readings it's possible to contact deceased relatives for clients and sometimes the deceased are surrounded by their former pets. In one reading I asked the client if her deceased mother loved dogs, as she was surrounded by 11 dogs. Seated on an old armchair, she sat smiling as the dogs lay placidly at her feet. Behind her across the top of the seat back lay an enormous ginger cat, snoozing. The client identified six of the dogs and the cat from their descriptions. Some she had grown up with and others she remembered from photos of her mother as a child with her pets.

In relationships with their children, parents can exercise control, as it is not an equal relationship. Children challenge their parents occasionally but they are not equal when it comes to control over the relationship. The child may easily be the adult's equal spiritually or even spiritually more advanced. However, the adult still bears responsibility for the child's need for food, love and security.

People who have experienced a loss of love or the inability to control the flow of love to themselves, have probably found it a painful and frustrating experience. Children with an emotionally unstable parent have limited control over the treatment they receive. They might decide that all people are unstable or unreliable.

As an adult, people with such an attitude sometimes attract partners who confirm to them that others are unreliable. Relying on an unstable or unreliable partner for a primary source of love is a recipe for emotional starvation. When relying solely on other people to fulfil you emotionally, there is a risk of paying a high price for fulfilment. Accepting emotional fulfilment from many sources increases the likelihood of lasting fulfilment, for when one source of love is lost or threatened, it is not as painful or tragic.

When becoming aware of how much love and support there already is in your life, before including other people, you may not rely so heavily upon others for fulfilment. When realising that love is giving and receiving, it may be a surprise to notice how much receiving you do in comparison to giving.

When next in a garden or a park, become aware of all the trees and plants. Notice them as they exchange sunlight and nutrients from the earth for oxygen for you to breathe. Herbs, fruits and vegetables go one step further, giving themselves that you might eat them and live. Every insect, each bird, bee and beetle has a purpose and contributes something as well as taking from nature.

Often we breathe, eat and make use of all the earth's resources without thinking about what we are giving in return. Instead of leaving this earth better for having been here, sometimes we expect to receive abundantly and contribute nothing. Imagine how secure it is possible to feel when meeting your love requirements through spirit, friends, animals, plants, your partner and through nature.

We each have preferred ways of receiving fulfilment, so keeping an open mind about what fulfils you is an asset. Narrow-mindedness tends to eliminate valuable sources of happiness or fulfilment. Valerie consulted me for assistance with setting and achieving personal goals. The most pressing of these goals was to experience a continuing, loving, personal relationship.

I asked her to clearly define the type of person she believed suited her in a love relationship. She quickly and confidently defined the perfect man for her. We spent time discussing this and a final draft was drawn up. Valerie's perfect man would be:

single
available
heterosexual
over 185 cm tall
dark-haired
muscular in build
confident
sports-minded
a sexual athlete
financially secure
kind and generous
without previous ties or commitments
possessing a slap-stick sense of humour
able to respect her need for independence.

"I like tall men!" she stated, to underline her priorities. The reasons for listing the desired qualities were twofold. Firstly to help Valerie accurately identify her needs and secondly to enable her to clearly recognise this man when he appeared.

In the universe, like often attracts like or at the very least, people who share the same perceptions of life are attracted to each other. Opposites attract and complementary types can work well together but it is still necessary to share fundamental beliefs about life to fit together.

A part of our task was to see if Valerie had many of the qualities she desired in a partner or if she possessed complementary characteristics to those qualities. For example if Valerie wasn't single, available, heterosexual, possessing a slap-stick sense of humour and independent, she may not have a good chance of enjoying a relationship with the type of man she had described to me.

Selecting an incompatible type of man may result in him being out playing cricket, enjoying himself and giving her plenty of independence, while she pines for him at home. To Valerie, romance might be dinner at an intimate restaurant by the sea, followed by an evening stroll. Her incompatible partner may think that romance is tuning up the motor of a 1956 sports car and taking it for a drive; alone.

Valerie told me what she believed was the type of person who might fulfil her love needs. Although she enjoyed the company of friends and pursued her own interests, her future partner was to be the man with whom she would be most intimate. I read the list back to her and she seemed satisfied with it. I suggested that sometimes what we think we will enjoy and what we actually enjoy can differ but Valerie was adamant. This list represented her ideal man.

In the months that followed Valerie dated a variety of men but none of them was 'the one'. About ten months later she wrote to me from overseas, describing the man in her life. According to her letter it was a serious relationship. Several months later the couple visited during their honeymoon world tour.

At first meeting, Donald seemed a wonderful choice for Valerie. He matched her in many ways and they even looked alike. However Donald was not as Valerie had listed her ideal man to be. He was about five centimetres shorter than her and his sense of humour was not slap-stick.

Five years later Valerie is very happily married to Donald. I wonder how many people go through life searching for love and fulfilment in a particular package while it awaits them in a different form. Valerie's sought happiness based on the previous man or men who had fulfilled her. With a clear sense of purpose, an open mind and assistance from those in spirit, the results can be surprising. This does not mean that you can ask spirit to help you and then to sit around expectantly while doing nothing constructive to meet a partner.

'Trust in God and tether your camel' is an old saying that applies. Trust in God to keep your camel safe and protect it from straying and do what you can by tethering it to a pole to ensure it's still there when you return. It is necessary to do your share to fulfil your desires. Ask spirit by all means and then do what you can to help the situation eventuate, unless those in spirit suggest otherwise.

There are other possible relationship obstacles to overcome, even when life has delivered a dream partner. Many people are so attached to the notion of romantic love that when the time comes for a relationship to move from the initial romantic stage on to levels requiring more commitment, they experience difficulties doing so. Some people never progress to love's deeper levels, preferring instead to terminate relationships and start afresh, with renewed hope of the promise romance holds.

Fortunately, romantic love does not last, for while perceiving life through the veil of romance, vision is usually impaired. Romantic love is what we do to ourselves, for it does not even require anyone else. Stars of stage and screen have been loved romantically by individuals who have never come closer to them than a photograph. No genuine interaction has taken place at all between such people and those whom they idolise or love in absentia.

Romantic love has its place, however, for in real relationships it can bring people together with the opportunity of forming deeper relationships beyond the romantic stage. By spending a short time carefully observing someone, even a stranger, it is possible to ascertain that person's level of emotional maturity. Some people show it in their faces. I have a friend who although in his forties, has the face of an 11-year-old boy. He often demonstrates behaviour that is similar to a child's.

Other people show their level of maturity in their dress sense, although this is not a reliable guide because someone else may be choosing their clothes for them. Another friend of mine dressed like a 16-year-old right through his twenties, complete with the same hairstyle he had at 16. Others show their emotional development in their movements or body language.

I recently worked with a client who, although in his late twenties, struck me as being about 12 years of age emotionally. I sensed very little personal power in this man. He displayed no sexual energy and his dress and attitude were those of a 'good boy'. When faced with a choice, he often asked others what he should do.

If someone continually exhibits behaviour associated with a child of a particular age then that person may have experienced upheaval at that age, interrupting emotional growth and development. At that time, some awareness or sense may have left the physical body. To continue growth and development requires the return of the senses. The senses are still attached by a thin silvery cord of energy, only they are 'not in residence' within. It's possible in mediation to trace these cords of energy out to those 'lost' parts and retrieve them. There is generally no harm in being emotionally younger than you are physically, especially when seeking a relationship where a partner nurtures you.

Society seems to adapt to people who are emotionally still children in adult bodies. Media and entertainment cater to those with the attention spans of four-year-olds, with magazines containing more photographs than words and television infotainment programs rarely producing a story that extends more than ten minutes.

A great part of the transition from childhood to being an emotional adult is shifting from seeking others to meet personal desires to meeting individual needs. Finding inner peace and fulfilment requires looking for personal solutions.

Some people juggle their lives like circus clowns, snatching small traces of fulfilment along the way. Others chase short-term fulfilment without any thought for the long term, while other people completely deny their immediate needs, with a promise of fulfilment later in life or in the after-life. We each have our own convictions. Maybe short-term fulfilment is as it states—short term. It has its place and but it still leaves unaddressed issues.

Denial of short-term rewards can increase desire and frustration but when coupled with long-term plans it can be useful. However, continuous denial can result in a deadening of awareness in a bid to dull inner desires.

A composite mix of denial, application and planning can be fruitful. Think of some of the habits, routines and possessions we replace love with when are unable to receive it.

The list includes the following:

Food: especially sweets, cakes, pastries, soft drinks, chocolate;
Alcohol: to deaden the hunger or to give courage to face life;
Sports: to shift the focus and to feel a sense of fulfilment from achievement.

This is not suggesting that food, alcohol or sports are wrong, only that sometimes people substitute them for love. Perhaps when consuming sweet food it may be beneficial to consider putting sweetness into your heart instead.

Years ago I shared a house with a friend and each week we shopped together for food and household items. After entering the supermarket he selected two packets of chocolate biscuits and opened one immediately. By the time we had covered four aisles, half the packet was eaten.

I often teased him about this while I ate the remaining half packet on the one-kilometre drive home. No chocolate was safe around us. This instant temporary mood improvement fulfilled us for a short time but the following day we were again empty and emotionally hungry.

Gradually he sought to deny his cravings for sweet foods and hear his cravings for love or emotional sweetness. As he reduced his chocolate intake and found sources for inner fulfilment, he felt good for longer periods of time. He believed that chocolate promised him happiness but it delivered only a temporary heightened state without changing or improving his circumstances.

We both learned that when craving chocolate it was time to ask ourselves honestly, 'What do I really need right now?' In response to that question, I had to open my heart and myself to a variety of new ways of fulfilment. It was difficult at first, finding my real needs in the moment but eventually I compiled a list of activities and people that nourished me emotionally.

While learning about the universe it becomes easier to find our place within it. This includes work that enables us to grow and develop. Instead of working to live, it is possible to work to grow and to strengthen personal weaknesses. Work can be an opportunity to develop an inner quality that is currently lacking. The standard of work produced with love and enjoyment compared with work completed with longing, regret or complete boredom is starkly different.

Tamara is a chef in a restaurant. After more than twenty years spent cooking for strangers she dislikes her job and the industry generally. She no longer has any passion for her work and each time I eat in her restaurant I leave feeling hungry. It's not that there is insufficient food but that I am not nourished by her cooking. Perhaps it is better to have less food, prepared with love, than a lot prepared carelessly and indifferently.

Discovering more sources of love and fulfilment is likely to develop a greater sense of inner confidence and security. This allows taking risks that others may not pursue in their lives. It becomes easier to leave an unrewarding job or a relationship if you have other sources of income or personal fulfilment. Taking those first tentative steps requires courage and commitment. It's easier when there are other sources of nourishment to support you through the process.

Choices are simpler when mastering difficult lessons that may obscure life purpose. In developing other sources of love and fulfilment I gradually became less demanding of people, while expecting less of them. Consequently, I am now free to enjoy others at whatever level they choose to operate from.

This has made life easier, yet occasionally I still have to remind myself not to ask more of someone than he or she presently chooses to give. Giving and receiving love does not need not be confined to displays of affection but can include smaller gestures such an email or a telephone call.

I am thrilled when receiving letters from friends, sometimes re-reading them at a later date. Instead of saving the act of giving for a huge opportunity, consider giving continually in a dozen smaller ways. There will still be sufficient to give when the bigger opportunities present themselves. Love increases in value when given away.

Pursuit of spiritual development doesn't require avoidance of love relationships. When evolving spiritually, relationships often advance personal growth. Eventually a person is likely to choose a partner from a soul group, which includes people who share soul purpose, even if unconsciously.

Attending to spiritual needs doesn't have to interfere with fulfilling emotional needs, because a loving relationship also provides divine growth. Spiritually destructive relationships are more likely to be avoided when valuing spiritual progress. Although this may limit an initial choice of partners, it is likely to result in more rewarding loving relationships in the long term. As the future arrives minute by minute, it may be wise to prepare for it.

When spending time with people from our soul group it's like coming home to our spiritual family. Although each member of the group is unique, they share a common spiritual bond. A soul group might spend time meditating together at an ashram or riding waves at dawn on a local beach. Although surfers may merely nod a brief hello during a two hour quest for the perfect balance on a flawless wave, this pursuit bonds them together. As the sun rises steadily, footprints in the sand are all the remains of their shared passion, until they return before dawn the following day. Before departing, each individual usually glances back at the swell, people still in the water and waves breaking around the shoreline as if to capture a moment that will live with them throughout the day.

35
Confirmation of Accuracy

How does a person effectively differentiate between imagination and accurate information while meditating, when the difference between a poor meditation and a good one can be slight?

In a poor meditation there is a tendency to feel restless or experience difficulty leaving daily concerns behind to focus inwardly on personal guides and make a clear connection with spirit. In a good meditation, establishing the connection with guides and with intuition is easier and it feels natural. There is no struggle as daily concerns are temporarily relinquished to focus clearly on guides and receiving information. It is an effortless glide into peaceful silence.

To confirm accuracy, ask guides for details about your life that are likely to occur within a few days, to have physical proof or confirmation in the physical world. If the information your receive occurs, you can be confident that it was a deep, accurate meditation. This is especially effective when looking ahead two or three years if you don't want to wait that long to be proven wrong due to a poor meditation or connection with guides. The short term information requested means that there is only a three day wait to know if what you've been told about the coming years is accurate. If the short term information isn't accurate, simply meditate again, using the same process. Confirmation of accuracy can occur by accident sometimes, as with Christine and myself during a meditation session at her house in 1991.

Christine asked me to meditate and then instructed me to visit her living master, by tracing the psychic cord from her body back to him. I did this and a few minutes after I had met her master in meditation I returned to wakefulness and to the room.

"How was it?" Christine asked.

"It was good. I could see him clearly but he was younger than I had imagined from your description."

"What did he look like?"

"He was in his late thirties and wore a dark, neatly trimmed beard. His face was soft and his eyes were intelligent and curious."

"How old would you say he appeared to be?" she asked, with a puzzled expression.

"Oh, about 35 to 38 years old I guess. His hair was dark but there was a touch of grey in his beard."

"You traced the cord I showed you out to this master?"

"Yes, exactly as you showed me. Why?"

"Well, the man you're describing is not my master. My master is an old man with a white beard that trails down to his chest."

"That's not the man I saw. The man I saw would not be more than forty years of age and his beard was shorter and dark."

We were both puzzled about this. A month later when I had returned to Australia Christine telephoned me to say she had discovered that when we completed the meditation the old master had died and a new, younger master had since been initiated to take over. The new master had taken on the responsibility for the deceased master's followers as a part of his initiation. I attended the next meditation meeting of his devotees in Sydney to purchase a photo of both the old and the new master. The new master was the man I'd seen in meditation and the late master was as Christine had described him.

Another confirmation occurred with Christine when she described to Amanda why she was experiencing difficulty in achieving high meditations. Christine asked Amanda if she'd been attending any psychic development groups. When Amanda asked why, Christine described a woman who had a link to Amanda that attached to Amanda's channel above her head. Christine traced the link out to a woman who strongly resisted Christine's attempts to cut the cord. The woman Christine described had attended Amanda's previous psychic development course and was using Amanda's energy source to further her own development. At the same time it was almost impossible for Amanda to receive the energy she required for high, clear meditations. Christine's description of Amanda's previous fellow student was immediate confirmation of accuracy, although confirmation of what is seen in meditation usually requires patience.

Another example of confirmation occurred a couple of years ago. I was feeling low and dispirited, so I ventured into meditation for some reassurance that things would eventually be okay again. My guide laughed at me and stated confidently, "Soon you'll be offered an opportunity beyond your dreams and that will only be the beginning. It will lead to other opportunities and you won't look back."

I felt reassured by his words and soon overlooked the content of my meditation in my day-to-day living. Several weeks passed and one day I realised that a business opportunity had come and it was to change my life and open the way for many other opportunities to follow.

I don't consult my guides simply for predictive purposes as often it is more important for me to know what I most need to learn in the present. After all, the power in life lies in the present. It is sound practice in meditation to request proof when doubtful about the accuracy of information received. If you are requesting proof during every other meditation, something is wrong. Guard against using meditation time for future predictions, as guides are sent to point the way in times of crisis, not to remove any hint of surprise life might offer. The higher the meditations, the less likely the guides are to answer mundane questions such as career or relationship issues. Although these issues are an integral part of life, higher guides are able to put this lifetime into context with many lives. Current issues are really only one grain of sand in a desert, which stretches as far as the eye can see.

Life needs to be experienced first-hand and each individual is responsible for personal decisions. Although guides in spirit can assist in times of crisis or clouded thinking, each individual is ultimately responsible for personal actions. Years ago, a friend of mine who had relied heavily upon her guides for every decision in her life, told me that she had lost faith in them and fired them.

"You what?" I asked incredulously. "How can you fire your spirit guides. You didn't hire them in the first place. Are they due for severance pay?"

It turned out that her guides had not told her what she wanted to hear about a man she was infatuated with, so she cast them aside and pursued him anyway. Several weeks later the man in question returned overseas, never to be seen again. My friend's desire to be in a relationship with this man clouded her judgement. Although she was receiving accurate information from her guides, she refused to believe them. However, they were proven correct within the month.

It's not easy to hear that you are capable of actions for which you criticise others. One particular guide who insists that I am aware of the part of me that is similar to those who upset me. I was feeling mistreated by my dance teacher when, in meditation, a guide helped me to see that my teacher was only doing to me what I had often done to my own students. I refused to accept this until he began a story that went:

"There was a young man who wanted so much to perfect a student that the teacher refused to acknowledge the student's good points until that student improved his weaker points. The student struggled and gave up in confusion but this teacher was unrelenting, believing that the student could do better. He insisted that the student wasn't leaving the room until he had mastered the techniques. The student simply wanted encouragement but this teacher wasn't going to give him any until he reached a higher standard."

I knew the student he was referring to and had been firm with him during private lessons. I argued with my guide that it was only to bring out the best in that student and that later the student had thanked me for doing so.

"And later you will thank your teacher also."

"I doubt that very much," I muttered but now upon reflection I admire my dance teacher for showing me what I was capable of doing and how undisciplined I was as a student. Not all the news spirit guides give is palatable. Generally the sign of a good meditation is a glow you feel within, during and after the meditation. If tense or burdened by the demands of life, a centred meditation offers peaceful feelings within yourself and your surroundings. This helps you to be more effective in your work and personal life. Information received during a centred, deep meditation is usually accurate.

Write down a brief list of what was covered after each meditation, as important information can be forgotten or overlooked. Date the list so that you know when the meditation took place. In meditation I have seen complete books that I may write and then forgotten most of the content a week later. Without written evidence these glimpses of universal truth can be easily lost in the demands of daily life.

During a meditation Katie noticed a large, stubborn cord protruding from the back of her neck, off to one side and away from her. As a test during a group meditation session, I suggested that with Katie's permission we all enter meditation and examine Katie and trace that cord outwards to its conclusion. Katie gave her permission so that we were not energetically trespassing into her aura. We spent ten minutes examining Katie and then shared the results.

Emma was first, confessing that she felt as though she was making it all up. I encouraged her to tell us what she has seen, despite her reservations. She described an old man at the end of the cord. Caroline agreed, saying that she felt that the ages two and three years were significant. Next Katie confirmed the same old man, as did Kim. Sharon saw him as both a young man and an older man.

Gabrielle described an old man and another cord appearing from the base chakra in the form of a tail. I saw this also, stemming from Katie's right ovary and outwards down into the earth. Kevin also confirmed an old man and a woman who looked bitter. He also noticed the cord became a hard branch of a tree. He saw the cord as being very long and wondered if it meant that it stemmed from a long time ago.

Margaret also confirmed an older man, with a very long cord. Leo saw an older man and another figure who had the body of a human but was covered in hair. (This is likely to represent a part of a person that is deteriorating as a result of being away from its channel for a long period of time.)

I also saw a young man and an older version of the same man, with a wizened old woman whom the cord passed through on its way to the man. Jacinta saw the cord but was unable to determine where it ended.

In all, eight out of ten students saw the same images, without prompting. Katie confirmed the older man as her grandfather and the woman as her grandmother. Emma seemed surprised that what she felt she was making up was confirmed by almost everyone else in the room.

Sometimes it is difficult to determine whether you have a good clear connection or if you are imagining. In time and with regular practice, it is possible to notice the subtle differences in your own state of being between imagining and gaining clear insights. Taking notes after each meditation ensures a record of all that is said. This offers proof later when what is foreseen in meditation, occurs in reality.

36

Paths up the Mountain; a metaphor

Each person is faced with a challenge of climbing a mountain. Some know the way to the top, others have a sense of the journey ahead of them, while a few are completely oblivious to the challenge. Here is a simple example of what 12 different people find during their journey up that mountain. Each person climbs a mountain in search of different goals and experiences. See which metaphor applies to you.

Adam begins his journey with a desire to please others. Soon he realises that to climb the mountain he must learn to ignore the fact that some of those people he'll leave behind at the base will miss him. At first Adam placates his friends and family. He promises them that he'll return within a certain time and that he'll send word that he is well. They insist that they cannot cope without him and ask who'll complete all the tasks he usually tackles.

Eventually his desire to reach the mountain top overcomes his need to please others and he finds the courage of his convictions. He departs and gradually his belief in himself is rewarded as he ascends the mountain. With each setback he initially thinks of returning home, to safety and security. Eventually he tells himself that he is past the half-way point, so he might as well attain his goal. When he finally glimpses the views from the top of the mountain he is stunned at how many other peaks are visible. He sits in wonder at the vistas laid out before him and resolves to climb some of the other nearby peaks.

Barbara is also a people pleaser, feeling that she alone can meet their emotional needs. When her desire to climb the mountain surfaces Barbara chastises herself for her selfish motives and to distract herself, she rows with her family. The ensuing brawls affect her health and she feels incapable of making her way to the mountain top unaided. Barbara feels that someone else must help her to reach the summit but she also believes that it is selfish to expect this.

Carl also wants to traverse the mountain but to do so, he must surrender his independence and reach a group consensus that it is right that he does so. This is not easy, as Carl, like Barbara, has a very demanding family.

Carl reasons with Barbara's family until they accept that it is okay for Barbara to climb the mountain. Carl agrees to accompany Barbara and in doing so, surrenders some of his independence, as Barbara is physically incapable of travelling at Carl's speed. Despite their squabbling, Carl discovers a calm, patient approach to Barbara, so that her health is strong enough for her to accompany him. As they ascend, Barbara gradually notices that the process and the views are much more rewarding than quarrelling with Carl.

Daniella is independent, organised and an excellent administrator. She decides that it is also imperative that she climb the mountain. In doing so, she discovers that she can only reach the top if she surrenders to nurturing offered to her along the way.

Halfway up the mountain Daniella became ill and was nursed by a local woman. As her health deteriorated, Daniella became allergic to almost all of the local foods and she survived by being spoon-fed by a local mother. This was a test for Daniella, who prided herself on her independence. She was ashamed at having to be fed like a small child, yet felt the local people loved and nurtured her like one of their own family. Because she was bedridden, the children spent time with her, teaching her games. As she was embraced by a new family, her practical, structured life in the valley seemed like a distant dream to her. It was a chance to be like a child, without incessant demands and responsibilities.

Edward only wants to blend in with the people who are content to live on the plains. His secret desire to climb the mountain troubles him, for he feels that it is his ego that prompts him to want to be different.

He attempts to organise a group of people who want to travel up the mountain together but gradually each member of the group finds other goals and commitments.

He tries valiantly to live a fulfilled life on the plains, helping others pack for their treks up the mountain but this only fuels his desire to reach the summit himself. As another winter is spent in the shadow of the mountain Edward's desire for the views from the peak grows deeper, until one day he sets out. As he makes his own path to the summit Edward realises that the mountain is, in fact, a path to his courage, his individuality and his creative expression.

Franjelica is searching for one clear truth and decides that it exists at the top of this glorious mountain. To reach the summit Franjelica must overcome her sensitivity to the harsh realities that lie along the path. At first setback Franjelica weeps and asks God why she has been chosen to feel all the pain in the world. At the second hurdle she weeps less. Eventually she decides that tears only cloud her vision of the path ahead. The obstacles begin to strengthen her resolve as she realises that traversing the path is the price of the view.

Gil is independent, self-righteous and cares little for the feelings of others. He decides to climb the mountain to get away from the demands of the people who claim to love him. It's his chance to escape and be free from his family. Discarding his tools one afternoon, he spends three days packing and purchasing supplies before walking out of his life and into the promise of glorious views and crisp, clean air.

With his strong legs he is soon striding past fellow travellers, pleased with himself for not bringing company that might slow his pace. A few days into the trek Gil stops to rescue a young woman from a startled snake and they fall in love. Suddenly Gil is torn between his need to trek to the summit quickly and his desire to spend time with his new love, who has no desire to reach the summit. His heart is heavy as he pleads with her to accompany him in his quest but she ignores his pleas. When he asks her why she will not accompany him, she reminds him that he has already left a small son behind.

This boy will spend his days searching for love, support and meaning in other men's faces, because his real father decided that a personal quest was more important than his responsibilities. As Gil wearily treads his path alone, he reflects upon the words of his love and realises that words and actions have consequences. To reach the summit he must see how each of his actions has affected others.

Hannah had a comfortable life as a merchant's daughter, affording her anything she desired. Although she had a childhood filled with gifts and pampering, Hannah realised that comfort is no substitute for inner peace. She decided to climb the mountain but Hannah did not wish to do this via the path, as others had done.

Her devoted father offered her guides, cooks and horses but for her, this trek was to be the ultimate prize, which required a mammoth effort. Hannah knew that she'd need to surrender her personal comforts and improve her physical fitness to achieve this goal so she made a careful plan. After many months of training, Hannah set out with ropes, tackle, climbing boots and food rations and proceeded to climb straight up the side of the enormous, rugged mountain. Along the way she spied the roads and paths beneath her like tiny ribbons. The wind turned to ice and tried to force her from the smooth cliffs and the mossy slopes. To reach the summit Hannah had to learn to give all of herself to her goals and in doing so, to find inner depths previously hidden.

Ingma was too interested in talking about how he was going to conquer the mountain to actually do so. Ingma proclaimed loudly to all who listened that it was going to be named Ingma Mountain after he had conquered it. Ingma often looked out of his little window above the bakery in the village, pondering which path would be more suitable and what season most agreeable for such an honourable task as this. He discussed his plans until he lost his voice.

He raised the subject of renaming the mountain at each and every meeting of the villagers at the town hall. Each month the villagers met and every month Ingma spoke of his intended endeavour. Small children thought that Ingma had already climbed the mountain.

The day finally came and Ingma set out on his journey. To reach the summit Ingma had to learn that words do not make deeds easier and that actions are needed to complete plans. As he climbed, Ingma discovered that true independence sometimes involves a departure from the community or the mainstream. As the view became more expansive Ingma became more nervous about being away from the safety of his community. However, when he reached the summit he discovered a small community of climbers who shared a common bond, having conquered the mountain.

Jennifer never even thought of climbing the mountain. She sat cosily sipping tea in her garden with her back to the mountain. Jennifer loved the comforts of home and had no intention of ever leaving them behind. As she grew up fewer and fewer people were prepared to replicate the love and nurturing she had received as a child. She desperately wanted to be like a child again but it seemed that the whole village wanted her to be grown up.

She took a job as an infant school teacher to be amongst other small people but the children wanted her to be in charge of everything. Jennifer soon became resentful of having to be the responsible one. Then one day a small boy called Michael asked if Jennifer could take their class up to the mountain top to see for themselves what lay there.

Jennifer was horrified at the suggestion and promptly told the class a story about the hideous dragons that lay in wait for any who dare venture to the mountain top. Michael was undeterred and asked Jennifer every day for a year. To escape this and life's other demand's, Jennifer loved to sleep. She slept for 10 or 11 hours each night and her dreams allowed her to recreate life as she felt it should be, until the nightmares began.

The first bad dream was of Michael departing for the mountain top alone. This was soon followed by a dream of Jennifer attempting to rescue Michael and becoming lost herself. The dreams continued for weeks, until some nights Jennifer was afraid to go to sleep. One day she awoke feeling resolute. There is only one thing for it, she told her cat Jemima. I'll have to climb that mountain myself, to be able to make a map that others can follow. In this way I can ensure that people who choose to climb it will return safely. Over the next two years Jennifer made careful plans, finally setting out for the summit in the school holidays. Michael came out to see her off, pressing a slice of warm chocolate cake into her hand, to help fuel her for the journey ahead. The soft sticky icing began melting into her fingers as she walked, so she ate it immediately.

In carefully climbing to the summit Jennifer had to leave behind the security of her childhood and operate from a sense of responsibility for those who were weaker or smaller than herself by making a map for them. It was a stressful process but she reminded herself that it would be more rewarding on her second or third attempt as she'd have a reliable map to guide her.

Kyle held a deep desire to climb the mountain to prove to everyone how special he was. He was desperate to show others that he was chosen for greater things than the other ordinary

Fig 9.
Your spiritual
master is found
above your guides
in your channel.

villagers and saw the mountain as his opportunity. As a child Kyle refused to play with the other children when they did not allow him to win all the games. He didn't like playing with ordinary children as he felt he was special. He held a big party which was his send-off up the mountain. Everyone in the village came and brought him gifts. "At last," he said to himself, "At last they recognise how special I really am."

Kyle set off up the mountain carrying all of his presents but soon found himself exhausted from bearing such a heavy load. One by one he reluctantly discarded the gifts to progress further. When he realised that the less he carried the faster he moved up the mountain, he generously gave away anything his didn't need. At night he entertained fellow travellers with songs by the campfire while discovering the social element of travelling.

To reach the summit Kyle had to discover that we are all special, which is what makes us the same. He only noticed this when he had discarded all of his precious gifts and personal belongings, even his guitar. He stood unburdened by expensive clothing and accessories and to his surprise, no one judged him poorly for his lack of possessions, rank or station. At the summit he felt self-confident and filled with awe at the beauty of the vista. He also felt small amidst the enormous and wide ranging view which stretched out before him. Satisfied at the result of his endeavours, Kyle decided to teach others how to climb this mountain as a way of building self-reliance.

Loretta was prepared to climb the mountain only if she could prove beforehand that the trip would be worthwhile. Loretta reasoned, read and researched all she could about the mountain and about mountains in general. She became so knowledgeable about the mountain that she lectured often in the town hall on such topics as 'What motivates people to climb mountains' and 'Is the promise worth the pain?' and 'Mountaineering: defying death or desiring a deity?'

Loretta was the expert on a mountain that she had never climbed. She had not climbed it, because she was unsure of what awaited her if she climbed it. The day came when she couldn't bear it any longer. She was terrified of becoming an object of ridicule about her growing obsession, so she set out.

It was very difficult for Loretta, for this was the first time in her life that she had stepped into the unknown, with only her faith to guide her. To reach the summit, Loretta had to accept that there are some things in this universe that cannot be rationally understood. She was called to challenge what she could not understand with words or measurements. She needed to trust what she could not see or prove.

At the top of the mountain each person found answers. They found each other and more importantly they discovered inner strength, self-confidence and personal inner peace. For some, inner stillness resulted from glimpsing the view. For others, it stemmed from a deep sense of self confidence in discovering personal capabilities. They might have encountered each other at the foot of the mountain but they chose this particular challenge. Later, some became guides to the remaining villagers ascending the mountain; others lived at the top, while a few moved on to other mountains in pursuit of other lessons and opportunities.

Perhaps life is an opportunity to climb a mountain or even a series of mountains. With each summit comes a deeper personal understanding of ourselves and our strengths and talents. Sometimes the conscious reason for commencing the journey conceals deeper spiritual motives. The knowledge and understanding gleaned from each sojourn is what is taken from life after the physical body has been discarded. It's like a documentary that serves as a record of each person's unique journey.

37
Spiritual Healing

Some ancient civilisations believed that ill-health in the physical body is caused by imbalances in the spirit. Today this belief flourishes and along with it, the number of spiritual healing methods; from simple laying on of hands, to meditation and the more traditional method of prayer.

According to its practitioners, spiritual healing has enjoyed various degrees of success. This accomplishment differs according to the actual methods employed, the illnesses treated and the attitude to those methods of the person being healed.

Reiki healing is a method of channelling spiritual energy through the hands into the body of the client. There are methods for channelling Reiki at a distance to facilitate healing where the client is far away. People who teach Reiki (or initiate Reiki channels) insist that the person giving or channelling Reiki energy cannot be drained psychically by the client. They believe that Reiki practitioners are channelling universal energy, so their own reserves are not depleted.

Perhaps this is not entirely accurate. I have clients who are Reiki practitioners who explain that they find themselves becoming considerably drained psychically by clients when channelling Reiki. Some are drained emotionally and physically. What is the point of healing others if you risk depleting yourself proportionately? You may be giving personal energy to clients who are not necessarily any wiser as to why they were ill or imbalanced in the first place.

Sometimes healing allows people who can afford it to continue to avoid their paths in life. In practising psychic healing, practitioners are effectively opening themselves to the energy of the illnesses that clients carry with them. There is a risk of taking on the energy of the illness or becoming weighted down with another person's karma.

To understand the goal of healing others it is necessary to appreciate a possible purpose of illness. Perhaps on occasion illness serves to remind us that we have departed from our path in life. It is likely that before physical symptoms of ill-health manifest themselves, they take the form of emotional symptoms, such as stress or emotional exhaustion. In the death of a newborn child, I have seen instances where the child lived only a few days to prepare the parents for when that soul returned again as another child to those parents. On rare occasions when a child dies, the parents grow spiritually and the karma between the child and parents is fulfilled.

Before emotional symptoms manifest themselves, they sometimes take the form of mental signs such as thoughts, worries or beliefs about life. Before mental symptoms manifest they may take the form of spiritual indications such as emptiness, a lack of purpose or a lack of inner fulfilment. Spiritual symptoms are easy to overlook as there aren't rashes or physical pain demanding treatment. When spiritual symptoms are ignored they often manifest as mental symptoms.

Mental indications such as mental confusion, fuzzy mindedness, depression or obsessions can also be ignored or accepted as a part of life, until they become emotional symptoms, such as worry, nervous mannerisms or fear.

If emotional signs are continuously ignored, people may experience physical symptoms such as tightness in the stomach, a nervous sweat, skin rashes or in severe cases, stomach cramps or vomiting. This is an extreme example but even low-level emotional disturbance can have physical effects, such as when a person sits an exam, awaits results of a test from a doctor or anticipates an event with dread. The levels of energy are detailed from the finest (spiritual) to the densest (physical) in the following diagram:

Spiritual energy

⇩

Mental energy

⇩

Emotional energy

⇩

Physical energy

Mental energy affects emotions, disturbing balance and affecting the physical body. Patricia consulted me for hypnosis for confidence in her high school exams. She was a diligent student who felt that she was slipping behind in her final year. She had been told repeatedly that this year was more difficult than all her previous years and she was beginning to doubt her own abilities.

When she thought about exams she began to worry. Her thoughts in turn affected her emotional state, tightening her stomach and reducing her appetite for food. Her emotional imbalance began to be affect her physically, disturbing her sleeping patterns, leaving her feeling flat and anxious about success in her forthcoming exams.

A more severe example was a client I worked with recently, who sought help to heal her skin complaints. Lee had consulted medical doctors, skin specialists, natural therapists and as a last resort, she was consulting a hypnotherapist in search of a cure.

Lee described how the scars on her face and arms were the result of operations to remove lesions and frankly, she looked a mess. What disturbed me more than the scar tissue and blotchy skin was the look of exhaustion and aloneness in her eyes. The number 19 flashed before my eyes and I felt prompted to ask her what had occurred in her life at the age of 19 which may have disturbed her. I was particularly looking for something that remained unresolved within her mind or heart.

She thought for a minute and shook her head. The number flashed across my mind again so I became quietly insistent.

"Is there any little thing? Even something which might seem insignificant after nine years?"

She pondered a moment longer and blankly asked me, "I was raped when I was 19 years old. Would that count?" I felt numb. How could she possibly think that being raped was an insignificant event in her life? Unless perhaps she didn't want to give it any thought at all.

"Exactly how long have you had the skin problems, Lee?" I asked gently.

'About eight years now. Yes, eight years."

"Could it be possible that there is some unresolved issue concerning your experience at 19 years of age?"

"Oh, not really. You see, he was a friend of mine at the time."

"Okay, so he was a friend at the time. Did you want that to happen?"

"No. I even told him so."

"What happened after that incident?"

"I forgot all about it really."

As was obvious from the lifeless look in her eyes, this man's actions had the effect of steering Lee away from her spiritual path in life. This is without the enormous mental and emotional anguish that appeared to have been given no outlet since the rape occurred.

The only avenue open to Lee to express her feelings appeared to be physical skin lesions. The operations did not cure her because they were treating the symptoms, not the cause. So were the other therapies she had sought. This is not to dismiss these healing modalities, for each has its own strengths. Had Lee found a suitable cure for her skin lesions without resolving her spiritual, mental and emotional imbalances, it is likely that other physical symptoms may have manifested.

I suggested that she undergo some regression through hypnosis to the time of the rape, to resolve her feelings. She refused and I offered her hypnosis for increased assertiveness and self-worth to reduce the damage caused by her 'friend' breaking her trust when she was 19 but Lee couldn't bear to think about it any longer. She couldn't face the possibility of more pain, even though it might bring eventual peace. She discontinued her sessions. I felt saddened that her 'friend' couldn't see the years of devastating damage he had caused through his selfish actions.

Spiritual healing offers answers to some health problems that stubbornly refuse to disappear when treated with orthodox methods. However, it might offer more for the client than for the healer.

When I challenged Christine about the need for spiritual healing arguing that healers serve a necessary purpose, she cited the example of her healer friend, Mosely. Mosely worked as a spiritual healer and was justifiably proud of his career. One day he called in to have a cup of tea with Christine. Despite being long-time friends, they fell into their usual argument about the value of spiritual healing and the side effects upon the healer.

To prove her point, Christine scanned his auric energy field for residual energy from the clients he had seen that day. She surprised Mosely with a clear and detailed description of each client and their health concerns.

Moseley suggested that Christine had linked into him psychically to trace the events of the day. She explained to him that she didn't need to, for he had taken into his aura plenty of the energy and hence the karma, of the people he had healed. She described his auric field as being choked up with emotional debris from clients. Mosely was healing his clients but in doing so he was also removing their opportunity to learn a lesson before returning to health again.

"What about medical doctors? Surely you cannot argue that they are interfering with the karma of patients when healing them?" I argued.

"In some instances it may be a doctor's karma to heal others. Perhaps he is balancing a lifetime spent causing others pain, or taking their lives. In saving the lives of others, he is now redressing this karma."

"So how do you know that psychic healing is not balancing the karma of the healer?"

"Medical doctors don't work with spiritual energy, they deal with the physical body and if it is not your karma to live or to return to health, then even the most experienced doctor cannot help you." This explains why sometimes a routine operation can go wrong whereas the most complicated procedure can go off without a hitch.

"Through watching other healers I have proved this to myself. I also resisted this concept when I first heard it from a master in meditation," she stated patiently.

"So where does this leave me if I can't heal others?"

"It leaves you with more spiritual energy for yourself and for your own purpose," she said.

"So what is the answer for people who need spiritual rebalancing?"

"There are masters everywhere who offer paths to self mastery, whereby they can rebalance themselves and remain keenly aware of their spiritual purpose in this life."

"And what about me? What am I left to do if I can't heal people?"

"You will write about it and in doing so ignite the desire in others to discover a spiritual path for themselves."

I realised that she was right. It occurred to me that whenever I spent time away from healing, or psychically reading for others, I had limitless energy. However, soon after I returned to healing and readings I felt continuously tired and listless.

In a meditation course Gabrielle, an enthusiastic student said that she wanted to continue her method of psychic healing. I tried to encourage her to see the bigger picture. She explained that she had seen positive results from the healing she had offered to others so I used a fish tank as a metaphor to illustrate her lack of perception of the bigger picture.

If I noticed that a fish in a tank was ill and plucked it from the tank, I might be able to rescue it. If I closely examined the tank it may become apparent that the cause of the illness lay in the water, which had become toxic for that fish. If I examined only the fish the long-term solution to the problem may not be located or identified. If I examine both the fish and its environment, decisions regarding the cause of its ill health may be based on a greater amount of information.

The same applies to the human spirit. If a person does not know the complete history of the spirit of a client, how can he or she know that the psychic healing is of benefit in the bigger picture. Perhaps is it simply robbing that spirit of a valuable lesson that must be learned for purification. It is impossible to know the complete history of a spirit, so any help is based upon limited knowledge or assumptions. Occasionally psychic or spiritual healing is perfectly acceptable, especially when the client has exhausted other means of healing. It sometimes offers rapid results but there is always the possibility that it is tampering with karma.

The other side to psychic healing is the dross factor (described earlier) when negative energy contained within the auric field of the person being healed can travel back to the healer. Gabrielle argued that she was meticulous about psychic hygiene but being sceptical, I remained unconvinced, especially when she freely admitted that, as a telephone tarot reader and healer, she sends psychic cords down the phone to complete strangers. When not knowing who or what is at the other end of the telephone, it is more prudent to exercise caution than to jump in.

Telephone caller identity service is a good example. If you telephone friends, they can receive your telephone number on a screen before answering the call. In calling for a conversation you inadvertently give them information about yourself. Psychic cords are similar.

Gabrielle is content to continue her healing, which is her personal choice. She has seen effective results with her clients and feels that she is making a difference to the lives of people who consult her. She offers her services based on practical training and with good intentions but there is a risk that she might take on the energy or the karma of people she heals, despite her rigorous cleansing procedures. Most of us have enough karma already without taking on the karma of others.

As there are many paths up various mountains, spiritual healing may simply be one of these paths. It can be a fine balance between sharing the load to help someone ascend their mountain and taking on another person's burden. Perhaps the answer to this is to teach others how to heal themselves so that each person is responsible for her or her own life journey.

38
The Energy of Beliefs

Having examined how the physical body and the auric or emotional bodies are composed of energy, it is time to examine thoughts. When thinking, a person creates thought forms which have energy that corresponds to the thought. They are weak or strong according to the intensity and frequency of the thoughts.

Thoughts and attitudes have energy. Love, hatred, fear and hope all have recognisable energies. When first forming opinions of people and situations, the accompanying energies anchor those feelings.

Sometimes very powerful thought forms are created around certain events and no matter how much we attempt to change our circumstances or our attitude to those events, we feel thwarted. One way to change powerful core beliefs is to examine how and when they were originally formed, being aware of the energy created as they were formed. It is possible to establish a new thought pattern or attitude regarding the person or situation. An extreme example is provided by a friend of mine who wanted to change an entrenched belief.

Jason wanted to transform his attitude to money. He wanted to earn enough to live comfortably. In his early thirties he was living week-to-week without knowing if he'd have enough money to pay his bills. He tried working harder, getting a second job and training for a better paid position but as his income increased, so did his overheads. He was still scraping by when he realised that the cause might not be entirely physical.

He consulted a counsellor and together they discovered what might have prevented him from earning sufficient money for the lifestyle he desired. Eventually they concluded that Jason's attitude to money was that it was contaminated and that it corrupted people. Deep down, Jason was convinced that if he accumulated money he would also become dirty or corrupted by that money.

After many months with his counsellor, it emerged that there were several incidents in childhood where Jason formed very strong opinions about money and its association with corruption. When he was young, his father had been injured in the workplace after his boss insisted that he work a double shift. After the injury his father lost his job and the company took no responsibility for the accident. His father wanted to purse the company legally but without money for legal fees, he was stuck. As a child Jason decided that money corrupts people. Watching his father struggle to feed the family, Jason feared that the pursuit of money led to greed and pain.

His counsellor was able to help him to realise that no one suffered in the process of his earning his present income. He was eventually able to grasp the concept of clean money. It took some time for Jason to consciously form a new energy association around money but ultimately he did, resulting in an increased income and an improved lifestyle. For many months he had to consciously notice money being honestly earned and spent to challenge and gradually replace his negative beliefs about money.

In Jason's situation, although he wanted to establish financial stability, his subconscious mind believed that it was morally wrong to have enough money, as it had negative associations around money. He had to realise subconsciously that it is possible to earn money in a clean manner and then he needed to go through a ritual to change his subconscious mind's attitude that an increased income was morally wrong.

Jason decided to give part of his additional income to someone deserving. This confirmed to his subconscious mind that having more money was good, especially if the money was honestly earned and shared with someone less fortunate. He effectively demonstrated to himself that additional income benefited both himself and others. He also had to demonstrate that he did not plan to earn or to spend money immorally.

Gradually his income increased until he enjoyed the lifestyle he desired without inner conflict.

Repetitive or obsessive thoughts can create strong thought forms that linger with a person or in the location where they are formed. If an individual is continuously entertaining the same thoughts over a period of time while sitting in a particular chair, it is likely that a stranger sitting in that same chair will find his or her thoughts influenced by existing thought forms. This can work positively or negatively according to the thoughts themselves.

It is possible to learn to recognise thought forms associated with particular homes or rooms when visiting friends or strangers. When inspecting houses for sale recently I walked into one house and was immediately engulfed by sadness. It felt as though dreams had died there and that the owners were about to divorce.

This is why meditating in the same place improves meditation. When sitting in your meditation place, the thought forms awaiting you are those which you have built up through repetitive meditation and they are likely to assist you into a more serene meditation. It's possible to enjoy a deep, relaxing meditation anywhere, such as when travelling on holiday or for work but by meditating in the same place when at home you strengthen the positive energy for meditation in that place.

Thinking creates a thought form of energy. A vocalised thought creates a stronger energy form. Actions associated with intense thoughts or feelings often produce the strongest thought forms. When preparing for a difficult situation it is possible to plan ahead by creating anchors that encourage thought patterns for support through a difficult experience. An anchor might take the form of a jacket which provides confidence for a job interview or a serve of your favourite ice-cream to remind you of better days.

Anchors are usually associations for emotions. George has his own business and occasionally he requires a positive anchor when business is particularly stressful. He then seeks out a Ferris wheel at a fun fair which reminds him of days spent at the fair with his father. To him the Ferris wheel has accompanying feelings of safety, being with his dad and pleasure resulting from the rides.

Without positive associations from the past to draw upon, you can set up a new thought form or anchor to provide confidence or courage to face life. A friend of mine, Judy was booked for an operation to remove a small skin cancer from her face. It was a delicate operation, and she was told it could take up to six hours without anaesthetic. Judy had to be conscious throughout a complicated procedure that she expected to be uncomfortable or very painful. She asked for some hypnosis to help her control the pain.

I taught her a self-hypnosis technique whereby she was able to take herself into a light trance during the operation and temporarily deaden the nerve sensations in her face. The thought form was that she could control her pain levels temporarily and the association was the self-hypnosis procedure. Each time she used the hypnosis procedure she strengthened the thought form and increased her control over her pain.

Judy practised her self-hypnosis technique diligently for several weeks prior to the operation. She was experiencing a continual tingling in the area of the skin cancer, so in practice sessions she knew that when all tingling sensations stopped she was in the hypnotic state and her face was numb. It was important for her to have evidence of the effectiveness of hypnosis before the operation, as she'd be under great stress in the theatre at that time she required confidence in the technique. True confidence comes from experience and she had several weeks of experience to draw upon, confirming that she'd feel nothing during the operation. As the operation proceeded, she did not feel any pain or even the tingling she had been experiencing for months.

She was delighted with the results and so was her surgeon. Judy had built up a strong thought form through continuous repetition of the self-hypnosis exercise. As the thought form strengthened she felt less and less of the facial nerve information while in the hypnotic state. Had she not diligently practiced the exercise and strengthened the thought form, she might have been less successful in numbing the pain during the operation.

Every day our thoughts are producing thought forms that are influencing our lives. Your surroundings can anchor you to your usual thought patterns, whereas unfamiliar surroundings encourage different thought forms. This is why it is essential to holiday occasionally in unfamiliar places. This allows a period of time without the influence of usual routines and thought forms.

Motivation is another point to consider. Judy was motivated by the looming operation to practice thinking in a particular way. She wanted the operation to be successful so that a repeat operation and further intrusive surgery would not be required.

When finding something that is motivating enough to change your thinking, the thought forms of energy that surround you change and your physical reality alters accordingly. It may not be necessary to require hypnosis to create a trigger for a desired outcome. Meditation and hypnosis are similar states and any suggestion you give yourself in meditation can have similar powerful effects, especially if it is combined with an action or ritual to convince your subconscious mind of its validity.

Ritual has been used for centuries to strengthen beliefs and attitudes and it is still used this way. During a marriage ceremony there are several rituals that symbolise the underlying commitment, including the wedding rings, the witness and the ceremony itself.

It is not enough to tell yourself that you are now going to change your life. It is necessary to make some physical change or repeat some physical ritual to let your subconscious mind know also. Judy practised a self-hypnosis exercise every day and that 15 minutes she spent lying down with her eyes closed as she went through the ritual strengthened her confidence that she could control the nerve sensations in her face.

Meditation offers powerful opportunities for self-suggestion. It is important to be outcome-oriented when deciding upon a suggestion. Decide what outcome is personally desired and give yourself a positive suggestion accordingly. There is no need to focus on how the outcome is achieved, for that is the task of the subconscious mind. It does as it is told, as long as you are not telling it to do something to which it is morally opposed.

When planning auto suggestions during meditation it is essential that these are worded positively. The subconscious mind takes things literally, so negative wording may cause more problems than it solves.

An example of negative wording is when parents tell their children "Don't get run over." They intend to make their children safe but the child must think about being run over by a car before they can apply the 'don't' part of the statement. Positively worded, the same intention might be stated "Stay safe." In this way children form thoughts or images of safety and as they are already safe, staying safe means simply continuing to be what they are.

39

Guilt and Auric Awareness

The auric or emotional energy field is composed of fine energy. It is subject to influence from other fine energy fields, such as thought form energy. Nursing guilt about past words or actions can weaken the auric energy field and allow disease to take hold.

As the subconscious mind is moral and unable to justify words and actions the way the conscious mind can, it seeks to redress guilt through punishment. Pain and illness are some of the ways the subconscious mind makes atonement for past perceived misdeeds. This is not suggesting that all pain or illness stems from guilt but that guilt can weaken the natural auric resistance to illness.

Even if your actions were not wrong, if your subconscious mind determines that they were wrong, it can harbour guilt. Guilt brings punishment, so a way to remedy such guilt is to resolve past incidents associated with guilt. When there is guilt about current actions, it is important to change behaviour or attitudes held in the subconscious mind.

An example of conflict between the conscious and the subconscious mind occurred with a client recently. Joan had a comfortable lifestyle with a sound business, two children and a large house that she had recently renovated. On the surface her circumstances appeared to be exactly what she wanted. Subconsciously, however, Joan felt undeserving of this lifestyle and no matter how much she rationalised her situation, she sabotaged her way of life. Although she had worked diligently to build up her business and to spend time with her family, she could not shake the feelings of inadequacy, which led to her attempting to destroy her life through alcohol.

Alcohol addiction began to destroy her relationships with friends and family and gradually eroded her ability to manage her business. Everyday business issues that ordinarily took an hour to resolve were taking days and disgruntled customers left to support her competitors.

After discussions it emerged that Joan felt guilty about her success, resulting in subconscious sabotage of her business, her health and her relationships. Despite her conscious efforts to succeed, her subconscious mind was driving her towards a lonely, unsuccessful life.

To resolve this guilt Joan searched for ways to ensure that others benefited from her good fortune. She began by providing training to her staff to help them to thrive. She then offered her time and management skills to a local charity, while working through counseling to resolve subconscious feelings of inadequacy.

When there is conflict between the conscious and the subconscious mind, it needs to be addressed. If ignored, the subconscious guilt may lead to illness or pain. Georgia's situation provides an example of the subconscious mind causing pain to prevent behaviour that it perceives as wrong.

Georgia was raised in a conservative family with strong religious beliefs. This began to cause her problems when she decided that she was more interested in love relationships with women than with men. Her subconscious mind was convinced that this was wrong, despite her rational conscious awareness that her actions were not hurting anybody.

After commencing a relationship with Elaine, Georgia developed a lung complaint that confined her to bed periodically. Doctors were puzzled, as tests did not reveal any particular ailment and the symptoms mysteriously disappeared overnight. The more Georgia pursued her relationship with Elaine, the more frequent were the bouts of illness, until she became physically unable to continue the relationship due to her poor health. Although her physical symptoms were real, the cause lay in the conflict between her conscious and subconscious beliefs.

In consultation we discussed her attitude to being gay. She appeared to be at ease with her lifestyle but intuitively I sensed conflict. Eventually she admitted a deep sense of guilt at disappointing her parents in their hope for grandchildren and a shame about her sexuality. Her guilt was preventing her finding happiness in a relationship with a woman, so it was necessary to resolve the guilt that might have been causing her ill health and disrupting her life with Elaine

The Kahunas believe that when offending another person, it is necessary to resolve it with that person, not with God. This makes sense when considering the negative thought form energy that an angry or resentful person may be directing towards you, even unconsciously. This negative energy can subtly disturb your personal energy field.

The first step for Georgia was to encourage her parents to voice their disappointment and to lay to rest any resentment they held about her sexuality. Georgia attempted to discuss her sexuality with her parents several times but they avoided the subject. Eventually she learned to meditate and she started her preliminary discussions with them in meditation. After some months she was able to talk with them separately to ask them not to resent her for her choice. Her parents were also feeling guilty, thinking that they must have 'done something wrong' for her to turn out this way. They eventually accepted her sexuality and she affirmed in meditation that her sexuality was okay as long as she did not hurt others. Gradually the guilt she harboured in her subconscious mind dissolved and her health returned to normal.

As a result she is able to enjoy a rewarding relationship with Elaine. When offending others, harbouring guilt over your actions and refusing to seek forgiveness, this guilt can weaken your auric energy resistance to illness, which in itself is an energy form. The Catholic tradition of confession of sins is designed to remove guilt so that a person can proceed with his or her life unhindered. The only difference here is that, instead of confessing to a priest, you are confessing to the offended party directly to restore the harmony between you both.

It may not even take the form of confession. It might simply be the admission that you recognise that your words or actions were unfair or inappropriate. It can also take the form of taking some action or making a sacrifice that helps to redress the source of your guilt.

An inner part of each of us knows when we have been unfair and it finds a way to balance the unfairness. A person may consciously choose to redress past hurtful actions or allow the subconscious mind to exact a payment. The conscious choice might involve an act of charity, giving of time, energy, expertise or financial support. A subconscious choice might involve ill health, deprivation or loneliness. It's important to know that choices are available.

40
Your Journey

Almost all of the answers a person seeks to questions lie within. The techniques outlined in this book are tools to use in your own journey. What you discover on that journey is unique to you. Your higher self or the part of you that is spiritually evolved is better placed to advise you about your current circumstances and your life direction than anyone else. This part has been with you since the very beginning and has already glimpsed outcomes that you haven't yet imagined.

As we are all spiritual masters in the making, the more contact that is made with the higher self, the more guidance is offered in life, both spiritual and practical. By strengthening this connection with the higher self through meditation it is possible to look within for answers to life's bigger questions. Decisions about a new job, a home purchase or a love relationship are often actually decisions about happiness, regular meditation can offer a constant source of joy and support throughout life.

Whether asking for guidance, stilling the mind for inner peace or cutting a psychic cord or releasing someone from your life, meditation can be a powerful tool for self-development and personal happiness. Even a short daily meditation can be nourishing emotionally and spiritually.

During courses I conduct on these techniques, students display many different approaches to the journey. They vary from individuals who have difficulty sitting still for each meditation to those who can clearly see their spirit guides the first time they enter meditation.

Patience is necessary. It is possible to meditate, cleanse and bring down the light for months or years before being able to see spirit guides or meet a master. The reasons for the delays can vary. Some students experienced difficulties seeing guides or psychic cords when in meditation whereas others quickly improve their visualisation abilities and are able to see cords and guides some of the time. Their abilities strengthen with practice.

In one course there were two students who could not see cords or guides in meditation at all. I asked my guides why this was so. They explained that in Jascinta's life so far Jascinta had seen too much that has disturbed her and she held a fear that seeing in meditation might mean glimpsing more painful images. Gradually, as she heals herself of her painful past, Jascinta is likely to see more clearly in meditation.

My guides explained that Sally was currently unable to see in meditation due to a history of poor diet and recreational drug use. As her health improves she can also expect to see clearly in meditation.

There are many valid reasons why a person might experience difficulties in clearly seeing guides or psychic cords when in meditation. When one student complained that she was unable to even sense the light entering her, I asked her to describe the technique she was using to enter meditation. She had shortened the meditation to suit herself and in doing so had inadvertently left out some important parts of the procedure.

Practice builds strengths and abilities, so it is important to give yourself time to practice. Meditating with others can be beneficial, both for motivation and for group energy taking you higher into meditation. Even people who have great difficulty in meditating usually find it easier when surrounded by others who are meditating. You may choose to get together with a few friends to practice the techniques or locate an ashram or a meditation centre to practice with a larger group.

If you conserve your spiritual energy to get high in meditation, when experiencing a clear, meditation you might feel so good that you'll want to share your excitement and energy with others. By remembering to cut cords afterwards, you can always achieve another high meditation and be filled with bliss again.

Clear meditations often arrive in a row, for a few weeks or even several months. Suddenly meditation is easier, clearer and more profound. When asking questions in mediation, the answers seem to arrive in your mind more rapidly and in a crystal clear form that is easily understood. This might be the result of a change in circumstances, such as the departure of a work colleague who has been draining or distracting you, the resolution of a longstanding problem or simply a change of season.

If you've been diligently practicing meditation, make the most of these opportunities when they arrive. It's an example of preparation meeting opportunity producing brilliant results. When this occurs, record your findings in a diary for later reference. It can inspire you when you feel despondent during a period of fuzzy meditations.

The more experience you have with meditation the easier it is to re-set yourself when life's demands bring chaos. A goal of inner peace takes 70 minutes when inexperienced but can be achieved in ten minutes with practice. The more rapidly you return to balance the better your decisions and the less upheaval exists within or around you.

41
Twenty Years Later

After I returned to Sydney, the first three months were precisely as Christine had predicted. My clairvoyant readings were crystal clear and I was able to tell clients their date of birth, date they were married, the dates of birth for each of their children and the ages of the important milestones throughout their lives. Gradually this ability faded, as Christine had said it would. She explained that psychic readings are actually a low form of use of spiritual energy and the more psychic readings one gives, the more difficult it becomes to enjoy high, clear meditations.

Throughout 1992 I wrote this book longhand, wondering how I might fit this new knowledge into my everyday life. Slowly life returned to normal, as I wrote other books, the first being published in 1995. When I felt spiritually empty, I'd open the manuscript and read a few chapters. It was a reminder and often I'd lay awake at night struggling to find a balance between the need to earn a living and the desire to write, teach and meditate every day for the rest of my life.

This book was first published in 1999 and in the year before it was released I ran some courses, to test-run the material before publication. When I gave public talks on psychic cords I expected to be faced with scepticism or disbelief, just as I had felt when studying with Christine but instead everyone seemed to know what I was talking about. Perhaps I was the last person alive to discover psychic cords?

In 2006 I designed a pure clairvoyance reading for clients which uses no tools. In these readings I begin by tracing the psychic cords from the client to people presently or previously in her life, describing how each person has shaped her life. I then scan back to childhood and through each year of her life, going beyond death to see who'll meet her when she passes through that final door.

This sometimes brings tears of joy, sadness or relief, as it did when I read for Fiona. I described her father standing, waiting to meet her after she let her life go. He held her tightly for a moment and then said "I'm sorry. I'm sorry about your education."

When I told her this she burst into tears, explaining how he was an old fashioned man. He had paid for her three brothers to attend university but refused to pay for her higher education, explaining that she was likely to marry and have children and that it was probably a waste of money. Each of her brothers bought farms, stayed in the country and worked the land. In her twenties Fiona held down two jobs while saving to put herself through university using her education as a foundation for a successful career in the city. Her father died before she graduated but he was still keeping track of her progress from the other side. Hearing this in her reading meant that Fiona didn't have to wait her whole life to realise that her father knew that he was wrong not to support her as he did her brothers.

Over the decades one of the most frequently asked questions is about love relationships. This makes sense as love relationships can bring the greatest joys and some of the deepest pain in life. From the reader's point of view, the most challenging part of giving predictions about love relationships is encouraging people to release what doesn't work for them and try a different relationship. Sometimes clients who have relationships filled with drama and power struggles might find stability tedious. Conversely, people who cling to dull routines for fear of loss or loneliness may find it almost impossible to summon the courage to discover a life away from the routines that they have built into their lives.

Some people grow up in bad situations and despite their best endeavours, repeat what they know. A partner comes along who fits the childhood impression of life and like a familiar song on a radio, they sing along to a well-known tune. Just because a person seems familiar, doesn't necessarily mean that he or she is right for you. Training yourself to like something that you've never had before takes courage, time and dedication and sometimes the support of a counsellor, a coach or a good friend can help ensure success.

As a younger man I was attracted to passionate bold, independent women who invariably found me too routine or uninspiring as a partner. One day, after a partner had stormed off into the distance and I was re-examining our relationship I found myself asking "What's wrong with this picture?"

It occurred to me that I had to become a bold, passionate and independent person or choose a less feisty partner. A calmer partner was the easier option because passionate lives are usually filled with arguments, tension and frustration, none of which looked appealing to me. Thoughts of weekends away camping and waking at dawn to be the first out hiking through the country filled me with dread, whereas the possibility of a weekend away by the fire reading a book with a partner who enjoyed the same pastimes began to seem much more appealing.

Instead of searching for another passionate, independent partner, I focussed instead on finding someone more sedate. I realised that what we focus on grows, whether it is happiness, spiritual growth, fears or hardship.

This means that instead of spending time and energy concentrating on what you don't want in your life, focus instead on what you want. If your goals seem too distant or overwhelming, focus on the next steps towards those goals. Early in life I wanted to be the best clairvoyant in the country but that was before I realised that this is an impossible goal to measure. Surely anyone can be the best at something for an hour in one day of his or her life. I believed that being the best at something might make me happy. Instead, I have chosen to focus on happiness and in doing so I discovered a dozen ways to be happy without the need to compete, either with myself or with others. What unique hobbies, practices, interests or places make you happy?

Your journey is individual and I hope that you realise that the first steps on a long journey are usually the slowest. The pace quickens with time and practice. I wish you the very best with your personal journey.

42
Glossary

Ascended master. The spirit of a person who lived on the earth in earlier times and mastered their spiritual lessons, e.g. Buddha, Jesus, Mohammed.

Chakra. A Sanskrit word meaning wheel or disc. Usually refers to the seven main wheels of energy located in the head, throat and down the spine. See Chapter 11.

Channel. A path of energy (spiritual) that passes through and around the physical body from the head to the feet (see Fig 1).

Clairvoyance. Clear seeing. It usually refers to the ability to see that which is invisible to the naked eye, e.g. to see ghosts and in the mind's eye, events from the past and the likely future.

Cords. Invisible tunnels of energy that link people to each other. They can be seen with clairvoyance. See Clairvoyance (see Fig 8).

Groundedness. The awareness of the physical body, physical needs and the physical world. Being connected to the physical environment.

Home. The destination for the soul or spirit of each person. (See Realms.)

Karma. The universal law of cause and effect that states that each cause has an effect and that each effect or symptom also has a cause.

Living master. A living Master is someone (still alive) who has attained spiritual mastery.

Manifested spirit body. A body image that resembles the physical body in size and appearance but which is composed of etheric or fine energy, making it visible only clairvoyantly. When we desire someone or something we often form an energy cord to that person or object and a part of us remains there for a period of time.

The appearance of the spirit body or etheric image we leave with that person or situation resembles our physical body at that age. If for example, a traumatic situation occurred at four years of age you may have a cord linking you to that incident. By returning to the incident it is possible to collect your spirit body image and return to the present, closing off the psychic cord that links you to that incident.

Master. A living person, male or female, who is spiritually adept and is prepared to assist others in their spiritual development.

Meditation. The act of quieting the mind and centering the physical, emotional, mental and spiritual energies within your physical self.

Soul rescue. The act of assisting a soul that has permanently left behind its physical body after physical death but is unable to reach its final destination. (See Home.)

Psychic. A generic term for people who perceive spiritual energy through second sight, second (extended) hearing or feeling more acutely than others.

Psychic blocks. An inability to sense psychically due to a blocking wall of energy, self-doubt, failure to calm your conscious mind or innate scepticism.

Realms. The eight levels or planes of existence that souls return to between lives on the earth plane. Traditionally the more evolved a soul, the higher the plane it may pass to in the realms. Souls for the earth plane are created on the fifth realm. The fourth realm is the true home of mind. The third realm is under the dominance of time and space. The second realm is more dense than the third and the first is even more dense.

Above the fifth realm are the infinite realms. The Creator began to extend him/herself from the eighth realm downward and in the fifth realm humans were created. This is why we are all gods in the making, as our source of energy extends from the eighth realm. As we didn't come down to the earth plane independently, we need to return together with those who know the way (guides and masters).

Spirit guides. Non-physical helpers who are available to guide us spiritually.

Thought forms. Clusters of energy created by thoughts, e.g. fear or dread in a dentist's waiting room resulting from many people thinking fearful thoughts while waiting.

Traveller. A spirit body that resembles the physical body which travels regularly away from the physical body to explore the universe. This is sometimes referred to as the Astral body.

Glossary